FRENCH EXISTENTIALISM

A CHRISTIAN CRITIQUE

FRENCH EXISTENTIALISM

A Christian Critique

F. TEMPLE KINGSTON

Professor of Philosophy
Canterbury College
The Assumption University of Windsor

UNIVERSITY OF TORONTO PRESS

Copyright, Canada, 1961
University of Toronto Press
Printed in Canada
London: Oxford University Press

TO THE MEMORY OF
GEORGE FREDERICK, MY LATE FATHER

Foreword

A GREAT DEAL has been written about Existentialism in recent years, but this work of Dr. Kingston's seems to me to occupy a unique and important place, and this for two reasons. First, in my opinion he seems to raise those questions about the Existentialist movement which most immediately spring to the mind of any intelligent Christian who finds himself confronted with it. Is the movement a reaction against Christian orthodoxy as such, or is it an attempt to recover certain Christian insights which Christians themselves have largely forgotten? If it is the former, how are we to explain the Christian existentialists, such as Kierkegaard and Marcel? If it is the latter, how are we to explain the atheist and antitheist existentialists, such as Sartre and Simone de Beauvoir? Is it possible, in view of their radical opposition, to consider Christian and atheistic existentialism as two species of the same genus? Or is it only by a misleading and equivocal use of words that the same label—"existentialism"—has been applied to both? And, granted that there can be a Christian existentialism, is it essentially Protestant or is there a genuinely Catholic type which can appeal to authentic, if perhaps partly forgotten, principles of traditional, and even of Thomist, theology and philosophy? To ask and investigate such questions as these has been a large part of Dr. Kingston's task in this book, and arising out of it is the second feature for which he is to be warmly commended. He has made a consistent attempt to form a sympathetic and critical judgment upon the whole movement from the standpoint of Christian orthodoxy, to get beneath verbal formulas to the realities which they express or (only too often) conceal, to sift the true from the false, to distinguish deliberate denials of the Faith from unintentional distortions of it, and to see how even denials may sometimes be explained, if not approved, as reactions from the timidity and mediocrity of Christians who were resting on their predecessors' laurels. M. Maritain has remarked that the devil's chief activity is to do in his way, which is not a good way, what good folk omit to do because they are asleep. That this is so is one of the most important lessons that Dr. Kingston has to teach us, and his book deserves an enthusiastic welcome, not only as a penetrating examination of a remarkable movement in literature and philosophy, but also as a salutary and astringent essay in the application of Christian ascetical theology.

Christ Church, Oxford   E. L. MASCALL
October 5, 1960

Contents

Introduction

In *Existence and Analogy* (p. 64), E. L. Mascall suggests that it would be interesting to discuss the existentialism of St. Thomas Aquinas in relation to contemporary philosophies known by the same name. In the past, Catholic philosophy has been dominated and distorted by an essentialist, Cartesian interpretation of St. Thomas and many have come to regard him as a Christianized Aristotle and his philosophy as a completely idealist, rationalistic and closed system. The dominant place given to atheism and freedom in Sartre's writings can only be fully understood as a reaction against this essentialist Thomism. In contrast to such an interpretation, Etienne Gilson, Jacques Maritain and Eric Mascall maintain that Thomism is not a closed system, "a museum piece," but a living philosophy, capable of facing the great issues of the twentieth century. By emphasizing the element of mystery in the act of existing and in the pure act of Being, they claim to have rediscovered the true wisdom of St. Thomas which has been obscured for many centuries.

At Dr. Mascall's suggestion and under his wise supervision, this study was undertaken, as a thesis at Oxford, to explore this relationship. Instead of dealing with each existentialist writer in a separate chapter, as has been done in many other works on existentialism, I have chosen the chief topics of existentialism and compared the writings of the existentialists in relation to these topics.

The problem of what to compare and how to compare it is difficult in the case of the existentialists for several reasons. In the first place, since they base their philosophies on the act of existing which cannot be thought *ut exercita*, it may be questioned if there is any ground for comparison at all. In the second place, since they stress the individual act of existing, one must consider whether it is possible for the philosophy to be expressed in terms that can be universally understood, that is, communicated to other men. Furthermore, since man in this life is in a constant state of becoming, his life may be regarded as a journey on which he finds ever newer experiences and gains greater insights. The philosopher's thought is enriched and expanded as his search for truth progresses through the years and growth and development are evident in the thought of all the existentialists, including Gilson and Maritain.

The third and most important difficulty arises from the fact that though the word "existentialist" has been applied to and used by both Christians and non-Christians, a careful distinction has been made by the philosophers themselves between the Christian and the non-Christian types of existentialism. In *Existentialism and Humanism* (p. 26), Sartre, recognizing this distinction, feels that what they have in common is a belief that existence comes before essence. However, Sartre's distinction is doubtful to say the least since he classes Heidegger with the atheists, a classification which may well be questioned; and he classes Jaspers with the Christians and it is very doubtful whether Jaspers is a Christian. Furthermore, his statement that what all existentialists have in common is that "existence precedes essence" may be only an agreement in name since Marcel, Gilson, Maritain and Mascall would strongly disagree with Sartre's interpretations of the words "existence" and "essence."

From the Christian point of view, a general distinction has been made between authentic Christian existentialism and inauthentic atheistic existentialism, a distinction which Jacques Maritain points out in his *Existence and the Existent* (p. 13).

Let it be said right off that there are two fundamentally different ways of interpreting the word existentialism. One way is to affirm the primacy of existence, but as implying and preserving essences or natures and as manifesting the supreme victory of the intellect and of intelligibility. This is what I consider to be authentic existentialism. The other way is to affirm the primacy of existence, but as destroying or abolishing essences or natures and as manifesting the supreme defeat of the intellect and of intelligibility. This is what I consider to be apocryphal existentialism, the current kind which "no longer signifies anything at all." I should think so!

However, according to this definition, some might doubt whether Marcel and especially Kierkegaard (both of whom are Christian) could be classed with authentic existentialism. Also, some might doubt whether Sartre who is so concerned to create his own essence and intelligibility could be classed with inauthentic existentialism.

Gilson suggests that the real difference between Christian and non-Christian existentialism lies in the knowledge of God's existence. Describing existentialism of the Sartrian type as a religious philosophy without God, he reflects that St. Augustine's *Confessions* would have been much the same had the author been left to his own devices, without the saving grace of God.[1] Mascall would seem to be in complete agreement with Gilson's point when he writes that though all existentialists are concerned to emphasize the ultimate significance of the individual as an active and willing being, "the Sartrians see him as creating himself by acts of sheer self-asserting unconditioned decision, while for St. Thomas he is a creature deriving his existence from the will of God and therefore morally bound to use his own will in accordance with the end for which God has created him."[2]

There are some who feel that Thomism has no right to be called an existential philosophy, and if it is, they insist that a sharp distinction be made between Thomistic existentialism and all other forms. The existentialist interpreters of St. Thomas Aquinas might accept this distinction for the reason that they believe, with justification, that Thomism has a prior right to be called an existential philosophy because the unique contribution of St. Thomas to philosophy was his approach to existing and being. It would be wrong to suggest that Thomism is characterized by an intellectualism while all other forms of existentialism are characterized by a voluntarism because in Thomism due emphasis is placed on both the intellect and the will.[3]

Many Christians writing about the non-Christian existentialists, Sartre, Merleau-Ponty, Simone de Beauvoir and Camus, have

[1]E. Gilson, "Philosophical Movements in France," *The Listener*, February 6, 1947, p. 251.
[2]*Existence and Analogy*, p. 64.
[3]*Ibid.*, p. 64.

tended to deplore their approach completely, but I feel that it is important to try to interpret their works as fairly as possible. The philosophies of the non-Christian existentialists are based on the *cogito* of Descartes. Their approach is primarily psychological, and in the field of psychology they have contributed much to human thought. On the other hand, considered metaphysically, their writings appear to be woefully inadequate. Thus, in comparing God in Christian or non-Christian interpretation, it must be always remembered that Sartre and his followers are working on a psychological level whereas the Christian existentialists base their assertions upon a metaphysical foundation. Therefore, what we must compare are attitudes to interpretations of reality.

At the same time, although many have criticized the writings of Gabriel Marcel for being vague and unrelated to the contemporary situation, it is clear that, by a method of contemplation, Marcel sees much more deeply into the core of reality than do many others. It is only through Marcel's or a like penetration into the mysteries of life that human beings can realize the unity and truth of their existence. Epistemology which has failed to penetrate these mysteries has been necessarily inadequate.

Well aware of these difficulties, this study seeks a basis of comparison on four levels: first, the common situation; secondly, the possibility and means of communication; thirdly, the chosen methods of philosophy; and fourthly, the attitudes and interpretations in relation to similar subjects. Although the French existentialists have been greatly influenced by Kierkegaard and by contemporary existentialist thought in Germany, Switzerland, Italy, Spain and the United States, the study is limited to the existentialism of contemporary French writers. France in the last fifty years has experienced some of the most crucial events of her history and this common setting for both Christian and non-Christian serves as a basis for comparison as to why from a similar situation, one man turns to Christianity and another to militant atheism. Though the examples are taken from French writers, the general themes mirror all existentialist writings and reflect the critical situations not only of the French but of all men seeking for a renewal of life in this oppressive and divided world.

There are so many to whom I should like to express my thanks. Many at Oxford gave me so generously of their time and wisdom, but I am especially indebted to Dr. Mascall who has added one more to his many kindnesses by writing the Foreword to this book. The experience of serving during the past year on the faculty of the first Anglican College ever to be affiliated with a Roman Catholic University has been a truly interesting one. I am most grateful to the Basilian Fathers for their open acceptance of me into the university community in the true spirit of Saint Thomas Aquinas. To the Principal of Canterbury College, the Rev. Dr. R. S. Rayson, I express appreciation not only for his advice and kindness in reading over parts of the manuscript, but above all for his leadership as a man of God, and as a devout servant of the Church.

I do want to thank Miss Elizabeth Chalmers, Assistant Editor of the University of Toronto Press, for the great care she has taken in suggesting improvements in style and expression, and also the Rev. Stanley Smith, the rector of St. Andrew's, La Salle, for proofreading. I am most grateful for the grants in aid of publication provided by the Humanities Research Council of Canada (out of funds provided by the Canada Council), and by the University of Toronto Press Publications Fund.

Finally, I do want to thank my dear wife who has been so patient and helpful.

Though all these have helped with the improvement of this book, I alone am to blame for its inadequacies.

F. T. K.

April 30, 1960

FRENCH EXISTENTIALISM

A CHRISTIAN CRITIQUE

Chapter One

THE WORLD SITUATION AND THE
HUMAN CONDITION

EXISTENTIALISM was first recognized as a valid and also a notorious
school of philosophy during the Second World War, especially
after the defeat of France. The fall of France was a matter of vital
concern for every Frenchman and it would be difficult to overestimate the impact of France's defeat in 1940 upon the French mind.
To many, it was a blind force which had overcome them, for
which they could discover no reason. To most, the defeat of France
by its traditional enemy—Germany—was deeply humiliating. For
almost every Frenchman, the sudden collapse of his country came
as a shock which brought him to an awareness of his own existence
in the midst of a world-shattering situation. Indeed, the whole
world was involved in this situation as Jacques Maritain writes
in *France, My Country, through the Disaster* (*A travers le désastre*): "There is no nation today which is not involved in this
tragedy, not one which can say that the misfortune of France is
not also, to some degree, my misfortune and that I am completely
innocent of this misfortune."[1]

There had been trouble within France in the years before the

[1] J. Maritain, *A travers le désastre*, p. 37.

war. The Front Populaire, supported by Russia, sought to disorganize and paralyze the political life of the country by strikes, riots and the general spreading of suspicion and unrest. The Spanish Civil War also caused much dissension as people supported one side or the other. As a result, the important national interests of France were obscured. Worst of all, despite the obvious discords, the majority of the French people were sunk in complacency. They avoided the issues of war and, relying upon others to carry out their obligations, they would not accept national and international responsibility. As they lost confidence in their political leaders, they came to depend more on military leaders and the Maginot Line, a symbol of the lethargy and irresponsibility of the French people. For the ordinary Frenchman, victory was never in doubt and therefore the shock of defeat was greater. According to Maritain, France was defeated not because her people loved peace and freedom but because they took peace and freedom for granted. Deep down they saw the danger and yet, because they did not wish to bestir themselves, they refused to acknowledge the challenge to their security. Maritain believes that basically the fault of the people was a self-satisfied love of self.

In the three volumes of *The Roads to Freedom* (*Les Chemins de la liberté*), Sartre illustrates this characteristic of the French people in the years before the actual moment of French defeat. In the *Age of Reason* (*L'Age de raison*), the first volume, there are few references to and little direct concern with political affairs. Though his acquaintance Gomez has gone to fight in Spain, the Civil War affects Mathieu (the chief character) only very slightly.

> Mathieu sipped his sherry, and said: "It's excellent."
> "Yes," said Daniel, "it's the best drink they have. But their stocks are running out and can't be renewed because of the war in Spain."[2]

Towards the close of the book the interest in Spain becomes a little greater.

> And he said aloud: "Two evenings ago, I met a fellow who had joined the Spanish militia."
> "Well?"
> "Well, and then he became deflated. He's down and out now."

[2]J.-P. Sartre, *The Age of Reason*, p. 271.

"Why do you tell me that?"
"I don't know. It just came into my head."
"Do you want to go to Spain?"
"Yes, but not enough."[3]

In *The Reprieve* (*Le Sursis*), world affairs enter more frequently into the consciousness of the characters. The Munich crisis is the background of the story and this threat to the peace of France and the complacent lives of the characters suggests disastrous possibilities. Yet they do not see the possibility of war as a challenge to any eternal values, but only as an act of blind fate which will force them to serve in the army and perhaps be killed. Their situation is changed by this outward force rather than by any cause to which they are attached. When these events are thrust upon him, Mathieu experiences frustration, a frustration which springs not only from the threat of German aggression but also from the fact that largely unknown and uncontrollable forces determine French policy. In all this, the individual feels forgotten. Some individuals in positions of authority, such as Stalin, Hitler, Mussolini, Chamberlain and the French politicians, are considered, but not Sartre, Mathieu and others like them. Sartre and Mathieu might well ask, with a certain resentment, why they are not as important as these leaders, just as Ivich does: " 'All over the world they are asleep, or in their offices preparing for their war, not one of them has my name in his head. But I am here,' she thought, resentfully. 'I am here, I see, I feel, and I exist, no less than Hitler.' "[4]

Throughout *The Reprieve*, the seriousness of the threat of war becomes more and more apparent, and more and more ominous because the chances for peace depend upon the personal relations of the leaders at Munich who have no more chance of realizing a true reconciliation than have Mathieu or Ivich in their relations. Although some are overjoyed at the promise of peace in the Munich agreement, Sartre sees that it is only a sham. Because it is built upon a personal relationship, it will be no more lasting than any other agreement made between persons. The sexual act between Ivich and her lover, which takes place at the same moment as the

[3]*Ibid.*, p. 358.
[4]J.-P. Sartre, *The Reprieve*, p. 327.

meeting at Munich, ends in betrayal and the Munich agreement will end in the same way. According to Sartre, that is the nature of all human relations, diplomatic or otherwise.

Iron in the Soul (*La Mort dans l'âme*) covers the brief period between the collapse of the French forces and the actual German occupation. It is a period when present existence is nothingness hovering between an annihilated past and a future which promises only total oppression. Mathieu, who, like Sartre, is a soldier in the French army and conscious of defeat, expresses his frustration and despair: "In Paris, the Germans lifted up their eyes to this sky and there read their victories and their to-morrows. But as for me, I no longer have a future."[5]

This despair comes hand in hand with a disgust at everything, the self included, because it is in part the self that is responsible for this calamity and defeat which has come to pass. The individual has only his own existence left because he no longer has honour, security, or purpose.

Gabriel Marcel would say that absolute disgust and feeling of nothingness expressed by Sartre and his followers at the moment of defeat results from the limited resources of which they avail themselves. Depending only upon the self and its power, they are sunk to nothingness when the self is reduced to all but its bare existence at the moment of defeat. Marcel compares Sartre's opinion of the limited resources of the self to that of a poor man who wants to make his funds last as long as possible, because when they give out he will have nothing.

Like Sartre, Marcel has made no direct comments upon the situation leading up to the French defeat, but as we see Sartre's attitude in his novels, so we see Marcel's in the plays written in the years immediately before the war. However, the political events of Europe are only dealt with as they affect the personal lives of the characters. In *Le Dard*, Werner, the central character, criticizes Eustache who considers world affairs only on the level of the problematic, and he himself seeks a transcendent, mystical level of activity in being through art. "What are you doing against injustices? You go to meetings; you shout: down with capitalism!

[5]J.-P. Sartre, *La Mort dans l'âme*, p. 38.

down with Fascism! and Heaven only knows what else besides" (p. 50). Werner suggests that some people seek to build up and invent injustices against themselves in order that they may gain meaning and justification on the lower level of existence. That was the method of Hitlerism. Werner, an exile from Nazidom, returns to Germany not in a spirit of suicide but in a spirit of self-sacrifice that, in fully facing up to his situation, he may transcend it in an eternal realm through complete loyalty to his suffering compatriots.

After the defeat of France, the atheist existentialists worked actively in the Resistance movement. Although some Christians acted in the Resistance in fellowship with the non-Christian existentialists, by far the strongest and most active members were the Communists. As a result, the non-Christian existentialists formed a close association with the members of the Party and at one point Sartre sought membership in it. However, he was rejected by the bulk of Party members. The majority of the Christians sought not so much a practical as a spiritual Resistance. As a result, the non-Christian existentialists accused the Church of collaboration during the occupation even as they attacked the reactionary position of the Church in Spain. Yet both Christian and non-Christian existentialists were opposed to the Vichy government though for different reasons. The non-Christian existentialists attacked the Vichy government more as a tool of the forces of reaction and oppression, whereas the Christians were generally opposed to Vichy as a betrayer of France and a collaborator with the ungodly forces of Naziism.

The Resistance spirit of the non-Christian existentialists, aimed not so much at freeing France but at the general liberation of man, is best expressed in Sartre's *The Flies* (*Les Mouches*) and *Men without Shadows* (*Morts sans sépultures*), Simone de Beauvoir's *Le Sang des autres*, and Camus' *The Plague* (*La Peste*) and *L'Etat de siège*. In these works, this spirit is directed not only against the German occupation but against oppression and authority in all its forms. In *The Flies*, Orestes, the chief character, in whom we can see Sartre himself, reacts not only against political domination but against God himself in the person of Jupiter. Orestes declares that he must create his own laws because it is his fate (as indeed it should be the fate of any man), to reject any authority beyond his own consciousness. Tyranny in any form can only have a hold over men who are not aware of their freedom. Jupiter says to Egisthe: "The grievous secret of Gods and kings is that men are free. They are free, Egisthe. You know it, and they do not know it."[6]

For Sartre, the German occupation of France was not something that could have been avoided. It was a force that bore upon his situation necessarily as the laws of nature bear upon any physical object to determine it. It brought to one's attention the real issue of life itself. But if the essence of life is to resist inexorable forces of oppression, is there any hope for man?

According to Sartre in *The Flies* and Camus in *The Myth of Sisyphus* (*Le Mythe de Sisyphus*), men have one slight chance of hope and that is to express freedom in a world where human freedom is almost totally destroyed. The individual must seize his opportunities, however few they may be, to impress himself upon the world of his experience, not only upon his own private possessions, but also upon the oppressor, seeking by some small means to determine the very one who determines him. That is why aid to escaped Allied prisoners, or blowing up a train, or the uprising of the Resistance movement in Paris several days before the entry of the Allied armies, had such a tremendous psychological effect upon the existentialist mind. Existence was at stake in revolting against the Germans and yet self-respect and existence were also at stake in accepting the occupation. The only chance to really "exist," to play at being men, was by some few deeds of reprisal against those who sought to eliminate self-respect.

Objectively, it would seem apparent that the part played by the existentialists in the Resistance movement has been greatly exaggerated. The risks to which the resisters were subject is indeed obvious, yet it does not seem that the non-Christian existentialists, at least, did very much to hamper the Nazi war effort. At the time of the Paris uprising of the Resistance, Sartre acted as a roving reporter for *Le Combat*.[7] In his articles for that paper, he describes

---

[6] J.-P. Sartre, *Les Mouches*, p. 101.
[7] August, 1944, in a series entitled, "Un Promeneur dans Paris insurgé."

the general confusion which existed even in the organization of the Resistance. The members of the movement were unaware of the position of the American armies and there were many conflicting reports that the Allies had or had not yet entered Paris. Some of the reprisals which took place in these last few days before the liberation are worse than all those which occurred during the four years of occupation. For example, Sartre describes a German soldier's burning to death in a car set on fire by some French. The French people gathered about and seemed to rejoice in the misery and terror revealed in the face of their former oppressor. Finally, a Frenchman takes pity upon the German and shoots him. Again, Sartre describes a simple Parisian citizen who came to cheer the entry of the Allies and was shot by a stray bullet of the retreating Germans. The whole situation is absurd, a reign of terror as the prelude to a restoration of freedom.

At the same time, many Christians assisted the Resistance movement and the non-Christian existentialists recognize this. Camus says that he did not make the role of the Church in *The Plague* as hateful as he might have because he respected those Christians who were fellow-workers with him in the Resistance.[8] In *Iron in the Soul*, Sartre, in showing sympathy for a young French priest who attributes the defeat of France to those Frenchmen who refused to accept their responsibilities,[9] suggests a respect for Christians who are aware of their responsibilities as resisters. However, Christians generally were not as active in the Resistance as were other groups and many were accused of collaborating with the Germans or at least of adopting a neutral attitude during the Occupation, a charge levelled at both Gilson and Marcel. Yet despite his frequent trips to America before the war, Gilson remained in France during the Occupation and, in a letter in *Esprit*, explained that he did not go to America because to do so he would have had to receive permission from the Vichy government and he had no respect for Vichy. "I remained in France during the whole occupation because the way to America was by way of Vichy."[10]

[8]A. Camus, *Actuelles-chroniques*, p. 247.
[9]Sartre, *La Mort dans l'âme*, p. 236f.
[10]*Esprit*, April, 1951, p. 594.

Although Gabriel Marcel, like Gilson, remained in the unoccupied zone of France, he too was no supporter of the Vichy régime. On the other hand, he did not fully approve of the Resistance movement and in his plays, *L'Emissaire* and *Le Signe de la Croix*, he presents four general criticisms of it. First, he feels it did more harm than good by dividing the people and causing unnecessary suffering in the form of German reprisals.[11] Second, he suggests that Russians or even Anglo-Saxons, aiming at the ultimate control of French policy, had inspired the Resistance by sending agents into France.[12] Third, Marcel questions the motives of many of the members of the Resistance and he suggests that, feeling guilty at the fall of France, they sought justification for themselves by organizing activity against the Germans. He doubts if any cause upon earth can be absolutely justified or utterly condemned. "One pretends to oppose facts; one only opposes opinions."[13] It is interesting to note that both Merleau-Ponty in *Humanisme et terreur* and Simone de Beauvoir in *Pour une morale de l'ambiguité* are aware of this criticism and they maintain that no justification was found until after final victory. The fourth criticism, and the one with which Marcel is most concerned, concerns the nature of true resistance. Through the characters of his play, *L'Emissaire*, he questions whether the resistance of the members of the Resistance is the best kind of resistance.

Clement: Was your fiancé also in the resistance?
Sylvia: No. Well, that is . . . Not in the usual meaning given to the word.
Clement: The meaning given by whom?
Sylvia: By those who have taken part in it.[14]

Marcel believes that he carried on a true resistance by writing *Homo viator*, and other articles denied publication by the Vichy government, encouraging French people to rediscover their true dignity as human beings. Writing of the spiritual decadence which had taken place in France and other countries in the preceding fifty

11G. Marcel, *L'Emissaire*, in *Vers un autre royaume*, p. 55.
12*Ibid.*, p. 48.
13*Ibid.*, p. 70.
14*Ibid.*, p. 39.

years, he indicated that, in the machine age, men have come to be regarded as mere tools, and therefore what is needed most is a recovery of human character. Character, in the most profound sense, is to be recovered not so much through passive obedience as through faithfulness. Yet the self must be very careful in choosing that to which it will be faithful. One is a fanatic if one is faithful only to principles which are excluded from any re-examination and discussion. Furthermore, modern society, which tends to classify people by their opinions, destroys true faithfulness since to change one's opinion is to risk being regarded as inconsistent. However, to rebel against the opinions of others merely for the sake of rebellion is no better than mediocre conformism. Because society is such as it is, there is an urgent need for men to be truly human by being faithful to their own existence, which Marcel defines as "the particle of creation which is in me, the gift which has been granted to me for all eternity, to participate in the universal drama, to work for example, to humanize the earth, or contrarily to make it more uninhabitable."[15]

For Marcel, then, true resistance is shown not by blowing up bridges and shooting Germans, but by each individual's probing into the mystery of his human being, and when he has discovered a soul, remaining ever faithful to it. It is only as individual Frenchmen rediscover the spirit within them that the spirit of France will be rediscovered and revitalized.

Furthermore, it is only through faithfulness that persons are treated as beings, not as things or ideas. The fault of treating other people as ideas is clearly exemplified in anti-Semitism. The Nazis sought to embody all their own weaknesses in the Jewish race. By persecuting the Jews, they tried to destroy their own frustrations. France also has been plagued by anti-Semitism and both Marcel and Sartre are concerned with this problem; in fact, Sartre's *Childhood of a Leader* (*L'Enfance d'un chef*) suggests that he himself was at one time a supporter of the anti-Semite movement.

In his *Portrait of the Anti-Semite* (*Réflections sur la question juive*), Sartre demonstrates that anti-Semitism is based not upon a consideration of the individual worth of each Jew but upon a con-

[15]G. Marcel, *Homo Viator*, p. 182. (Written in 1942.)

cept of the Jew. The anti-Semite, usually a man of little talent, seeks to justify his own mediocrity by attaching himself to a cause. Thus anti-Semitism is founded on a desire to create a class struggle through which the frustrated individual can find a meaning for his life. Sartre distinguishes this struggle, which is regarded as the war of good and evil, from the class struggle in Marxism. "A Marxist does not regard the class struggle as the conflict between Good and Evil: it is rather a conflict of interests between human groups. . . . The revolutionary's aim is to change the organisation of society."[16]

The hatred of the anti-Semite for the Jew is also distinguished from the hatred of the French for their German oppressors. "The objects of hatred were oppressors, hard, cruel and powerful men who had arms, money, might on their side, and were able to do much more harm to the rebels than the latter could even have dreamed of doing to them. Sadistic inclinations play no part in such hatreds. But since the anti-Semite finds Evil incarnate in men unarmed and so little to be feared, he is never in the painful necessity of proving himself a hero: to be an anti-Semite is amusing."[17] The anti-Semite seeks to justify his cruel and sadistic tendencies and to avoid responsibility at the same time. He knows that he is doing evil but tries to justify his actions by regarding himself as a deliverer of the people. In *Le Signe de la Croix*, Marcel shows that the anti-Semite seeks to justify his persecutions by pointing out the faults in the idea of the Jew, for example, his exclusiveness in his religion.[18] In the play, Marcel condemns the attitude of certain Christians who refuse to shield Tante Lena because she was not French but a German Jew.

Sartre, indeed, blames Christians for the origin of anti-Semitism because they talk of the Jews as the murderers of Jesus. (Yet he destroys the point that he had made by saying in a footnote that Jesus was really killed by the Roman soldiers as an agitator; for, *in Sartre's terms*, if it could be proved historically that the Jews not the Romans were the actual murderers of Jesus, then anti-Semitism by Christians might be justified.) In his anti-Christianity, Sartre

[16]J.-P. Sartre, *Portrait of the Anti-Semite*, p. 34.
[17]*Ibid.*, p. 38.
[18]P. 172, Simon's speech.

himself appears as the frustrated anti-Semite and treats Christians in accordance with his idea of Christians in general, and not as they are. Sartre's portrait of the anti-Semite's attitude to the Jews closely parallels Sartre's own attitude to Christians in the latter part of the essay.

In the face of anti-Semitism, both Sartre and Marcel observe that many Jews take one of two paths. The first is for the Jew to become an anti-Semite himself. He is made so aware of the faults of his race that he is constantly on the look-out for any characteristics which distinguish him from other men as a Jew. In *Le Signe de la Croix*, Odette says, "In the majority of Israelite families, there is an anti-Semite. Here, I am the one who holds this role and I hold it with conviction" (p. 143). Sartre writes: "And he who, a short time before, did not even notice the ethnic characteristics of his sons or nephews, now begins to watch every move of his co-religionists with the eyes of an anti-semite."[19]

The second recourse of the Jew in the face of persecution is rational philosophy and mathematics. "If reason exists, there is not one French truth and another German truth, just as there is not one Negro truth and another Jewish truth. There is only one truth, and he is best who discovers it. In the sight of universals and eternal laws, man is himself universal. There are no longer either Jews or Poles, there are men who live in Poland, and others who are designated on their papers of identity as being 'of the Jewish faith,' and an agreement is always possible between them as soon as it is related to the universal."[20] The works of the Jewish philosophers Spinoza and Brunschvicg may be classed as typical examples of this tendency. Bergson, who was a French Jew, is regarded as a notable exception. Marcel has taken note of the rationalism of Brunschvicg and much of his philosophy has developed in reaction to it.

In the political philosophy of Sartre since the war, the same consciousness as that of the persecuted Jew is revealed. His consciousness is that of a defeated Frenchman, a member of a nation which is in great confusion and which has lost almost all of its former greatness. Sartre seeks a rational view of man akin to the

[19]Sartre, *Portrait of the Anti-Semite*, p. 86.
[20]*Ibid.*, p. 93.

Marxist ideal in which Frenchmen can be regarded as equal to all other men.

Since the war, the oppression of the Germans has been replaced in French consciousness by a double oppression—the Communists on one side and the Americans on the other. The alternatives of Communism and Americanism are unacceptable to both Marcel and Sartre because with either one they would have to abandon their own ways of life, becoming either Russians or Americans. They would lose their identity.

For Christians in France, facing the constant threat of being overrun by Communists, there is a natural desire to leave France for safety in the New World. When Gilson became a permanent member of the staff of the Pontifical Institute of Medieval Studies in Toronto, he was much criticized by many French intellectuals for "abandoning the ship." Gilson's letter in *Esprit*, in which he defends his move, has already been noted. He feels that the greatness of France must not only abide in France but also be spread throughout the world if it is to survive.[21] Gilson notes the great opportunities he has in Toronto for spreading his French training across the world and he criticizes strongly the small-mindedness of so many in France who feel that loyalty to France requires the localization of things French in France. "The true France is not made up of these mediocre persons, tiresome in their vanity and jealousy, who organize themselves into mutual admiration societies in Paris and play the comedy with such self-conceit that one wonders how they can believe it, since they are the actors and the authors of it."[22]

In the play *Rome is Elsewhere* (*Rome n'est plus dans Rome*), dealing with a professor who leaves France and then condemns his own departure, Marcel seems to have Gilson in mind. Marcel believes that in understanding the actions of another we must always see what there is in ourselves which would have prompted us to take the same action. But, though he considers the possibility of leaving a weakened and threatened France, yet he still seems to

[21]In *Etienne Gilson—Philosophe de la Chrétienté*, Jacques Maritain says that Gilson went to Canada as a Christian missionary: "Il savait bien qu'il travaillait pour un motif apostolique" (p. 11).

[22]*Esprit*, April, 1951, p. 595.

regard Gilson's action as a flight. "This problem of flight has obsessed me for some time: it has furnished the theme for a play I finished some days ago."[23] It would be a good thing for Frenchmen to go abroad under ordinary circumstances when one is not so aware of being French. But in these days, when all that is best in France is threatened, Marcel feels that one is most aware of being French and, therefore, one should stay to work for the preservation of France. His position can be understood through his consideration of the Jewish problem. In *Le Signe de la Croix*, Simon, a Jew, has never been consciously aware of his race until he sees another Jew being persecuted. Then he feels he must identify himself with the one who is persecuted. This is not a turning to Zionism, which he regards as an unreasonable nationalist cause, but rather it is the discovery of a mystical unity and fidelity. "From the moment a Jew from Poland whom, in ordinary times, I would have avoided—perhaps not despised, but avoided—from the moment he lives in this country and is persecuted, I have no longer the right to turn from him. He has received something like a sacrament and I ought to share it as one shares Holy Bread." (P. 223.)

A similar realization of the suffering and shame of the French people has led Marcel to support a right-wing political policy through his participation in L'Action Française. Marcel writes in the Postface to *Le Signe de la Croix*: "What has been impressed upon me during these terrible years, and what I had not yet clearly seen in 1938, is the fact that persecution changes all relationships, that it creates a bond and that in refusing to recognize this bond, one runs the risk of sinking into betrayal" (pp. 231–2). Marcel's Christianity becomes associated with his belief in France, in a Gallicanism like that of Bossuet. He desires an authority based on power and truth under which men can find a deep and sure basis of unity. In this regard, Marcel mentioned in an interview[24] that he hopes for the restoration of the French monarchy. He points out that even though the people of the Netherlands underwent a most difficult time during the German occupation, yet they, unlike the

[23]*Ibid.*, p. 590. Without doubt this a reference to *Rome is elsewhere*.
[24]January 13, 1953, Paris; also found in G. Marcel, *Les Hommes contre l'humain*, p. 32.

French, were able to preserve their spirit of unity through their common attachment to the Crown.[25]

For Sartre and his followers, there is no appeal to a higher authority. Indeed, they seek to renounce any authority but the will of the free man. Consequently, it is the free man who must resolve the overwhelming problems that confront him.

The non-Christian existentialists reject Americanism. Although they fully appreciate the American support of democracy, yet they feel that the form of democracy that the Americans recognize is the American way of life and this, they believe, the Americans try to impose upon others, France included. The non-Christian existentialists want democracy, but they see that true democracy is a government created by the people from their own situation and not a form superimposed from outside. Furthermore, they make a point of showing the weaknesses of the American system. That is one of the purposes of Sartre's play, *The Respectable Prostitute* (*La Putain respectueuse*). In *Le Combat*, with which Sartre was associated for a time and of which Camus was editor, there have been frequent references to the American negro problem. In 1945, Sartre went to visit the United States and Canada as a correspondent and wrote a series of articles entitled "Les Américains dans le souci." Evidently, according to the content of these articles, Sartre saw little more than the shallow and artificial life of Hollywood and New York and, therefore, his articles fail to give a just and valid account of American life. Concerning New York, he writes of the poverty, the wrecks of men in the Bowery and of the mad search for pleasure in New York nightlife.[26] His impressions are no more profound than those which Parisians receive of Americans on a gay holiday in Paris. In any case, Sartre finds many faults with American democracy and will in no case allow it to be imposed upon his life in France.

Sartre is much more sympathetic to Communism. The majority of those who fought with him in the Resistance were Communists. Furthermore, their atheism and materialism are held in common. In reality, non-Christian existentialism may be regarded as a Com-

[25]Marcel, *Les Hommes contre l'humain*, pp. 30–31.
[26]*Le Combat*, February 5, 1945.

munist heresy. Its chief distinguishing point is the fact of self-consciousness as evidence of the human freedom which is not to be betrayed by Party affiliations.

In *Humanisme et Terreur*, a discussion of Communism, Merleau-Ponty distinguishes between pure principle and the actual political situation and proposes to deal with Communism not on the level of principles but on that of humanity. He takes this approach as a result of his experience in the Resistance movement "where the risk is complete because the final meaning of decisions taken depends upon a conjecture which is not entirely knowable" (p. xiii). If Communism led to world revolution in which classes and exploitation disappeared along with the causes of war and decadence, then everyone would be a Communist—but is this so? Man is faced with a dilemma. If he uses no violence, then he succumbs to the powers that be. If he uses violence, then he succumbs to the powers of violence. By violence, Marx wanted to seize the human future and he thought he found the means in proletarian violence because he felt that by this means all humanity would eventually be encompassed. But what of Russia now? The proletariat plays an insignificant part in the Party Congress. The Marxist dialectic has been replaced by a scientific rationalism. Merleau-Ponty feels that the gulf between what the Communists think and what they write is greater because of the gulf between what they wish to do and what they actually do.

The value in Marxism is its criticism of capitalism.[27] But in Russia "one cannot be anti-communist, nor can one be communist."[28] The passage from Marxist formal freedom to real freedom has not been made. Furthermore, the Communist policies present frequent contradictions. In a conference at Geneva in 1946, they criticized formal democracy and then asked eastern intellectuals to revive the same democratic ideas they said were dead. Then there is the contradiction of a party which believes in revolution yet co-operates in the French government. The Communists seem to seek unity only with weak groups which they can dominate and they refuse to collaborate intellectually with any movement (in-

[27]M. Merleau-Ponty, *Humanisme et terreur*, p. xvii.
[28]*Ibid.*, p. xvii.

cluding non-Christian existentialism) of which they do not have control. Merleau-Ponty challenges the Communists to realize that all the world is not communist, and though there may be many bad reasons for not being so, there are also some good ones.

The non-Christian existentialists find their mission in France to be one of mediation between Communism on the one hand and Americanism on the other. In fulfilling it, they seek to restore the universal level of humanity, exactly the ideal of Karl Marx. They believe the Communists have betrayed this ideal in becoming just another faction in the historical dialectic. "We are in France and we cannot confuse our future with that of the U.S.S.R. or with that of the American empire."[29] In Hegelian terms, the non-Christian existentialists seek to present a synthesis for the thesis of Americanism and the antithesis of Communism, whereas the Christian existentialists would say that the synthesis exists already in God and it is up to men to realize this synthesis in their daily concrete experience.

However, the non-Christian existentialists feel that the Christians are not justified in establishing the basis of the human synthesis by an appeal beyond the human level to the authority of God. Indeed, they feel that an appeal to a higher authority will not establish human solidarity but upset it. They affirm that a politic must be justified not only by its good intentions, but also by its success; yet not every politic that succeeds is good. Though they may recognize good intentions of Christians, they feel that history demonstrates that the Church has not united man but has done the opposite. Luther's appeal to God, "Hier stehe ich, ich kann nicht anders," was no guarantee of the efficacy of his actions, but rather it disturbed Christian solidarity itself. The Christian morality introduced into the sphere of politics, which is essentially immoral, simply does not fit because love and forgiveness, according to the non-Christian existentialists, permit no advance in human justice. The result is that, where Christianity is practised, a pact is made with the infernal powers for the preservation of order. People choose God (Christian or of some other religion) and, loving the emphasis on sin in religion, they are easy prey for propaganda and

29*Ibid.*, p. xxv.

war. Merleau-Ponty denies that any man has rights. Rather man is thrown into an adventure the happy issue of which is not guaranteed and the agreement of human minds and wills is not assured in principle. Such an attitude reflects the living spirit of the French Enlightenment from the days of the French Revolution.

The non-Christian existentialists criticize Communism most strongly for its enslavement of men in the present in order to attain a future goal. The experience of the Resistance is compared to that of the Russian Revolution in which the hitherto uncontested was at last questioned. The French disaster separated formal legality and moral authority and a new opportunity was found for a social contract. Those not fit for responsibility sought formal legality in Vichy; but, though the Vichy government restored order, the time was not forgotten "when reason was violence and freedom was not honoured."[30] After the war, there was a tendency among Frenchmen to say that Laval and Pétain were evil incarnate in order to justify punishing collaborators. However, the non-Christian existentialists deny the existence of absolute good or evil, and feel that there is no neutrality in history nor is there any absolute objectivity. Thus, though all existentialists are agreed that collaborators should be punished, still they cannot be utterly condemned. Thus the Communists who take shelter in the historical dialectic are suddenly found to be instigators of a crime of inhumanity to which history has directed them, but 'they cannot seek excuses nor be discharged from a morsel of responsibility."[31] In Sartre's *Crime passionelle* (*Les Mains sales*), Hugo decides to sacrifice his life to give his own responsible meaning to it, rather than betray himself for the sake of the Party. The glory of the resisters supposes the contingency of history, wherein free men face an undetermined future and without which they would be blameworthy in politics or else fools. But the resisters, according to Merleau-Ponty, were neither fools nor sages, but heroes in whom reason and passion were identical. The human element in politics and history is all important.

With this in mind, Merleau-Ponty[32] sets down three rules for dealing with Russia. Rule one is that all those who write about

[30]*Ibid.*, p. 41.
[31]*Ibid.*, p. 43.
[32]*Ibid.*, p. 196f.

world affairs in a vague and abstract way and do not try to understand the other side are guilty of an act of war. Rule two is that humanism excludes war with Russia. For France to wage war on Russia, it would be necessary to silence the French Communists who made up one-third of the voters and elected men, including most of the workers. A war with Russia would be a far different matter than a war with Germany. Rule three is that a state of war does not exist and there is no Russian aggression because strategically Russia is on the defensive. If Russia were the aggressor, then the situation might be different.

Simone de Beauvoir[33] sees in the struggle between Russia and the United States the clash of two ideal systems in which the form of government had replaced the sovereignty of man himself. The adversaries of Russia tend to treat her as absolute evil by emphasizing the violence of the Party without endeavouring to understand the ends that the Party seeks. There is no doubt that there are more purges, deportations and political abuses in Russia than in any other country. One hundred and sixty million people provide a field for more injustices; but Simone de Beauvoir feels that the quantitative considerations are insufficient. As one cannot detach the means from the end, so the end cannot be detached from the means. The lynching of one Negro in the United States and the suppression of a hundred people in Russia are both evil. Yet she feels that lynching is an absolute evil, a perpetuation of race war that ought to disappear, a fault without justification and without excuse, whereas the suppression of a hundred men in Russia must be seen in the light of the cause it serves. The Party desiring to justify its violence unconditionally seeks to prove that the end is unconditional and that the crimes committed in its name are completely necessary. The ruse of Communism is to play on necessity.

The non-Christian existentialists recognize two kinds of opposition. The first is the refusal of the ends proposed, for example, anti-Fascism to Fascism or Communism to Americanism. The second is to accept the end but to criticize the means used to attain the end. They see in Communism the danger of ruining the ends by the means.

[33]In *Pour une morale de l'ambiguité.*

The non-Christian existentialists seek for a humanism akin to the ideal end of Communism. Sartre, who claims that there have been no great changes in his thought, has actually changed his position from the solipsistic despair of *The Diary of Antoine Roquentin* (*La Nausée*) through the negative Resistance spirit of *Being and Nothingness* (*L'Etre et le Néant*) to the optimistic humanism of *Existentialism and Humanism* (*Existentialisme est un Humanisme*).[34] On the other hand, Marcel, who claims that one's life and ideas develop as a musical theme, has shown no great change in presentation since his earliest writings in the years of the First World War.

Sartre arrived at his humanism through the experience of human solidarity which he found with his companions of the Resistance. Philosophically he justifies his humanism through the *cogito*, his starting point. In accordance with the principles of phenomenology, "consciousness is consciousness of something," and, in discovering one's existence in the *cogito*, one is necessarily aware of others who condition one's situation. Man's being in life necessarily depends on the opinions others have of him and the truth of oneself can only be found through the mediation of the other. Thus, one finds oneself in a world of inter-subjectivity. Though Sartre denies any human nature (which he believes could only be given by God, if there were a God), he speaks of the human universality of condition. Every man must be in the world, to labour and to die there, and every human act can be understood as an attempt to surpass these limitations, to widen them, to deny them or to accommodate oneself to them. Any man can be understood in these terms, even an idiot, a child, a primitive man or a foreigner.

Sartre sees a danger in treating man as an end in himself[35] since no one can have experience broad enough to judge man as such. Comte pretended to make a universal judgment on man and his humanism shut man in upon himself.[36] Marcel himself sees the danger that anti-Communists may turn to a Comtian humanism in a reactionary, self-satisfied Fascism. Sartre sees that man is always

[34]See article by J. Delhomme in *La Vie Intellectuelle*, June, 1946, p. 130.
[35]J.-P. Sartre, *Existentialism and Humanism*, p. 55.
[36]G. Marcel, "Le Drame de l'humanisme athée," in *La Vie Intellectuelle*, December, 1945.

in a state of becoming and it is only by projecting himself beyond himself that he can make mankind exist and it is only by pursuing transcendent aims that the individual can exist.

This relation of transcendence as constitutive of man (not in the sense that God is transcendent, but in the sense of self-surpassing) with subjectivity (in such a sense that man is not shut up in himself but forever present in a human universe)—it is this that we call existential humanism. This is humanism, because we remind man that there is no legislator but himself; that he himself, thus abandoned, must decide for himself; also because we show that it is not by turning back upon himself, but always by seeking, beyond himself, an aim which is one of liberation or of some particular realisation, that man can realise himself as truly human.[37]

In his humanism, Sartre reflects the spirit of Rousseau and of the anarchists who had such a great influence upon Marx. Underlying this, there is a basic faith in humanity's ability to solve its problems if given half a chance, unimpeded by rigid organization. Marx himself did not believe that the dissolution of capitalism would take so long and there must be many in Russia who are disheartened by the continuation of the rigid Party dictatorship. The non-Christian existentialists see the danger that Party methods may destroy the very ideal of a liberated humanity which they seek in common with the Marxists. If the rule of freedom is determined to come, then the Party is unnecessary. But it seems unlikely for Sartre and his followers either that the kingdom of freedom is determined to come or that the Party will achieve it. Freedom will only be achieved by free individuals responsibly working for the freedom of others.

But if this kingdom of freedom were achieved, what would it be like? It is sometimes said that if world communism were achieved, it would collapse because it is only an ideal, inapplicable in a practical world of human affairs. The non-Christian existentialists find their true role in the position of critics, analysing the faults of political systems around them. In this, they reflect the spirit of the Greek sophists. As long as there are causes for resistance, then men can be united in opposing these causes, but if the reign of freedom arrived,

[37]Sartre, *Existentialism and Humanism*, pp. 55–6.

we might expect that Sartre's picture would fall back to the situation of *The Diary of Antoine Roquentin* or *The Roads to Freedom.* Here are parasitic, bourgeois characters, living in a café society. Their sole concern is for their own introspective desires and opinions, isolated from everyone else, yet seeking to force their opinions on others; in short, men trying to be gods. The characters are rather like freed serfs who do not quite know how to use their freedom. They are uneasy in every situation, timid and afraid. Beigbeder compares them to fish out of water which gradually decay and die away.

Sartre calls his humanism optimistic, but if it is an optimism in the attainment of the kingdom of freedom, then it is surely false because this kingdom would no sooner be achieved than the characters presented would sink back into their complacency and petty rivalry, meet prey for a tyranny greater than before. Since his real basis for optimism is in the act of negating, the only hope, for Sartre, is that man can find some worthwhile purpose for which to work, in fighting against evil and tyranny rather than languishing about in the meaningless existence of a café society. In *The Chips are Down (Les Jeux sont faits)*, the only hope that Sartre allows for man in the face of inexorable fate is the hope of trying.

But Marcel affirms that this fatalism of Sartre is a sin and a source of sin. The aim of the philosopher is to defend man against himself, but the philosopher's great temptation is to inhumanity. After reading Mignet's *Histoire de la Révolution française* as a youth, Marcel did not feel any admiration for a spirit of revolt, such as that of the non-Christian existentialists, but rather he reacted against violence, disorder and cruelty, just as he has reacted against the horrors of Naziism and Communism in recent times. He affirms that his thought has always been ruled by a love of music, harmony and peace. Provided that men remain faithful to their beliefs, Christianity alone can bring peace and order to the world.

In *Men against Humanity (Les Hommes Contre l'Humain)*, Marcel seeks to analyse what it is that has brought such degradation to mankind in this century. Through his experience of the German occupation, Marcel realized how bureaucracy tends to degrade man himself—"each individual appearing more and more reducible to a slip of paper which will be collected by the central agency and whose component parts will determine the fate which will finally be allotted to the individual."[38] Through the reports of those who have returned from concentration camps, he sees a possible picture of the world in the future if such bureaucracy continues.

In the light of this, Marcel seeks to find how the idea of man in the mass is constituted, above all in industrial communities, and also how the masses are held together by a dictatorial or bureaucratic authority, the basis of which he discovers is servility and terror. Beginning here, he seeks a way to human dignity and fulness of life. Although, as Marcel recognizes, mechanical devices are not evil in themselves, yet if they are not mastered, they tend to be controlled by what he calls the man of refusal. There seems to be a connection between nihilism and technocracy in recent years and evidence of this may be seen in both Russia and the United States.

Marcel believes that when one reflects on the problems of the world, there is always a danger that the self will insulate itself and forget that it is in part responsible for the situation. Therefore, the light of the self must depend on something beyond the self which is, in the words of St. John, "the light which lightens every man that comes into the world." That is truly the most universal existential characteristic there is and man is only man in so far as he is lightened by this light. Apart from revelation, the ego has the free and active role of presenting no obstacle to the spreading of this light among all men.

Another threat for man comes through his use of statistics. Statistics are useful in the realms of the physical sciences, but they are dangerous when applied to man as man. Marcel, the neo-Socratic, seeks to base human reflection on one's immediate surroundings since beyond them there is always the danger of not being able to distinguish between being and not-being. He feels there is a tendency to avoid the local, immediate situation in France either by turning to statistics or by seeking to copy ways of life in other parts of the world. The tremendous growth in population in the last century has increased the temptation to deal with men

[38]Marcel, *Les Hommes contre l'humain*, p. 134.

statistically. At the same time, this overpopulaion has also brought men a proportionately greater responsibility for safeguarding the universal rights of men and acknowledging human value. These rights are in no wise to be understood as general maxims; they are rather revealed through the individual work of art. This universality is deep rather than wide. Marcel denies that the work of art is meaningful only to the isolated individual; authentic profundity exists only where a communion between human beings can be effectively realized. Self-centred individuals and men in the mass are excluded from this sphere of inter-subjectivity.[39] "It is only in groups that are restricted in number and animated by a spirit of love that the universal can be effectively embodied."[40] In this regard, Marcel deplores the tendency to level men down to a lowest common denominator, a tendency which started with the French Revolution. He sees the need for an aristocracy of small groups of men that will serve as an embodiment of human values. But there is always a danger that these groups, animated by this spirit of love, will become mere sects and then they will betray the universal love which they have tried to incarnate. One must be in a state of active openness, "disponibilité," towards other groups of a different inspiration. This involves the self in a constant adventure where uncertainty is necessarily implied because the systematizable is incompatible with the need that animates the mysterious meeting of spirit and heart. It is the true artistic spirit which can best counteract the crimes of inhumanity in our time.

Marcel affirms that there is no human being who is in such a situation that truth and love cannot become incarnate through him. But also there is no one who has not exercised his spirit of refusal, thus contributing to the blindness, mistrust and division in the world. The responsibility of each man is to find the sphere where he may best bear witness to the truth and love of the world. One of man's faults consists in wishing to persuade himself that this sphere does not exist and that his contribution to the world will be worth nothing. A greater fault, Marcel believes, lies in the

[39]It is important to note that Marcel's "intersubjectivity" involves a mystical communion among men, whereas Sartre uses the term for isolated individuals facing a common human condition.
[40]Marcel, *Les Hommes contre l'humain*, p. 202.

attitude of Sartre and his followers: "A more serious error still lies in a denial of this work and of shutting ourselves within a nihilist consciousness of a sterile freedom."[41]

One of the great needs of the modern world, and indeed of the world at any time, is a real unity. The unity through technocracy and the unity of the philosophic ideal are unities of the human imagination which do not exist but which men have tried to impose upon the world with disastrous effect. The non-Christian existentialists in their philosophy of ambiguity, seek to reach the unity of the philosophic ideal but despair of ever doing so, because they realise that this unity does not exist. All man can do is to try to make it exist. Marcel believes, with the non-Christian existentialists, that the unity of the world brought about by power will lead to its very destruction. He seeks a spiritual unity instead, a unity which will come about through the reflection of all men upon their experience in the broadest sense. Marcel deplores, for example, the professor of philosophy who has lost contact with the world and deals only in abstract ideas; for he has refused the world of being and replaced it with the world of his own ideas.

Yet the characters in Marcel's plays seem to represent a small clique of the bourgeois intellectual group, detached from the world of ordinary human affairs and concrete experiences. What Marcel seeks to do is to emphasize the importance of human reflection on the deepest personal level and, in making this emphasis, he fails to show its practical significance. However, when so many people live as machines from day to day without any meaning in their lives and when many who seek for meaning turn to the imaginary world of abstraction, Marcel points the way in which men can come to a realization of what they are, to find their dignity as creatures, based on the world as it is, on the level of Truth and Love, where, of course, one finds God Himself.

Let us summarize:

1. All of the existentialists admit that human beings in this century are threatened to an unusual degree in their very existence by abstract philosophies, by all-powerful totalitarian states, and by the misuse of scientific inventions.

[41]*Ibid.*, p. 204.

2. This awareness has been made especially vivid to the French philosophers by France's defeat in the war and by the present tension between Communism and American democracy.

3. The solution which the non-Christian existentialists offer is brought about both by an enlightened criticism and by an active resistance in the belief that every individual effort counts and, indeed, for the individual, his effort is all that really counts. The unattainable ideal lies in the values of the French Revolution—Freedom, Equality and Fraternity.

4. Marcel works towards a solution by revealing the sources of evil in our time, and by hastening the recovery of personal value through art, contemplation and friendly association which leads to a truly existential unity of every creature in the Light and Love of Being.

Chapter Two

TIME, SUICIDE AND DEATH

ALL the existentialists are united in their opposition to idealist philosophies which ignore space and time as necessary conditions of the human existence. In no way is the finiteness of the human creature more evident than in the fact that he must live an earthly existence, and, since things in time have a beginning and an end, that he must be subject to the mysteries of birth and death. Ignoring these fundamental facts, the idealists sought to transcend the time process by rational system and they imposed a rational pattern upon the course of historical events. In other words, they approached reality from a point of view which is only valid for God.

Unlike Kierkegaard, (and unaware of his writings), Gabriel Marcel began his consideration of religious intelligibility as an unbeliever. Yet even as he believed himself to be an unbeliever, Marcel found that he could not escape the influence of Christianity in any concrete situation. At the same time, though he opposed rationalism, he found its basic rules—the need for verification, the principle of universality and the supremacy of scientific certitude —to be major obstacles in his desire to justify an active faith. Rationalism must treat religion as a matter of pure reason or of pure emotion and, because of this, either the spirituality or the reality of faith must be sacrificed. Modern rationalism cannot consider faith without destroying it.[1]

Because of his initial difficulty with rationalism, Marcel tends to extremes of subjectivism and fideism in the first part of his *Metaphysical Journal* (*Journal Métaphysique*). He suggests that God who transcends all causal description, does not exist and that the human being can only attain to God by escaping causal determination in space and time and by resorting to the present absolute of the empirical tradition.[2] However, Marcel comes to realize that the counterpart of scientific realism does not have to be idealism or scepticism. Whereas science insists on truth by verification, Marcel concentrates on the spiritual character of nature and especially of human personality, which cannot be verified. Through this, he comes to assert the existence of God as the Unverifiable Absolute which makes possible a communion in the being of the spiritual realm. Citing a development of thought in Marcel's *Journal* which leads to his concluding article on "Existence and Objectivity," Marcel de Corte notes the evolution from idealism to realism.[3]

In his earlier years of philosophizing Marcel hoped that he could write a complete philosophical system, but as he proceeded, he realized that his very approach made this impossible.[4] It is a contradiction for a finite existing individual to attempt to place himself in some ideal position where the universe can be regarded in its totality. In the introduction to his *Journal*, he writes that "properly speaking, existence cannot be questioned, or conceived, or even perhaps known but only recognized as a land that one explores; and, without doubt, is not the language itself deceptive here?"[5] To base a philosophy upon abstract definitions and dialectical arguments is not only invalid but also sinful because it represents undue pride on the part of the philosopher in his capabilities.

[1] G. Marcel, *Journal métaphysique*, p. 51.
[2] *Ibid.*, pp. 48–9.
[3] M. de Corte, *La Philosophie de Gabriel Marcel*. See also P. Prini, *Gabriel Marcel et la méthodologie de l'invérifiable*.
[4] G. Marcel, *The Mystery of Being*, Part I, p. 1; *Du refus à l'invocation*, Introduction, *Homo viator*, p. 5.
[5] Marcel, *Journal métaphysique*, p. 11.

The world of being cannot be adequately explained or understood, in terms of reason, by a finite existing person. "Whatever its ultimate meaning, the universe into which we have been thrown cannot satisfy our reason, let us have the courage to admit it once and for all. To deny it is not only scandalous, but in some ways truly sinful. . . . This is the sin of Leibniz and Hegel."[6] Marcel's chief objects of attack have been the writings of the idealists, Hegel, Bradley and, in more recent years, Brunschvicg. Of these, Bradley has had the greatest influence upon Marcel.[7]

It is in his reaction against philosophical system and abstraction that Marcel believes he has the most in common with Sartre and his followers.[8] As in the opening pages of Camus' *The Rebel* (*L'Homme révolté*), the philosophical system which some men passionately seek to impose upon all men is seen to be the cause of much injustice in this century. "It is the philosophy which can be used for anything, even for turning murderers into judges."[9] In his *Portrait of the Anti-Semite*, Sartre also opposes the unreality and evil which result from unwarranted abstraction and, like Marcel, he finds it to be the basis of the hatred and mass hysteria of modern times.

Sartre's reaction against philosophical system and abstraction has been inherited from Kierkegaard through the German philosophies of Husserl and Heidegger, but primarily he reached his own conclusions in a consideration of the imagination. He regards a white piece of paper on his table and then turns his head away and imagines the same piece of paper. What, Sartre asks, is the relationship between the paper as he actually sees it and the same paper as he imagines it? In his consideration, he turns to three different concepts of the image—those of Descartes, Leibniz and Hume.

In resolving the Cartesian dualism of image and concept, Leibniz sought to regard both in the realm of thought, whereas

6G. Marcel, *The Philosophy of Existence*, pp. 92–3.
7Marcel, *Journal métaphysique*, p. 94. See also J. Wahl, Vers le concret, p. 225.
8Interview with Marcel, January 13, 1953.
9A. Camus, *L'Homme révolté*, p. 13.

Hume turned thought to a system of images. However, Sartre criticizes Hume for collecting the series of images without considering the existence of the consciousness which collects the images. As Descartes understood, the realm of thought cannot be understood in terms of images but only in terms of a thinking subject.[10]

Sartre believes that the problem of the imagination is chiefly a psychological one and opposes the traditions in philosophy which give a metaphysical basis to thought and thereby reduce the empirical to a position of relative unimportance. The essentialist interpreters of St. Thomas have followed these traditions, making thought man's dignity, and his physical nature his weakness.

The Cartesian idea of pure thought, that is, of an activity of the soul which would be exercised without the concurrence of the body, is an arrogant heresy. It is because of this that Maritain could reconcile Descartes with Protestantism. One can go back to Aristotle who wrote that one could not exercise the intellect without the help of the imagination; and also to Leibniz who, although Protestant, has always been much closer to Catholic thought than Descartes. That is why one must not reject associationism but only integrate it. Associationism is the body, it is man's weakness. Thought is his dignity.[11]

It is interesting to note how Sartre associates Christianity with the rationalism of Descartes and Leibniz and indeed it is this view of Christianity which gives him his terms of reference. Although he sees the importance of rational thought, he seeks to balance it with the other tradition of modern philosophy, namely the empirical. Indeed, the empirical method is prior to reason. "Far from the fact that our rational motives can make us cast doubt upon our perceptions, it is our perceptions which rule and direct our judgments and our reasonings."[12]

However, the psychological character of Sartre's approach is evident in the fact that the basis upon which the rational and empirical traditions can be correlated and unified is the individual consciousness. Consciousness can be explained by nothing else

[10]J.-P. Sartre, *L'Imagination*, p. 14.
[11]*Ibid.*, pp. 31–32.
[12]*Ibid.*, p. 107.

but itself. Therefore, "the only way of existing for a consciousness is to be conscious that it exists.[13]

On the other hand, Mr. M. B. Foster has clearly pointed out, in a series of articles in *Mind*, that from a Christian point of view the empirical and rational traditions of modern philosophy are not to be united by a psychological study of consciousness but by the Christian doctrine of creation. He points out the failure of these two traditions to grasp the importance of the created order and the material universe.

The failure of modern Rationalism was its failure to do justice to this un-Greek element, the failure of modern empiricism was its failure to do justice to anything else. The Christian doctrine on this, as on all other subjects, itself includes an element derived from Greek philosophy, and any doctrines from which all Greek elements are excluded is less than Christian. It is Christian to ascribe to God an activity of will, but it is not Christian to deny to God a theoretical activity or to ascribe to Him a blind activity of will. It is a consequence of the Christian doctrine of creation that the created world must contain an element of contingency, not that it must be nothing but contingent.[14]

Whereas Sartre opposes modern rationalism and positivism for primarily psychological reasons, the Christian existentialist bases his criticism upon the metaphysical foundation of the Christian doctrine of creation.

By the rational, mathematical approach, the mind determines the unchangeable laws of the universe. Metaphysics and the other sciences amount to the same thing; for all give an account of the rational nature of reality. The material world is the unreal or the unintelligible upon which the mind imposes its order and meaning. This rational, mathematical approach follows the Greek tradition. Matter is the infinite variety; the many is the rational order imposed on matter and the one is the philosophical principle of God as the perfect being who gives universal validity to mind and who assures the real existence of the world external to mind. But then God is only an assurance and man himself with an active reason can almost attain to the attributes of God. As E. L. Mascall writes

[13]*Ibid.*, p. 126.
[14]M. B. Foster, "The Christian Doctrine of Creation and the Rise of Modern Science," *Mind*, 1934, p. 468.

concerning Descartes, the founder of modern rationalism: "Descartes discovers an idea of God by looking into his own mind and tells us what he sees there."[15]

In tracing the philosophical background which leads to the development of contemporary French existentialism, there appears a definite pattern of thought concerning essence and existing which may be summarized as follows:

1. The essentialist interpreters of St. Thomas Aquinas and Descartes have argued from essence to existence through the deductive method, in which existence is regarded as an essential property or concept.

2. Kant, influenced by Newtonian science and yet desirous of establishing an order of freedom in morality, has shown the impossibility of arguing from philosophy to existence.

3. Hegel, giving absolute priority to reason, has argued from philosophy to exclude existence.

4. Kierkegaard, beginning from existence, protests vehemently against any possibility of philosophy. He does this in the name of Christianity.

5. The fifth step which follows logically in the pattern is to move from existing to philosophy, to open philosophy to existence, and this step has been attempted by various representatives of contemporary existentialism.

Jean-Paul Sartre and the non-Christian existentialists in France begin with individual existence and in the empirical tradition of philosophy and psychology they deny existence to any rational structure in the name of the freedom of the human consciousness.

Heidegger, though recognizing fully his own finitude, seeks to attain to a knowledge of a Being that has not been totally revealed. In his essay "What is Metaphysics?"[16] he begins with two propositions: (1) every metaphysical question always covers the whole range of metaphysical problems; (2) every metaphysical question can only be put in such a way that the questioner as such is by his very questioning involved in the question. The result is a philosophy of despair and solitude.

[15]E. L. Mascall, *Existence and Analogy*, p. 26.
[16]M. Heidegger, *Existence and Being*, p. 355.

Mascall, in a review of Gilson's *Being and Some Philosophers*, clarifies the non-essentialist aspect of Christian existentialism. The incessant vice to which philosophers have been subject from the first beginnings of philosophy down to the present day has been the assumption that the fundamental question with which finite beings confront the human mind is the problem of their nature rather than that of their existence, why they are the sort of things they are, rather than why they are there at all; furthermore, when this latter problem has been raised, it has usually been taken to be a case of the former. That is to say, essence has almost uniformly been given the primacy over existence, and since essence is existentially neutral, philosophers have tended either to eliminate existence altogether from their field of consideration, or else to regard it as a type or mode or accident of essence. This is very understandable, for essences are conceptualizable while existence is not, and the mind thinks by forming concepts before it makes judgments; in addition, when it does make judgments, they consist for the most part in the comparison or contrast of concepts. There is, however, one type of judgment which is totally different, namely the judgment of existence. If we are prepared to accept it as fundamental and irreducible it will provide us with the key to the understanding of reality. The only philosopher who has really grasped this (so the argument continues) was St. Thomas in the thirteenth century; even the most ardently professing Thomists have tended to fall more or less deeply into the snare of essentialism.[17]

In his book *Réalisme méthodique*, Gilson makes clear that, in following the philosophy of St. Thomas, he is pursuing a realist philosophy as distinct from idealist and he makes every effort to point out the unreality in the idealist system. He begins the fifth chapter (which has the amusing title "Vade mecum du débutant réaliste") by saying (p. 87): "The first step on the path of realism is to perceive that one has always been a realist; the second is to see that, whatever one may do to think otherwise, one will never succeed in it; the third is to affirm that those who pretend to think otherwise, think as realists from the moment that they forget to play a part. Then, if one wonders why, the conversion is almost accomplished." Gilson goes on to say that the greatest difference between the idealist and the realist is that the idealist thinks while the realist knows. For a realist, the knowledge always precedes

17*Journal of Theological Studies*, 1949, pp. 199–200.

thought, but the idealist begins with thoughts and then he is never able to know if these thoughts correspond with things or not. "To know is not to apprehend a thing as it is in thought, but, in thought, to apprehend a thing as it is" (p. 91).

Gilson affirms that the power of idealism is based on the strict logic of the system. "It is a doctrine which can survive only as logic, since the order and connection of ideas replaces the order and connection of things" (p. 93). Frequently the idealists have sought to strengthen their systems by attaching them to the scientific method, but Gilson affirms that method is deduced from science, not science from method. In a direct move to refute Descartes who has had such an influence on Thomistic interpretation in France, Gilson writes that no realist has ever written a discourse on method. "He cannot know how one knows things before having known them, nor can he apprehend how to know each order of things except in knowing them" (p. 55).

In chapter IV of *Being and Some Philosophers*, Gilson gives full credit to Kierkegaard for restoring existence to philosophy but blames him for presenting an abstraction of faith, as the idealists present an abstraction of reason. Man is so made that he can believe nothing of which he knows nothing and Christ is such that one knows nothing of Him without knowing that one ought to truly believe in Him. One knows that he speaks, one believes that His word is the word of God. Gilson realizes that the order of knowledge is greater than the order of concept and that it is possible to know what it is not possible to conceive. The judgment of existence is an act that affirms an act: an act of thought which affirms an act of existing. Like Kierkegaard and Marcel and unlike Sartre, Gilson rejects the *cogito* of Descartes.

Does this approach from existence make philosophy an easier task? No, rather it makes it much more difficult. How rich are our projects and hopes in comparison with our effective realizations! For Plato, existence in time impoverished essence. For Marcel, the basis of tragedy is the realization that our ideals have no existence in the broken world.[18]

If we begin from existence, is a rational metaphysic possible?

[18]See Marcel's plays *Le Monde cassé*, *Le Palais de sable*, *Un Homme de Dieu*.

Heidegger despairs and says that the question "What is meta-physics?" must always remain a question. Marcel, abandoning all hope of a rational metaphysic, bases his metaphysics on participation in the mystical communion of one being with another. However, Gilson, Mascall, and Maritain following St. Thomas, feel that a rationalist existentialism is possible. The world alone can have no meaning; but through God meaning comes to creation. The key to the meaning of creation is found not in an empty framework of the mind—for example, a being whose essence involves his existence or a being such as Kant's moral governor—but in *He Who Is*, the self-existing God who in His love has given existing to creatures.

In the nineteenth century, historical determinism became closely allied to a strongly rationalistic position in philosophy and the existentialists have been particularly critical of it in Hegelianism and Marxism. Also, Gilson has opposed an absolutism in historians of philosophy who treat the writings of a certain philosopher as abstract discoures on truth valid for all times. He affirms that a philosopher can only be truly understood in relation to his historical context. St. Thomas himself wrote when Aristotelianism was the prevailing intellectual climate and the profoundly true insights of his philosophical writings can only be understood in the light of this. The essentialist Thomists have tended to treat the Aristotelian references in St. Thomas's thought as absolute, as if he were merely a Christianized Aristotle. On the other hand, Gilson and Mascall affirm that the profoundly true insights of St. Thomas or of any other philosopher must be constantly related to current movements of thought if these insights are to be meaningful, and it is this task of reinterpretation which the existentialist interpreters of St. Thomas have set for themselves. Gilson has rediscovered not only St. Thomas but also most of the leading philosophers of the Middle Ages by seeing that they were human beings, living in a particular situation and facing problems which were particularly related to their own time. Through this approach, the existentialist Thomists have brought out several truths of St. Thomas and others which have been overlooked for hundreds of years.

Indeed, all the existentialists realize that they are writing not for all time but for their own time. The writings of the non-Christian existentialists especially belong peculiarly to the twentieth century. Berdyaev begins his chapter on "Sartre and the Future of Existentialism" by saying: "The extraordinary popularity of Sartre and the fashion for existentialism are symptoms of our time."[19] Sciacca in his *L'Existence de Dieu* (p. 7) affirms that it is the sufferings and insecurities of a time such as ours that give rise to a philosophy such as existentialism.

Marcel feels that the atmosphere of the present age may well lead one to an absolute despair or to an eschatological consciousness. So many self-confident people tend to rationalize the evils of this age away by saying that these evils are no greater than those of the past. However, Marcel believes that in this age there are reasons for pessimism which did not exist in any previous age. The non-Christian existentialists share this belief. The concentration camps, the mass movements of people, the vast increase in the population, accompanied by the new scientific discoveries, are all signs of a new insignificance of the individual from the worldly point of view. The atomic bomb is a symbol of man's ability to destroy himself and his kind completely. What will the future hold? "Without there being any question of prophesying or of simply giving way to a fatalism which, for my part, I consider unlawful and culpable, we must admit the extreme possibility that we are heading for catastrophes even more terrible, even more uprooting, than those which many of us have witnessed during the last thirty-five years."[20] Even if the end of the world does not come, man is certainly about to enter a new historical era and, in this, it is difficult to speculate what his future will be.

The way to men's salvation will not be found by mechanical explanations but through the unity of freedom and grace. By contemplating the impossibility of understanding how freedom and grace are joined Marcel is led to discover the value of grace as a gift which defies any natural laws of causality. Therefore, he

[19]N. Berdyaev, *Towards a New Epoch*, p. 95.
[20]Marcel, *The Mystery of Being*, Part II, p. 166.

opposes a rational dialectic of history as inapplicable to the relationship between God and the believer. Marcel refuses to regard God's power as a mere mechanical cause;[21] for on the level of prayer there is no mechanical explanation and no automatic response by God. In primitive religions men seek to gain power over their God by sacrifices. In prayer, one rather offers oneself to a free Being whose response may not be the one requested or expected. One says: "Thy will be done."

Because there are no cases, no precedents, and no objective comparisons, prayer becomes the level of hope. Here is found the spiritual event of the miracle of God's personal appeal to particular persons. Every prayer is unique. The rationalist seeks to interpret history from facts which move by a strict causality but, by such an approach, the acts of persons lose all their true and deep significance.

Whereas Marcel transcends historical determinism on the level of the mysteries of personal being, Sartre rebels against it in a spirit akin to Kierkegaard's. In the name of a free conscious existence which can say "no" to any force which threatens to overwhelm it, Sartre affirms free existence in the present. Though one may be determined in part by one's past, yet the free consciousness can always reject its past in the present, with the intent of imposing a new project on the future. In fact, a consciousness with a realization of its possibilities in the present is in revolt against its past. Thus Mathieu in the *Age of Reason* breaks a 3,000-year-old vase and afterwards thinks: "I did it, and I felt quite proud, freed from the world, without ties or kin or origins, a stubborn little excrescence that had burst the terrestrial crust."

In the face of historical determinism and the stress of the present age, Sartre recognizes outside of the individual consciousness no source to which one may appeal. On the other hand, Marcel believes that the self whose outlook is restricted to the realm of space and time cannot but become a prisoner of the senses and of the customs and prejudices of the world. He seeks, therefore, to make people realize that the ego in space and time is not the true ego. Only in

[21]Marcel, *Journal métaphysique*, p. 258.

the ego of love and prayer can the eschatological consciousness grow. The self should not prophesy when the world's destiny will be fulfilled but prepare for the event; and the preparation should be made not in mourning but in joy, as a response to an appeal which becomes more and more distinct.

Since for Sartre there is no recourse for men beyond space and time, time becomes one of the most noteworthy symbols of man's finitude and anguish in a meaningless world. As Simone de Beauvoir concludes her novel, significantly called *All Men are Mortal* (*Tous les hommes sont mortels*): "It was when the hour began to strike from the tower that she uttered the first cry" (p. 359). Human existence is completely coloured by history. "Everything which is moulded by human hands is at the same time carried away by the flux and reflux of history, formed anew by each new minute, and it causes around it a thousand unforeseen repercussions."[22]

The existing self finds that time has three dimensions, past, present and future. The past is what determines the human individual and gives him an essence, but the self always escapes the past by virtue of the present and the future. It is only at the moment of death that the self is no more than its past and therefore is defined by it. Sartre suggests that, in so far as the past defines the self, it can be sorted into a series of objectively determinable facts, but Marcel believes that the past cannot be so reduced. The climate of the age always affects the one who seeks to judge history and "this historically conditioned attitude is something which, for all of us, is quite inescapable."[23] A dehistoricized attitude is an abstraction because no one can escape from his local, temporal and personal circumstances. Rather the past must be approached like a work of art to which we must open ourselves, and make it our own, if it is to be truly meaningful.

Sartre defines the present as the infinitesimal instant, the nothingness, between the future which is not yet and the past which is no more. Yet only the present is. The present is not what it is (past) and is what it is not (future). It is this negation which

[22]S. de Beauvoir, *Pyrrhus et Cinéas*, p. 52.
[23]Marcel, *The Mystery of Being*, Part I, p. 160.

the individual consciousness brings into the world and consequently, it is the individual consciousness which brings the present into the world.

Also it brings the future into the world by means of the imagination and the will. Sartre agrees with Heidegger when he says that the human existence is always infinitely more than it would be if one limited it to the pure present because the future entertains all one's possibilities.

Because the human existence discovers itself to be trapped on the slippery ladder of time, there is always the tendency to escape, to fall off by committing suicide. T. G. Masaryk, in *Modern Man and Religion*, writes that suicide is a peculiar problem of the modern world. Furthermore, he believes that the temptation to suicide is greater in countries where traditional religion has been undermined by modern philosophy and science, as in France. Man is left in uncertainty and despondency about the basic issues of life in a society where contemplation is forgotten. He writes:

Is there a God?—We do not know. Is there a soul?—We do not know. Is there a life after death?—We do not know. Is there any purpose in life?—We do not know. Why am I living?—We do not know. Am I living, do I really exist?—We do not know. What then do we know? Is it possible for us to know anything at all?—We do not know. And this systematic "We do not know" is called science! And people clap their hands above their heads and cry exultantly: "The progress of the human mind is incomprehensible. We no longer need even faith in God, for science has observed that water boiling in a pot lifts the lid, and that rubbed resin attracts straw. . . ."[24]

In a world which leads to such despondency and uncertainty, death has come to mean a longed-for release.

Sartre believes that the temptation to suicide is very strong for the free man who realizes what tremendous responsibilities he has in such an inhuman world where God does not exist. Furthermore, men who find themselves abandoned, existing but through no choice of their own, must choose whether they will continue to

[24]T. G. Masaryk, *Modern Man and Religion*, p. 28. This work was originally written in 1896–8, but it was republished in 1938. Though written over fifty years ago, it may be regarded as a prophetic work which has a direct bearing on the contemporary human situation.

exist or deny their existence by committing suicide. Man, who introduces nothingness into being, must at some time consider the possibility of introducing complete nothingness into his own being —that is, suicide.[25] The moment when one considers suicide, one feels fear and giddiness. Fear is fear of the unknown state of death wherein the life and being of the self are destroyed. Giddiness is the anguish by which the self defies its own reactions to the situation. In fear the self faces suicide and in anguish the self decides to remain alive. Though the temptation to suicide provokes fear, it also offers a chance for the self to escape from its ambiguities of mind and body, and of past, present and future. Mathieu considers suicide in *The Reprieve* (pp. 326f.):

He clutched the stone with both hands and leaned over the water. A plunge, and the water would engulf him, his freedom would be transmuted into water. Rest at last—and why not? This obscure suicide would also be an absolute, a law, a choice, and a morality, all of them complete. A unique, unmatchable act, a lightning-flash would light up the bridge and the Seine. He need only lean a little further over, but he would have made his choice for all eternity. He leaned over, but his hands still clutched the stone, and bore the whole weight of his body. Why not? He had no special reason for letting himself drop, nor any reason for not doing so. And the act was there, before him, in the black water, a presentiment of his future. All hawsers cut, nothing now could hold him back: here was his freedom, and how horrible it was! Deep down within him he felt his heart throbbing wildly: one gesture, the mere unclasping of his hands, and I would have been Mathieu. An effluence from the river bemused his senses: sky and bridge dissolved: nothing remained but himself and the water: it heaved up to him and rippled round his dangling legs. The water, where his future lay. At the moment, it is true, I'm going to kill myself. Suddenly he decided not to do it. He decided: it shall merely be a trial. Then he was again on his feet and walking on, gliding over the crest of a dead star. Next time, perhaps.

It is in *The Myth of Sisyphus* of Albert Camus that the problem of suicide is given the most serious consideration. This work begins with the sentence: "There is only one truly serious philosophic problem: that is suicide. To judge that life is or is not worth living, is to reply to the fundamental question of philosophy." Camus wrote

[25]J.-P. Sartre, *L'Etre et le Néant*, pp. 58 f.

this in 1942 during the German occupation of France. Then, there was a strong temptation for many Frenchmen in moments of deepest despair to commit suicide, and Camus hoped to bring a new hope to such people. He affirms that suicide is not the answer. Suicide is merely a form of escape. The leap into the water is regarded as comparable to the leap into the faith of Kierkegaard or Jaspers. Camus believes that, when the world appears to be most absurd, then man can realize that the absurdity depends upon his judgment of absurdity. Yet when man judges the world to be absurd, he must also have an idea of what the world would be like if it were not absurd. Camus gives hope by saying that it depends upon man to bring meaning into the world.

For Sartre also, though there is always the possibility and, indeed, the temptation to suicide, suicide is not the answer. To commit suicide is to end one's life—the only thing of which one is master. Furthermore, the act of suicide, being an act of one's life, requires a meaning which the future alone can supply. However, suicide being the last act refuses a future and thus this act would remain totally undetermined. "Suicide is an absurdity which makes my life sink down into the absurd."[26] To commit suicide is to destroy all the projects one has tried to impose on the world.

Marcel writes that considerations of death, suicide and betrayal form a large and essential part of his writings and any philosopher who refuses to consider these is guilty of the worst kind of betrayal.[27] It is through suffering and the trials of life that one can reach the heights, because through suffering one may be led into a far deeper insight into the nature of reality and to an appreciation of the sufferings of others. However, to abandon oneself to suffering is to abandon oneself to absurdity.

At this point Marcel draws a distinction between suicide and sacrifice. The person who sacrifices his life gives all he has for a cause beyond himself. He makes himself totally available to a superior reality and, in doing so, he has recognized his being to be beyond his life, in an ontological hope. On the other hand, the person who commits suicide is one who denies his availability to others. "Suicide is essentially a refusal; a resignation. Sacrifice is

[26]Ibid., p. 624.
[27]Marcel, Du refus à l'invocation, p. 100.

essentially a union."[28] Whether he believes in eternal life or not, the one who sacrifices his life is acting as if he did believe in it, whereas the one who commits suicide is acting as if he did not believe. Yet philosophy cannot be based on an "as if" and, indeed, Marcel affirms that nothing can show us less the worth of a person than his opinions. He wonders whether atheistic justification, which the unbeliever seeks to give for his sacrifice, does not, in fact, prove the very truth that the unbeliever was seeking to deny.

The fact which brings man most acutely to an awareness of his own finiteness and of his captivity in a world of space and time is the fact of death, and death is a major consideration for both Christian and non-Christian existentialists. In *Sein und Zeit* Heidegger affirms that "Being unto death" is the essential characteristic of the human existence. At the moment of death, life stands as a completed whole and then sinks into nothingness. In his work *Le Problème de la mort chez M. Heidegger et J.-P. Sartre,* R. Jolivet notes the distinction between Heidegger and Sartre with respect to the problem of death. For Heidegger, death is full of logical significance and, indeed, determines the whole meaning of the human existence. On the other hand, Sartre affirms that death, being an existential fact like birth, can have no logical significance. Death like birth is absurd because there is no logical justification for it, and therefore death cannot be something personal but merely an absurd force which overtakes the self. This tendency to ignore the fact of death in Sartre's writings is an example of the psychological character of his philosophy as distinct from the more ontological approach of Heidegger.

However, it is interesting to note that Simone de Beauvoir seems to give greater emphasis to the influence of death on human existence. The death of her dearest friend, as recorded in her autobiography, *The Memoirs of a Dutiful Daughter (Mémoires d'une jeune fille rangée),* may be the reason for this. She writes in *Existentialisme et la sagesse des nations*: "Since every man dies, since everyone finally comes to an end, no other happening has so much importance; one would be at fault either to hope or to despair" (p. 32–3). Again she writes in *Pour une morale de l'ambiguité*: "Every living movement is a slipping towards death"

[28]*Ibid.,* p. 106.

(p. 177). The human being is characterized as a "small fly, scum, an ant until death."[29] In *Le Sang des autres* (p. 12), she pictures the death of a friend as something concrete and personal. "It is not my death. I shut my eyes, I remain motionless, but it is myself that I remember and her death enters my life: but I do not enter her death." When another person dies, the relationship with that person is forever solidified. Thus, in De Beauvoir's novel *She Came to Stay* (*l'Invitée*), the fact that Françoise poisons Xavière solidifies their rival relationship and Xavière's power over Françoise in life is in death made certain for eternity. The death of the other person is not a solution to human jealousies.

However, according to Sartre, it is necessary to notice the absurd character of death because it is always possible; yet the exact moment when it will come is never known. A man preparing for death might resolve to be brave and then find he has only an attack of 'flu. Sartre notes Christian wisdom in preparing for a death which might come at any hour.

Human life is a "reprieve" between birth and death. In death, I become a part of the meaningless and indiscernible mass of being, like any other physical object. "To be forgotten is in fact to be apprehended resolutely and for always as an element merged in a mass, it is certainly not to be annihilated but it is to take one's personal existence to be constituted with others in a collective existence."[30] Thus Sartre writes of Mathieu's attitude in *Iron in the Soul*: "Mathieu looked at him and did not look at the dead man; the dead person no longer mattered."[31] And, therefore, he concludes that "it is absurd that we were born, it is absurd that we shall die."[32]

In his consideration of death, Marcel seeks to find his way between what he regards as two false approaches. Spiritualists seek to deny gravity to death, and thereby remove any real tragedy from life. On the other hand, other people dogmatically affirm the absolute finality of death, and Marcel regards this view to be more in the nature of sin than of error. He sees a direct connection between the two erroneous views because man, disappointed by the

[29]De Beauvoir, *Tous les hommes sont mortels*, p. 359.
[30]Sartre, *L'Etre et le Néant*, p. 626.
[31]Sartre, *La Mort dans l'âme*, p. 101.
[32]Sartre, *L'Etre et le Néant*, p. 631.

consolation of pseudo-spiritualism, is apt to turn to absolute despair. We must have the courage to face the fact, especially in this age, that we are surrounded by possible sources of despair. If men in this age come to regard life as worthless, how much more will they come to regard life after death as absurd? Marcel records that, at the Philosophical Congress of 1937, Brunschvicg accused him of putting too much emphasis on his own death. Marcel replied that the question should be put on a different plane—that is, the eternal value of the loving relationship among persons. In a mechanistic universe, death is only the wearing out of a machine, but our universe is not a machine as yet, however much people are trying to make it such. Indeed, "it is on the ground of immortality that the decisive metaphysical choice must be made.[33]

Yet on what assurance does the belief in immortality rest? In an essay on "Valeur et immortalité" in *Homo viator*, Marcel asserts that the spirit of truth is to be identified with the spirit of fidelity and love. Furthermore, "value can be thought of as reality only if it is referred to the consciousness of an immortal destiny" (p. 211). In speaking of values and of immortality, there is always a great danger that the words will be reduced to mere abstract ideas. Yet Marcel constantly emphasizes that one is not to be so deceived by using words which inevitably fall short of the reality which they signify. He refuses to admit that a real survival of persons can be conceived without appeal to transcendence. "There is no human love worthy of the name which does not constitute in the eyes of him who thinks of it, at the same time an assurance and a seed of immortality; but on the other hand, it is undoubtedly not possible to think of this love without discovering that it cannot constitute a closed system, that it is transcended in every sense, that it requires basically, in order to be fully itself, a universal communion outside of which it cannot be satisfied, and is given up in the last analysis to corruption and ruin; and this universal communion itself can rest only in the absolute Thou" (p. 212). It is through a realization of values that we can foresee our destiny as human creatures. There is no certainty in this destiny as there is certainty in earthly empirical experience or in rational formulations of the mind. It is for the sake of such a narrow certainty that so many modern philo-

[33]Marcel, *The Mystery of Being*, Part II, p. 151.

sophers limit their field of study to the rational and empirical. Yet Marcel asks a fundamental question whether those who refuse to run the risk of eternity and of the beyond do not involve themselves in a path which can only lead them sooner or later to perdition? Though Sartre does not believe in life after death, it is noteworthy that he has pictured an after-life in two of his imaginary works—*In Camera* and *The Chips are down*. This has confused some people in interpreting Sartre's thought, and Marcel notes how a business man from Lille, having seen *In Camera*, thought that Sartre was not an atheist after all because he believed in the doctrine of hell.[34] Yet the hell which Sartre pictures is an earthly hell, limited in its terms by the defined limits of Sartre's whole philosophical approach. In Sartre's hell, the people have lost their means of transcendence in a free consciousness. Their life is an open book, being equal to the opinions which other people have of them. The Medusa-like gaze by which the free and living self regards others as objects and *vice versa* is now given eternal validity. In life there was an escape from the gaze of others in consciousness. In death, there is no escape. Thus H. J. Blackham writes of *In Camera* in his book *Six Existentialist Thinkers* (p. 151): "The moral of the play is not the cry of Garcin towards the end, 'Hell is . . . other people!' It is the horror of human consciousness if it could not break off, if it could not be new, if it could only go on reproducing the past, if it were really determined, a fate." In death, the self is solidified into what it has been on earth.

On the other hand, for Marcel, it is in death that a person can experience the full measure of freedom and virtue. On earth, one is always hampered by restrictions and limitations but in death the self is able to participate fully in reality. Thus a love that existed between two persons upon earth has even greater possibilities if one of the persons dies[35] and, of course, a full love can be realized at the death of the second person. It is in the realm where the saints are in communion that the person on earth longs to participate in love, hope and fidelity provided that he has not so narrowed his outlook that he refuses to open himself to the mysteries of Being.

[34]G. Marcel, "L'Existence et la liberté humaine chez J.-P. Sartre," in *Les Grands Appels de l'homme contemporain*, p. 147.
[35]For example, Marcel's play *L'Iconoclaste*.

In summary, we may list the following conclusions:

1. All the existentialists oppose an extreme rationalism in philosophy which becomes associated also with a deterministic view of history, but they do so for different reasons. Sartre bases his opposition upon a psychological study of the imagination. Gilson, Mascall and Maritain have been concerned to restore the truly realistic outlook of St. Thomas, and Gilson in particular has been concerned to rediscover the history of philosophy by rediscovering individual philosophers in their particular situations. Marcel seeks to rediscover the qualitative and personal aspects of Being.

2. Facing their situation in the present, the existentialists wonder what the future will bring. Contemporary man seems so overwhelmed by forces of oppression that the temptation to suicide is very great.

3. Both Christian and non-Christian existentialists deny that suicide is the answer. Sartre and his followers urge man not to abandon himself to despair and meaninglessness but to accept responsibility to bring meaning to life and if possible to bring meaning to an absurd world. Gabriel Marcel also urges man not to abandon himself to despair but to realize an appeal which comes to every person in an eschatological consciousness that the world can only end in the power of Being. The end of the world is not to be feared but to be awaited with joyful expectation.

4. However, though Sartre urges man to refuse suicide and to try to give significance to life, the task which he assigns is hopeless because death comes to every man at an unknown moment. When death comes, the self is forgotten as it is merged into the meaningless mass of things. Thus, death brings a measure of absurdity to every human activity.

5. On the other hand, Marcel affirms that it is in the light of immortality that the world of space and time attains to real significance. People bound by time are restricted but those who have died are able to make themselves completely available. Thus it is where the saints are in communion that true love, joy and hope are to be found.

Chapter Three

LANGUAGE AND COMMUNION

ONE of the most noteworthy characteristics of the writings of Marcel, Sartre, Camus and Simone de Beauvoir is that their philosophy is expressed not only in traditional discursive form but also in plays and novels. A question that we must ask is why philosophy is expressed in this way? It would be absurd for rational philosophers such as Spinoza and Leibniz to express philosophy in imaginative works because the subjective idea which the word embodies is reality for them and this reality is beyond any temporal process.

Simone de Beauvoir in an article in *Les Temps Modernes* (April, 1946) entitled "Littérature et métaphysique" affirms that "the novel is justified only if it is a mode of communication irreducible to any other" (p. 1154). The non-Christian existentialists make a distinction between the *cogito* pre-reflective and the *cogito* reflective. It is upon the ambiguity based on this distinction that their two methods of communication are founded. For the non-Christian existentialists, the pre-reflective *cogito* concerns an immediate awareness in sense experience, emotion and action that precedes any objectifying by the mind. This they seek to present by imaginative works such as novels and plays. The intention is not to lead people to ideas but rather to involve the reader or the spectator directly in the experiences of the characters. "That is the value of the good novel. It permits imaginary experiences to take place which are as complete, and as disquieting as real ones. The reader is questioned, he doubts, he takes part and this hesitating elaboration of his thought is for him an enrichment for which no doctrinal teaching could serve as a substitute" (pp. 1154–5). Thus there is no analogous connection, according to Simone de Beauvoir, between the novel and metaphysics. "In reality, 'to do' metaphysics is to be metaphysical, it is to realize the metaphysical attitude in oneself which consists in being presented in one's totality before the totality of the world" (p. 1158).

Gabriel Marcel in the Platonic tradition of philosophy may be distinguished from the non-Christian existentialists in his use of the drama. Whereas for Sartre the novel or play leads to a direct participation in a being which precedes any objective thought, Marcel seeks by the drama to lead people from their finite situation to an apprehension not of an idea (as in Plato) but of being itself. The participation to which Marcel calls one is not participation in emotion and immediate sense experience as in Sartre's plays and novels but a participation beyond sense experience and emotion and beyond subjective thought. This participation he calls contemplation.

Nevertheless, both Marcel and Sartre and his followers seek to define the limits of subjective thought, and Simone de Beauvoir says that the more this is done, the more metaphysics will be expressed in concrete and temporal terms. She notes (p. 1162) how Christian writers such as Claudel and Dostoievski have used the drama and novel because they realize that good and evil for the Christian is not abstract but concrete.

At the same time, the *cogito* finds itself to be capable of reflective thought as well as consciousness and thought inevitably produces a desire to create meaning for the almost infinite number of experiences in which the self participates. It is through the unity of the conscious self that the non-Christian existentialist pursues the impossible task of unifying that which is not able to be unified— thought and existence. In an effort to present both sides of the dilemma of the human situation, the non-Christian existentialists feel justified in expressing philosophy both in discursive works and in works of art. Thus, Simone de Beauvoir writes (p. 1160): "It is not a matter of chance if existentialist thought tries to express itself today, sometimes by theoretical works, sometimes by works of fiction: it is an effort to reconcile the objective and the subjective, the absolute and the relative, the non-temporal and the historical: it claims to grasp the meanings at the heart of existence; and if the description of essence enhances philosophy properly speaking, only the novel will permit one to evoke in its complete, singular and temporal truth, the original gushing forth of existence." That is why the title of Merleau-Ponty's book *Sens et non-sens* expresses the ambiguity of meaning that faces the non-Christian existentialists[1] and that is why Robert Speaight concludes, in an article in the *Listener*,[2] that imaginative works are much more an integral part of philosophy for the non-Christian existentialists than they are for Marcel.

The plays of Sartre in the French tradition are plays of ideas in which the characters are subordinated to the imaginary situation expressed.[3] Because of this, in Sartre's plays and novels, the people generally appear as stock characters who seem to lack the presence and depth of real people. On the other hand, the plays of Marcel are centred on persons.

In his autobiographical essay,[4] Marcel affirms that the characters in his plays take the place of friends he missed in real life and,

[1]In an article in *Sens et non-sens*, entitled "Le Roman et la métaphysique," Merleau-Ponty points out the metaphysical character of the literary work. At every moment, in every experience, man is metaphysical. He denounces Descartes' statement that metaphysics is only the concern of a man for a few hours each month. Rather it is the constant contact with the world that precedes all thought that is truly metaphysical and for this reason the efforts of literature and philosophy can no longer be separated.

In a discussion of Simone de Beauvoir's novel, *She Came to Stay*, Merleau-Ponty points out the essential ambiguity that arises in the problem of communication. Xavière represents the concern with the immediate, the vital, which precedes any word, and Françoise the concern with language and rational decision. Both are necessary and yet both are irreconcilable.

[2]R. Speaight, "Philosophy in the French Theatre To-day," *The Listener*, February 19, 1953, pp. 308–9.

[3]See the opening remark of Merleau-Ponty in his article "Le Roman et la métaphysique," in *Sens et non-sens*, p. 51: "The work of a great novelist is always borne by two or three philosophical ideas."

[4]*Existentialisme chrétien: Gabriel Marcel*, article by Marcel entitled "Regard en arrière," pp. 291 f.

therefore, Joseph Chenu affirms that it is possible to read some of Marcel's plays without seeing any association with philosophy.[5] Marcel himself writes that he did not see the connection of his plays to his philosophy till 1930, and then he realized that those which were not written from a philosophical motive were the richest in spiritual content.[6]

For Marcel, despair and pessimism result from basing one's hopes on a dream world of ideals and in his plays he tries to show that human beings are necessarily involved in the existing world. Thus the essence of the theatre for Marcel is to create beings incarnate, and philosophy according to him aims at exactly the same purpose. Chenu calls the working out of this purpose a movement from Idea to Spirit.[7] Marcel insists on the reality of the characters portrayed in the drama, yet he does not insist upon a static realism which would destroy the artistic style. Rather he regards his dramatic characters as superreal. The plays do not express something that the writings could not express as in Sartre and his followers, but the plays and the writings all add together to lead the reader toward the light. Because of what the light is, it would often appear that the plays are more successful than the writings and Marcel himself recognizes this.

Chenu strongly affirms the unity of theatre and metaphysics in Marcel. "If we add that, in order to be truly men to merit the act of existing, persons themselves ought to put their existence in question, at the very least to have a destiny which is not that of simple living creatures, but that of men gifted with consciousness, there will be no cause for astonishment to see the boundaries between the drama and metaphysics give way. Drama and metaphysics are two forms of a similar activity, two moments of the same elucidation of existence."[8]

In Sartre's thought, the world simply exists and to have any meaning, a conscious subject is required to sense it and to think about it. Thus it is the human consciousness which "reveals" being

[5]Joseph Chenu, *Le Théâtre de Gabriel Marcel et sa signification métaphysique*, p. 8.
[6]*Existentialisme chrétien: Gabriel Marcel*, p. 297.
[7]Chenu, *Le Théâtre de Gabriel Marcel*, p. 171.
[8]*Ibid.*, p. 178.

by setting up patterns and relationships and meanings for things.[9] At the same time, the human consciousness is only too well aware that it does not produce the world or bring it into existence, nor does its departure destroy the world. "Thus to our inner certainty of being 'revealers' is added that of being inessential in relation to the thing revealed."[10]

Furthermore, the contingency of the self is further heightened by the fact that the self can feel itself to be an object for another consciousness. A crucial problem for consciousness is its relations with other consciousnesses from which it seems so separated.[11] It is evident according to Sartre that the relation of my body with the body of another is a relation of pure, indifferent exteriority. If the consciousness is separated from the other by the body, then there is no possibility of immediate presence one to the other. If it is possible to go from my consciousness to the body of another, still one must go through all the thickness of the body to arrive at the inner consciousness of the other. Yet if animals are machines, why is not the man I pass in the street one? On his face I see only muscular contractions. For the psychologist, the existence of the other is taken as certain, whereas knowledge of the other is only probable. Sartre affirms that if the knowledge of the other is conjectural, the existence of the other is also conjectural. For Sartre, existence is measured by the knowledge we have of it and he affirms that, as the mind refuses solipsism, it builds up a dogmatic realism that is totally unjustifiable. The fundamental presupposition in the existence of another is of the "me who is not me." Thus there is negation in the constituent structure of the being of another, and the knowing subject can neither be limited by another subject nor limit it. Space separates my consciousness from that of another. It is

[9]This is perhaps best expressed by Simone de Beauvoir in the opening pages of her novel *She Came to Stay*, as Françoise enters the empty theatre. "When she wasn't there, no one was aware of the musty smell, the semi-darkness, or the dreary solitude; they didn't even exist. But now that she was there, the red of the carpet entered the gloom as a scarcely visible night-lamp. She had this power: her presence wrested things from oblivion and gave them colour and smell. She went down a flight of stairs and shoved the door of the room. It was like a mission that had been conferred upon her; it was up to her to make that dark and deserted room exist."

[10]J.-P. Sartre, *What is Literature?*, p. 26.

[11]J.-P. Sartre, *L'Etre et le Néant*, p. 227 f.

through a desire to unite one's own consciousness with another that Sartre claims philosophers such as Leibniz have posited the existence of God.

Sartre points out the errors that arise from Hegel's assimilation of knowledge to being. Consciousnesses are ontologically separated and no universal knowledge can be deduced in relating them. If Hegel believed he could overcome plurality of consciousnesses, it is because he never grasped the peculiar dimension of being-self-conscious. My relation to another is being to being, not knowledge to knowledge. Sartre writes: "The multiplicity of consciousnesses is by principle insurmountable because, without doubt, I am truly to transcend myself towards a whole, but not to set myself in this whole in order to contemplate myself and in order to contemplate other people."[12]

The appearance of another person in my world becomes an object of disintegration because I appear to myself no longer as subject but as object also. Thus Sartre says that what he feels immediately on hearing branches crack behind him is not that there is someone near, but that he is vulnerable. "I have a body that can be wounded —I am seen."[13] Yet the self cannot be an object for an object and after having the image of being object for another, the self perceives that the object is a subject. Therefore, at the appearance of another, I remain master of my own situation and yet there is a new dimension by which it escapes me. When another looks at me, I am in the midst of a world I cannot see. For example, the chair on which another person sees me sitting, I cannot see. The other holds the secret of what I am: he makes me be and possesses me by being conscious of me. Thus my being for another is essentially a conflict. While I seek to liberate myself from the control of the other person, the other person tries to be liberated from my control over him.

For Sartre, unity with the other cannot be realized because the assimilation of two isolated states of consciousness—mine and that of the other—will necessarily entail the disappearance of the character of otherness of the other. How then is communication possible between the self and the other?

[12]*Ibid.*, p. 300.
[13]*Ibid.*, p. 317.

Language is not a phenomenon added to the being for another, but rather it is the original being for another. In a universe of pure objects, language would not have been invented. Rather by language a subjectivity is tested as object for another since an original relation to another subject is presupposed.

It follows then that language is more than a formulation of words; it is an expression of the whole self because the body also takes part in its expression. "I am language, for the sole fact that whatever I may do, my acts freely conceived and executed, my projects towards my possibilities have externally a meaning which escapes me and which I put to the test."[14] One cannot conceive what effect gestures and attitudes will have, and, therefore, I never know exactly if I am expressing what I wish to express nor even if I am expressing anything at all. When I express, I can only conjecture the meaning of what I express. Yet what I express is the meaning of what I am since, in this perspective, to express and to be are one. However, the other is always there as the one who tests the meaning of the language. Language reveals to me the freedom or transcendence of him who hears me in silence.

Husserl by his eidetic reduction has made language an object before thought which could only play a substitute or secondary role in the process of communication. By regarding language in such a way or by accepting a conventional language, there is an inevitable loss in fruitfulness of expression. On the other hand, Merleau-Ponty affirms that language can become a living reality.[15] He distinguishes between language as an object of thought and language as one's own. This is not to say that one invents his own language and yet the language which we are taught in youth is a language that is historical in which some words become obsolete and new words are created. When we learn a new language, we at first seek for an exact correspondence of one word with another and yet when we come to use the new language, we use it for our own needs, in our own way. Merleau-Ponty claims a new conception of the being of language—a logic in contingency, "which, though it

14*Ibid.*, p. 440.
15M. Merleau-Ponty, "Sur la phénoménologie du langage," *Problèmes actuels de la phénoménologie*, p. 93.

always elaborates contingencies, is rescued from mere chance in a totality which has a meaning, an incarnate logic."[16]

Merleau-Ponty goes on to consider what light phenomenology has shed on the act of signifying and of the signified. If language is the common act of signifying and of the signified, there is a dualism between ideas of past expression and new meanings which are created in any act of communication. Every act of expression seeks to unite the two by projection into the future. "Every act of literary or philosophical expression contributes to fulfil the wish for the recovery of the world which is expressed with the appearance of a language, that is to say of a finite system of signs which claims to be able in principle to grasp every being which would appear."[17] Truth is possible in so far as a communication in the present becomes the truth of all past experience in the movement towards greater and greater comprehension. As an experience is transformed into its meaning, truth is established which is a kind of sedimentation of meaning to the present. However, no one is able to gain a universal, idealist view of truth because the future always escapes the thinking subject living in the present. Thus the ideal becomes actualized in the present and the present act of expression becomes idealized in the word. As distinct from psychology, history or dogmatic metaphysics, phenomenology seeks to establish the function of the mind within the living world of expression. "In the measure in which what I say has a meaning, I am for myself, when I speak, another "other," and in the measure in which I understand, I no longer know who is speaking and who is listening."[18]

For the non-Christian existentialists, there can be no finality of expression because of man's historical nature. It is only in the living present that the meaning of the past can be realized and that an understanding can be reached with another in the same world. It is through the use of the word that the self learns to understand. "There is finality only in the sense in which Heidegger defined it when he said approximately that it is the flickering of a unity exposed to contingency and which recreates itself indefatigably. And

[16]*Ibid.*, p. 96.
[17]*Ibid.*, p. 106.
[18]*Ibid.*, p. 108.

it is to the same non-determined, inexhaustible spontaneity to which Sartre made allusion when he said that we are 'condemned to freedom.'"[19]

In his *Being and Nothingness*,[20] Sartre asks when it is possible to use the word "we." Is there a time when the self is not in conflict with others? If "we" can be considered as a subject, it is through a common action or a common perception. A group of spectators watching a play may be considered a "we." A group may be sitting in a café watching each other in conflict when an accident occurs on the street and all conflicts disappear. "Nous prenons parti." The existence of the individual consciousness before the other was a metaphysical, contingent fact, but "we" is only a psychological one because it is tested by a particular consciousness only and because all in the café do not have to be conscious of "we" to make "we." To be regarded by another as part of a "we" involves the self in a feeling of humiliation and impotence as one who is glued to an infinity of strange existences. However, every situation of two persons with a third is a test of "we" and "we" becomes a regular experience in day-to-day life in the modern city, where one is necessarily involved with other people. "I thrust myself into the great human stream, which, without ceasing and as long as there has been a metro, flows into the passage-ways of the station 'La Motte-Picquet–Grenelle'"[21] Sartre affirms that such an experience of humanity is psychological not ontological and implies no real unification of one individual consciousness with another. Rather it is through the solitary conscious act that the self recognizes the existence of the other and establishes a dialogue with the other. The essence of connection between consciousnesses is conflict because the individual consciousness alone is transcendent to the world. The word "we" is essentially my word and all meaning essentially belongs to the individual consciousness.

In his book *What is Literature?*, Sartre presents the thesis that the function of the writer is not to communicate a truth to others, but rather to arouse the free consciousness of others. The literary

[19]*Ibid.*, p. 109.
[20]Sartre, *L'Etre et le Néant*, pp. 484 f.
[21]*Ibid.*, p. 496.

work becomes a meeting-ground for two freedoms—that of the writer and that of the reader. Both freedoms make demands, one on the other. "There is then established a dialectical going-and-coming; when I read, I make demands; if my demands are met, what I am then reading provokes me to demand more of the author, which means to demand of the author that he demand more of me. And, vice versa, the author's demand is that I carry my demands to the highest pitch. Thus my freedom, by revealing itself, reveals the freedom of the other" (p. 39). The writer's function is inextricably bound up with the idea of freedom and, by the very act of making the free consciousness conscious of the society in which it is found, it is bound by its very nature to question the established institutions and values of the society. Therefore, Sartre's function as a writer is inseparable from his political and religious views.

Sartre deplores the restrictions of Roman Catholic society from mediaeval times to the present. The literary work in the shadow of such a society has been only an inessential creation of praise, psalm, offering and pure reflection and, as such, Sartre believes it is alienated from true literary purpose.[22] The writer of such work is only a clerk as distinct from a true author because, by his non-reflective reflectiveness, he serves in every way to preserve the status quo. Sartre accuses Benda and Marcel of being mere clerks of the Catholic society and, consequently, of not being true writers.

Whether he identifies himself with the Beautiful or the True, a clerk is always on the side of the oppressors. A watchdog, or a jester: it is up to him to choose. M. Benda has chosen the cap and bells and M. Marcel the kennel; they have the right to do so, but if literature is one day to be able to enjoy its essence, the writer, without class, without colleges, without salons, without excess of honours, and without indignity, will be thrown into the world, among men, and the very notion

[22]If Christianity were a purely rational system of philosophy which was revealed in terms of matter and form, then the work of praise and thanksgiving would be sheer nothingness and meaninglessness before absolute determinism. On the other hand, if the Christian existentialist is correct in maintaining the precedence of being and existing to any categories of form and matter, then the act of praise and thanksgiving, the act of worship, is the most existential act of all wherein the creature freely recognizes his total dependence on the one who makes him. Sartre's criticisms of Marcel and Christianity in general fall away because he falsely and idealistically accepts his idea of Christianity to be what Christianity really is. Christianity is not an ideology: Christianity *is!*

of clerkship will appear inconceivable. The spiritual, moreover, always rests upon an ideology, and ideologies are freedom when they are being made and oppression when they are made.[23]

In the nineteenth century and even as late as the First World War, there was an excuse for idealistic complacency, but in the days of the Second World War, and since then, horror and misery have become everyday occurrences. One may dream of the utopia of a classless society and even work to that end. However, if in previous days the average situations in which men lived led to a Romantic literature of the natural man, in the time of the Resistance, men had to make a decision between abjection and heroism. Humanity was a thin flame kept alive in the heart of each resister. Therefore, Sartre concludes that the literature of this age must be one of extreme situations and he writes: "What are Camus, Malraux, Koestler, etc., now producing if not a literature in extreme situations? Their characters are at the height of power or in prison cells, on the eve of death, or of being tortured or of killing. Wars, coups d'état, revolutionary action, bombardments, massacres. There you have their everyday life. On every page, in every line, it is always the whole man who is in question."[24] This literature of extreme situations is perhaps nowhere more clearly seen than in Sartre's own

[23]Sartre, What is Literature?, p. 117. By Sartre's restricted phenomenological method, the only authority that is recognized is that of the individual consciousness and consequently any authority beyond this, Sartre feels, is the result of a false universalizing of this individual consciousness into an idealist structure. Furthermore, that Christianity has only too frequently been presented in an idealist way is all too true and in reaction against such a presentation. Sartre's criticisms are justified. In the measure in which Marcel's writings have been negative against idealism or against Sartre, he himself does appear to be a clerk of such a system. There is a tension for Marcel, as indeed there is a tension for any Christian, to protect the beliefs which he has against abuse and denial and at the same time, for that part of him and others that is unbelieving, to preserve the freedom needed to find the light. Camus writes of this tension in Marcel (Actuelles, p. 215) in a talk to some Dominicans on the unbeliever and the Christian. "I believe that M. Gabriel Marcel would be better off to leave in peace the forms of thought which arouse him to error. Marcel cannot be called democratic and at the same time request the prohibition of Sartre's plays. Marcel's position, tiresome for everyone, is to defend absolute values, such as decency and the divine truth about man, when the immediate question is to defend the very values which will permit men like Marcel to fight in the future, and at their ease, for the absolute ones."

[24]Ibid., footnote, p. 228.

plays and novels. Characters at the height of power—*Lucifer and the Lord* (*Le Diable et Le Bon Dieu*); in prison cells—*The Wall* (*Le Mur*) or *Men without Shadows* (*Morts sans sépulture*); on the eve of death or torture or killing, wars, *coups d'état*, revolutionary action, bombardments, massacres—*The Roads to Freedom* (especially, *Iron in the Soul*), *Crime Passionelle*, *The Respectable Prostitute*, or *The Flies*. These are the experiences of existence which precede essence and which defy any conceptualization or presentation in rational terms. It is a metaphysic of such human situations as these that men face in this present revolutionary age, and which Sartre believes can only be expressed in a literary work.

According to Marcel, no matter what the situation, be it extreme or quite simple and ordinary, its ultimate significance can only be found through an appeal to a transcendent reality, and he questions under what conditions the self can make this appeal. Marcel ignores the question of language as such in favour of a discussion on the preliminary condition of communication. If the self is too absorbed in itself, its sensations and its preoccupations, it will be impossible to blend with the message of the other.[25] Marcel believes that to receive communications persons must be in a state of availability ("disponibilité") analogous to the state of the senses prepared to receive sense experience of the other. As freely as people are able to see one another, so must their minds be open to one another.

In a meditation on the verb "recevoir," Marcel concludes that this verb must not be taken as a synonym of mere submission.[26] For Descartes, the state of receiving was considered as the passivity of a wax seal. However, it is difficult to express true receptivity in rational terms, for it implies a qualitative harmony of the self with its surroundings. Marcel believes that certain experiences, which philosophers have regarded as unworthy of consideration to this time, may be full of significance. Such are the experiences of homesickness of a child on a trip or the feeling in a hotel room of being "chez personne." It is on the personal level of homeliness, "chez quelqu'un," that receiving truly becomes giving. True recep-

25G. Marcel, *Du refus à l'invocation*, p. 119.
26*Ibid.*, p. 120.

tivity is the participation with the other in a profoundly personal experience such as receiving friends at home. "To give hospitality is truly to communicate to another something of the self."[27]

Marcel believes that it is in art more than in any other sphere that receptivity and giving are identified. It is through the work of imagination that a unity of experience is discovered of which our immediate sense awareness supplies only an indistinct and intermittent presentiment. The scientific and idealistic approaches have tended more and more to make an absolute separation between one's self and one's life and Marcel sees a common element in idealism and modern scientific materialism in that they both refuse to recognize the incarnation of the self. Such an approach not only separates the self from its life, but also creates a barrier between the self and others which Sartre finds so difficult to overcome. Marcel affirms that "I communicate effectively with myself only in the measure in which I communicate with the other, that is to say, in the measure in which he becomes a "thou" for me, because this transformation can only be realized thanks to a movement of interior calm by which I put an end to the kind of contraction by which I draw back into myself and with the same movement deform myself."[28]

However, when a true personal level of communication is achieved, "we" pass from one world into another. Not only is the self in a world as one among others, but the transcendence of the self is found in a deep and tender love. Marcel suggests that the expressions "never enough," "always more," "ever nearer," best express the change in perspective. The other person, the "thou" can always be regarded impersonally as a "you," but then one falls back to the objective level of uncertainty and doubt. However, Marcel feels that in a certain sense the other person can never be completely reduced to a mere object of experience and he believes this is most clearly seen in the experience of the death of the other.

Marcel recognizes the temptation for himself as indeed for any philosopher to create a system in which communication could be

27Ibid., p. 123.
28Ibid., p. 50.

effected in rational terms.[29] However, he recognizes that in such a system there is no true communication because there is no difference recognized one from the other. Rather such a system assumes an exterior agreement of thought with itself as in a mathematical proof. Marcel affirms that a true community is possible only when persons mutually recognize each other as different, and as existing together in their very difference. "What brings me nearer to a being, what binds me effectively to him, is certainly not to know that he could verify and ratify an addition or a division that I could have done on my own. Much rather, it is to appreciate that he (like me) has undergone certain trials, that he is subject to the same vicissitudes, that he has had a childhood, that he has been loved, that other beings have depended on him and have set their hopes in him; it is also to realize that he is called to suffer, to wither, to die."[30] This bond of communication is maintained by a common recognition of weakness, but this weakness changes in the light of a common destiny. It is on this personal level that true fraternity is possible as distinct from the rational abstract definition of fraternity put forth in the name of democracy, especially in France. The idea of divine fraternity is not, as Brunschvicg and other idealists have said, only an anthropomorphism; it is through divine fraternity that an existing, authentic and effective community can be realized.[31]

Marcel believes this personal communication does not transcend the natural order but is an intimate part of it. All philosophies based on abstraction have so transcended the natural order, and depersonalized man, that the religious life is made unintelligible and must be explained away in terms of psychological urges or sociological forces. It is only where thought is based on the living, concrete experiences of being itself that any true measure of community and, therefore, communication is possible.

In this connection and by his concrete approach, Marcel affirms the great value of the use of examples, not as a help to the expression of an idea which is fully understood, but as an appeal to one's

29Ibid., p. 7.
30Ibid., p. 14.
31G. Marcel, *Homo viator*, chapters on "Le mystère familial" and "Le vœu créateur comme essence de la paternité."

inner being to grow into holy participation.[32] A concept of such participation cannot be translated into a language of outer objects; its transcendence being within and without, it requires a creative work of art for its true expression.

Marcel's sensitive soul is the soul of the artist, and the arts hold a great attraction for him. Even more than drama, music seems to inspire his insight into the ontological. In a meditation in *Being and Having* (*Etre et avoir*), he writes (p. 136): "Through a phrase from Brahms (in one of the Intermezzi, op. 118, I think) which has been in my head the whole afternoon, I have suddenly come to see that there is a universality which is not of the conceptual order; that is the key to the idea of music. But how hard it is to understand!" Through Werner in *Le Dard* (pp. 52–3), Marcel presents the view that interest in music is related to fulness of living. "If music diminishes, if music is impoverished, then life also diminishes, it becomes paltry. Without music, one no longer lives, one only exists." Marcel says that it is the supra-rational type of unity that he finds in music which he seeks to present in his plays.[33] This is especially evident in his play *Quatuor en fa dièse*.

The central theme of Marcel's plays is communion and consequently the plays centre on hindrances to mystical unity. As a result, the plays contain an intense psychological introspection into the things which separate one person from another and this accounts in part for the rarefied atmosphere of his theatre. Roger Troisfontaines was troubled about this same point and asked Marcel about it. He records Marcel's reply in his article on "La Notion de présence chez Gabriel Marcel" in *Existentialisme chrétien* (p. 211). " 'I do not ignore the positive aspect of existence,' he replied to me, 'but I speak of it in another register. Intimacy, happiness, fellowship flow freely into musical voluntary.' " It is easier in a play to show what separates persons, but it is more difficult to point out the positive life because each person is different and each person has his own vocation to pursue. This is the difficulty which Marcel finds in the drama that he does not find in music or in contemplation as such. Troisfontaines writes (p. 213): "For Marcel so delicate, so

[32]G. Marcel, *The Mystery of Being*, Part I, p. 116.
[33]*Existentialisme chrétien: Gabriel Marcel*, p. 297.

sincere, drama arises when falsehood, unkindness, pride, daily vulgarity, betrayal or false fidelity thwart the communion between persons and interior transparency."

A noteworthy method of expression which distinguishes Marcel from the other French existentialists is his use of the diary. Kierkegaard used this method quite frequently also. Marcel's *Metaphysical Journal* and *Being and Having* are written as the record of his day-to-day reflections. From one day to the next, his train of thought may be entirely different. Indeed his philosophical essays also have the character of personal meditations. Such methods of expression are in keeping with his whole approach.

The tendency is for words to become very stale; for they can never reconstruct the real experience. "Grace and salvation are no doubt commonplace words, like their peers, birth, love and death. They can none of them be tricked out anew, for they are all unique. The first time a man falls in love, or knows that he is to be a father or to die, he cannot feel he is hearing stale news. He would more likely feel that it was the first time anyone had ever loved or had a child or prepared for death. It is the same with genuine religious life. Sin, grace and salvation as words may be old stuff; as facts they are not, since they lie at the very heart of our destiny."[34] Marcel wonders if religious truths cannot be expressed in fresher terms which would convey more to Christians in this century.

I believe that there is a danger in thinking that philosophico-theological ideas such as we find in St. Thomas Aquinas for instance (not doctrine, for that is another story) are suitable for everybody in our day, just as they stand. I am inclined to say that they are suited to some minds, but not all; and that the profoundly true intuitions expressed in the Thomist formulae would gain greatly in force and intelligibility if they could be presented in fresh terms; in words that were newer, simpler and more moving and more closely in tune with our own experience and our own ordeal.[35]

It is, of course, this reinterpretation of St. Thomas in present-day terms that Gilson, Mascall and Maritain have so adequately presented.

[34]G. Marcel, *Being and Having*, p. 200.
[35]*Ibid.*, p. 200–1.

Marcel believes that his writings will serve as the key to his message. The only way that anyone else could be led to grasp his message is through the reality which he portrays. Thus Emmanuel Mounier writes of Marcel's problem of language: "Marcel while stressing throughout all his works the impossibility of writing his philosophy in coherent language, finally comes to rejoice in the fact that he can't. This impotence shows that thinking is an approach, rather than a systematization, a laying of foundations, rather than a construction of an edifice, a clearing of the ground, which is always being restarted without any progress being made. It is not so much a question of building up as of digging down."[36] In contrast to Jean Wahl, Marcel says that lives are only sources of philosophy —they do not really constitute a philosophy. On the other side, Marcel is in decided opposition to the idealists who present their philosophies as the systematic explanation and outline of the truth.

It is in his reaction against the completely abstract use of language that Marcel has most in common with the non-Christian existentialists. Both are concerned with the problem of communication. However, whereas Marcel affirms the impossibility of true communication through the use of objective language, Sartre and his followers face the task, which they recognize is impossible, of uniting objective language to the world of immediate consciousness which cannot be objectified. For Sartre language is always subordinate to concrete sense experience. For Marcel, sense experience and objective thought can only be unified in the concrete realm which can be neither sensed by the senses nor objectified by the mind. The distinction is seen in exaggerated proportions in a comparison of the other-worldly characters of Marcel's plays and the completely worldly and lonely characters of Sartre's plays and novels.

However, perhaps it is through the mediating position of St. Thomas's doctrine of analogy that the distinction between communication in Marcel and Sartre may be more clearly visualized. Otherwise we are in great danger of comparing two incomparables.

For St. Thomas Aquinas, the intellect in the act of perceiving identifies itself with the form of the object of sense experience. This identification of the intellect with its object may be translated into

[36]E. Mounier, *Existential Philosophies*, p. 14 .

a word which signifies the universal concept. At the same time, any object existing in space and time is in a state of becoming and this becoming of an object defies conceptualizing. Nevertheless, because an object is becoming, it is; therefore, it is possible for the intellect to identify itself with the universal form of the object and for the self to speak of the object. However, the object escapes the spoken word and the concept to a certain degree—this degree being the act of existing of the object. Consequently, any word used in referring to a specific object is in a sense analogical because the object always stands outside its concept (and word). The sensible species is not the "objectum quod" but the "objectum quo."

It is the part of existing objects which escapes conceptualization that is the chief concern of Sartre and Merleau-Ponty and this concern leads them to the novel and the drama as modes of expression. They put such emphasis on the becoming nature of the object in space and time that they deny any possibility of accurately conceptualizing a universal form within the object. Consequently, a word, the product of a concept, has a completely equivocal character in respect to any existing object and situation, and the word must constantly be tested by the self and the other in the way and situations in which it is used in order that its validity may be established. This testing can only be done through immediate sense experience because, for Sartre and his followers, only that which can be seen can be recognized to exist. Any words which refer to something outside of sense experience are purely products of the mind and they have no existing object to which they can be referred for their validity. On the other hand, it is just this unseen realm which is the core of reality for Marcel and for him it is only through the unseen that the seen can be understood and appreciated. In brief, the question is one of the validity of theological language.

For the essentialist Cartesian Thomists,[37] the problem of theological language is really no problem at all. Since one can prove God's nature and existence by reason, the mind can have a clear and distinct idea of God and the appropriate words may most ade-

---

[37] A term to be associated with Cardinal Cajetan and interpreters of St. Thomas strongly influenced by him, Descartes and Wolff.

quately be applied in description of His nature. Indeed, for Descartes, language about God was more adequate than language about finite existing things which could only be perceived through the veil of sense experience. However to approach God's existence through His nature is not only to make God a product of the mind but also to determine Him by the laws of human thought. By this, God is seen to be in some way dependent on His creation because His rational nature would necessarily lead Him to create. Thus Gilson states in his *God and Philosophy* (p. 88): "It is quite true that a creator is an eminently Christian God, but a God whose very essence is to be creator is not a Christian God at all. The essence of the true Christian God is not to create but to be. "He Who Is" can also create if he chooses; but he does not exist because he creates, nay, not even himself; he can create because he supremely is."

God then is a completely self-existing being who had no need whatsoever to create the world. All the finite creature can apprehend about God is that God made him and that he is totally dependent on this self-existing Being for the fact that he is. The reason why God created the world is the great mystery and it is through an awareness of the fact that God did create the world that we seek to know something of God's nature and also seek to communicate this knowledge to other persons. It is at this point that the doctrine of analogy begins.

In the Thomist epistemology, knowledge is knowledge of something. By the senses, we receive an awareness of something and an image of that something and the active intellect abstracts the universals and identifies itself with the object—all this in the unified act of perception. By this epistemology, we are able to talk about these objects. But can these words apply to an object beyond sense experience, namely God? For some Protestant theologians such as Barth, God is a self-existent, absolutely transcendent Being and between Him and the world there is an absolute qualitative difference. Consequently, for Barth any words that we use for objects of sense experience could have no relevance for God. Indeed, Barth in his earlier writings affirms that one can only point to God's activity; to speak of it would inevitably involve one in contradictions.

On the other hand, St. Thomas would say that, though God is a self-existing Being, yet the fact is that He made the world and that He preserves the world. Therefore, there must be some connection, however slight, between God's nature and the nature of the world which He has made. If this be true, then our language which applies to the nature of finite objects may in some way be used to apply to God's nature.

The fact is that Christians do talk about God in terms that are not always contradictory and other Christians understand what is being said. As E. L. Mascall has affirmed, the doctrine of analogy does not seek to lay down rules for theological discourse. Rather it begins with the fact that Christians are able to talk about God in intelligible terms and seeks to find out how this is is possible. "In spite of all that has been said by the positivists, logical and other, we do in fact find ourselves talking about God, and talking about him in a way that is significant."[38] Here, undoubtedly, is an existential approach to the problem of communication as distinct from the essentialist Cartesianism of much modern philosophy. Even the French non-Christian existentialists adopt an essentialist attitude with respect to the question of theological discourse. Furthermore, the doctrine of analogy in a truly existential approach cannot be concerned only with the problem of language because language reflects things and things reflect their maker. Mascall makes this point in *Existence and Analogy*: "This is only what we might expect in a fundamentally realist philosophy, which holds that words are not merely noises and that thought is not merely about ideas, but that speech with its words and thought with its ideas are ultimately about things" (p. 96).

Aristotle distinguishes between three kinds of terms—univocal, equivocal and analogical. He gave little place in his writings to analogical terms because most finite beings can be described in univocal or equivocal terms. However, in Christian thought, analogical terms have received far more consideration because it is these terms which must be used in discussing transcendentals and God. The transcendentals in scholastic thought, as Mascall records,[39] were the six primary notions that transcended the cate-

---

38E. L. Mascall, *Existence and Analogy*, p. 94.
39*Ibid.*, pp. 98–9.

gories—*ens, res, unum, aliquid, verum, bonum.* It is on these trans-cendentals which cannot be categorized by human thought that Gabriel Marcel focuses his attention. It is because of his concern for this unified level of being that all his thought is analogical in expression. Thus, through the mediation of Thomistic thought we can see Marcel's approach to language in relation to that of Sartre and his followers. In particular, the basis for the differences in their opinions of the function of artistic expression can be distinguished clearly in Sartre's emphasis on the level of immediate sensation and emotion and in Marcel's emphasis on the six primary notions onto-logically transcending any logical categorization. Furthermore, this distinction shows clearly the psychological character of the approach of Sartre and his followers and the ontological character of that of Marcel and, of course, of St. Thomas Aquinas and his existentialist interpreters.

The question of analogy resolves itself into the question of being (*ens* or *esse*) since the other transcendentals may ultimately be reduced to this. Being cannot be regarded as a univocal term because there is nothing outside being from which it can be distinguished.[40] We can talk certainly of two distinct beings, but these differences must be instances of being itself because "if differences were not instances of being, they would be non-existent, and then no two things could be distinct from each other.[41] There-fore, though everything that exists is an instance of being, being may be differentiated within itself by the analogical variety un-veiled there. "Self-existent being and dependent being, actual being and possible being, substantial being and accidental being, real being and rational being, not in any pantheistic or monistic sense, as if being were some kind of cosmic material, a meta-physical modelling-clay appearing now in this shape and now in that, but in the far more profound sense that every being must

---

[40]It is this universal character of being which leads Heidegger to a considera-tion of nothingness because he believes that it is only through knowing what is not than one can know what is. Being is treated univocally and nothingness becomes a something which can be differentiated from being. Furthermore, it is because of this approach that he is led to despair of ever answering the question, "What is metaphysics?"

[41]Mascall, *Existence and Analogy*, p. 99.

be, and must be in some determinate way, and—the theist will add —in the sense that the way in which it has being depends in the last resort upon its relation to the self-existent Being which is the prime analogate of all."[42]

Marcel's interest in music and drama springs from his central interest in the participation of creatures in the transcendentals, which transcend all genera. It is here alone that true community and communication are possible. But when creatures are considered in relation to the self-existing Being who is spoken of in terms applied to finite beings the principle of analogy holds even more strongly. "Here if anywhere, the distinction between the *perfectio significata* and the *modus significandi* will hold; here, if anywhere, will the classical definition of analogy apply, namely that it is the application of a concept to different beings in ways that are simply diverse from each other and are only the same in a certain respect, *simpliciter diversa et eadem secundum quid.* It is noticeable that St. Thomas does not deny that analogues are equivocal but only that they are purely so."[43]

For Gabriel Marcel the uncertainty of God's nature becomes *The Mystery of Being* (*Le Mystére de l'être*) which is found by contemplation, not rational argument, by wonder and humility, not by objective thought. The more light is shed on the mystery, the more we know of other things and, at the same time, the more is known to be unknown. This knowledge for Marcel is communicated, as we have seen, largely by means of an analysis of the faults of limited views and by an outline of steps which may assist the unbelieving part in us to share in the light. Various uses of words may be used to express this, the test of them being their power of communication. Marcel's methods of expression for the knowledge he has gained has been largely successful and he is led to write in his "Regard en arrière": "You have proved to me that my thoughts were not my thoughts alone, that they were capable of assimilation, that they could become a common ground on which, one day, a fruit would grow which I could not foresee."[44]

[42]*Ibid.*, pp. 99–100.
[43]*Ibid.*, p. 100.
[44]*Existentialisme chrétien: Gabriel Marcel*, p. 291.

It is important to note how strikingly similar Marcel's views are to those of Gilson in his revised edition of *Le Thomisme*. Mascall outlines these views of Gilson in *Existence and Analogy*, affirming that there is no solution in terms of essences and concepts. He quotes Gilson: "We must observe, in fact, that in the case of God, every judgment, even if it has the appearance of a judgment of attribution, is in reality a judgment of existence. When we speak, with reference to him, of essence or substance, or goodness or wisdom, we are doing nothing more than repeating about him: he is *esse*. That is why his name par excellence is *Qui est*."[45] Nevertheless, St. Thomas does allow us to have some knowledge of God, but how are we to apply this knowledge? "Every effect of God is analogous to its cause. The concept which we form of this effect can in no case be transformed for us into the concept of God which we lack, but we can attribute to God, by our affirmative judgment, the name that denotes the perfection corresponding to this effect. To proceed in this way is not to posit God as similar to the creature, it is to ground oneself on the certitude that, since every effect resembles its cause, the creature from which we start certainly resembles God (S.c.G.1, xxix)."[46] However, whereas creatures can have accidental qualities, in God, all qualities are self-existing: we cannot talk about God without talking of his existing. No statement about God can be regarded as in the purely essential or conceptual order because it necessarily involves the order of existing and consequently of judgment.[47]

Let us summarize the existentialist approach to communication.

1. For Sartre and his followers, communication is necessarily ambiguous. An expression of immediate sense experience and of emotion is only possible in an artistic work and even then the sense experience and the emotion are necessarily individual in the participation of the existing subject. A rational imparting of meaning in language is only possible by a conventional agreement about the meanings of words and even then there is no completely adequate

[45]Mascall, *Existence and Analogy*, p. 117 (quoted from E. Gilson, *Le Thomisme*, 5th ed., pp. 155 f.).
[46]*Ibid.*, p. 118.
[47]Since Sartre has limited existence to the objects of sense experience, God for him can only be spoken of in conceptual, not existential terms.

communication since the meaning is particularized in the particular act of expression. Communion is impossible.

2. On the other hand, for Gabriel Marcel, true communication is only possible in a personal, spiritual communion. The work of art and the philosophical work are efficacious only if they lead persons toward such a communion. Direct communication by rational language is necessarily inferior and inadequate.

3. For St. Thomas and his existential interpreters, a rational communication is possible through rational forms in the existing objects of the natural world. However, existing escapes rational language, and, therefore, all language is in a sense analogous. Language about God in terms that apply to the created world is necessarily analogous; yet it has been proved effective by Christians through the ages. It is through the use of such analogous terms that men may be led to a knowledge of and a communion with their Creator.

It would seem that what Sartre and Merleau-Ponty seek to do for the language of sense experience, Gilson and Mascall seek to do for theological language: to bring language from the purely conceptual sphere and to show its necessary relation to existing. The value of such an undertaking cannot be overestimated in the face of the essentialist cultism in much of recent study among logicians.

Chapter Four

PHENOMENOLOGY

THE method of philosophy which the French non-Christian existentialists choose is phenomenology, which has been inherited from Husserl and Heidegger, and if the approach of Sartre and his followers to philosophy is to be understood their debt to these two German thinkers must be remembered. The Christian existentialists have also, in their own way, been interested in phenomenology. Marcel developed his own phenomenological method before Husserl's works were known and he is regarded by some as a more authentic phenomenologist than Husserl or the non-Christian existentialists.[1] Gilson affirms that the phenomenological method has effected the most profound study of the human "ego" since the time of the *Confessions* of St. Augustine.[2]

Greatly influenced by Descartes, Husserl chose the act of experiencing—the *cogito*—as the object of his research. His concern was not with existence but with the fact of consciousness in a desire to find the nature of pure consciousness and what elements enter into it. In other words, he searches for the "phenomenological residium"—what is left when all phases of phenomenon are gone.

[1]See the article by J. Hering on "La Phénoménologie en France," in *L'Activité philosophique contemporaine en France et aux États-Unis*, p. 85.
[2]E. Gilson, "Le Thomisme et les philosophies existentielles" in *La Vie Intellectuelle*, June, 1945, p. 153.

Husserl finds that all experience contains an essential relationship with an object. Consciousness is always consciousness of something, but there is no question raised about the existence of the object of consciousness.[3] In this approach, Husserl is greatly influenced by Brentano's study of the intentional character of consciousness. By knowing the essence of experience, one knows the relations of objects and, consequently, one knows the objects.[4]

Husserl is convinced that there is a real world, but he feels that all questions of existence should be omitted from philosophical discussion. Husserl does not deny existence, but he ignores it,[5] in order that he may concentrate on the act that is experience, because he hopes to establish a philosophy upon which all scientific study can be based. However, what in Husserl is an arbitrary limitation, in order that he may concentrate his attention upon the mind's awareness of its experiences, becomes in Sartre and his followers the basic assumption that only that which can be experienced by the senses can exist.

Husserl regarded his phenomenology as the first science,[6] essential to all other sciences and it may be regarded as a sort of metaphysic of the tradition of transcendental idealism. Heidegger, on the other hand, regarded phenomenology not as the first of all sciences but only as a method. Because of this, Husserl denounced Heidegger for degrading phenomenology to psychology in explaining only human existence, and not the essence of things.

Heidegger distinguishes between two ways of expressing being.[7] The first way is the existential or psychological approach which is characteristic of Sartre. The second way, which Heidegger adopts, and which is characteristic of Marcel's approach, is the existantial.

[3]E. Husserl, *Ideas: General Introduction to Pure Phenomenology*, pp. 56, 223 f.

[4]Brentano was a former priest of the Roman Church and his theory of intentionality is undoubtedly based on an essentialist, Cartesian-like interpretation of intentionality in St. Thomas Aquinas. In studying intentionality, he analyses the *cogito* of Descartes and bases intentionality not on the level of knowledge but on that of consciousness. Therefore, the basic dictum of Husserl is that *consciousness is consciousness of something*. In contrast to this, the existentialist Thomists reject the *cogito* of Descartes and base their epistemology on the assertion that *knowledge is knowledge of something*.

[5]Husserl, *Ideas*, p. 110.

[6]*Ibid.*, p. 182–183; Encyclo. Brit., Vol. 17, p. 702a.

[7]M. Heidegger, *Sein und Zeit*, p. 12, p. 235.

This involves an effort to understand not only one's own particular experiences of being, but being as a whole. However, a question put to being as a whole involves the very questioner who must be a being to ask the question. Man is the only being who can ask this question and, therefore, the study begins with the individual human being in his own concrete situation asking the questions of his own being. What in Heidegger is a basic starting-point to the study of being as a whole, becomes in Sartre the matter of ultimate concern. While Heidegger seeks again the vision of Parmenides, Sartre turns to a psychological study of human consciousness on the ground that for the human individual his thoughts and impressions are the only things that really matter.

Professor Merleau-Ponty defines phenomenology in the Foreword of his *Phénoménologie de la perception* (p. i).

Phenomenology is the study of essences and, according to it, every problem comes back to a definition of essences: the essence of perception, the essence of consciousness, for example. But phenomenology is also a philosophy which puts the essences back into existence and which does not think that one can understand man and the world in any other way than by beginning from their contingency. It is a transcendental philosophy which "brackets" the affirmations of the natural attitude of mind in order to understand them, but it is also a philosophy for which the world is always "already there" before reflection, as an inalienable presence, and of which every effort is to regain this simple contact with the world in order to give it finally a philosophical status.

It is the second aspect of phenomenology which distinguishes it from idealism because other things cannot be considered through consciousness in general but only as existing in particular situations. Though one's body is always involved with other material things in the world of time and space, the detachment of one's mind from this world is put into its proper perspective through the phenomenological method. Though the human consciousness is always tied to the world, yet the way to understand the world is for consciousness to withdraw itself by phenomenological reduction to an attitude of astonishment before the world. Husserl saw that the human mind is always to a degree transcendent to the world and, because of this, the world can never be completely enclosed within one's mind. The philosopher's task never ends because he too exists in the flow of time which does not cease when the philosopher makes his observations. That is why Merleau-Ponty believes that the phenomenological method leads not to idealism but to an existentialist philosophy (p. ix). From existence, by phenomenology, Merleau-Ponty seeks essence, not as an end but as a means towards an understanding of one's effective involvement in the world. The Vienna School of Positivism only aimed at meaning in the abstract, but those who use the phenomenological method propose to use meaning as a means of knowing and controlling concrete existing things.

Sartre and Merleau-Ponty both affirm that phenomenology opens the way for a solution to the problem of the image in dream and reality.[8] The empiricists found it impossible to distinguish one from the other, their fault being to regard perception as absolutely true, not as an access to truth. On the other hand, the idealists mistook their clear idea of what makes the world possible for what the world is. In a sense, the non-Christian existentialists turn the Cartesian dualism upside down. Whereas, for Descartes, the rational ideas of the soul were more sure in their presentation of reality than confused sense impressions, Merleau-Ponty in *La Structure du comportement* shows how the immediate sense impression is more of a key to reality than the rational idea. As Sartre affirms: "Since appearance is the absolute, it is appearance that must be described and questioned."[9] The mode of being of the objects of the reason is logical necessity and not reality.[10] Therefore, the existing world can never be understood completely in a rational form; instead, the contingent element in both the things of the world and in the person who thinks and observes these things makes them what they are.

Kant had posited a level of intentionality in the ideal unity inherent within the subject-object relationship. Merleau-Ponty notes the wisdom of Husserl in adding another level of intentionality, the natural and antepredicative unity of the world and life which exists before any subject-object relationship is established.[11]

[8]J.-P. Sartre, *L'Imagination*, pp. 138 f., M. Merleau-Ponty, *Phénoménologie de la perception*, pp. xi–xii.
[9]J.-P. Sartre, *Esquisse d'une théorie des émotions*, p. 10.
[10]M. Merleau-Ponty, *La Structure du comportement*, p. 289.
[11]M. Merleau-Ponty, *Phénoménologie de la perception*, pp. xii–xiii.

In his *The Emotions: Outline of a Theory* (*Esquisse d'une théorie des émotions*), Sartre compares these two levels of intentionality by relating them to a comparison of traditional psychology and phenomenological psychology on the question of emotion. For the psychologist, the emotion becomes a fact, conceptually defined. On the other hand, for the phenomenologist the basic tool is phenomena, not facts, and by means of his immediate sense experience, he constantly relates any ideas about emotions to actual, existing emotional experiences. Therefore, "emotion is not an accident, it is a mode of existence of consciousness, one of the ways in which it understands its Being-in-the-World."[12] Sartre concludes that the existence of emotion cannot be explained away necessarily and, therefore, the two levels of intentionality correspond to two levels of consciousness which can never be reconciled but must always remain in tension. "The fact that emotion is manifest in a particular way, and in that way only, shows without any doubt, the contingency of human existence. It is this contingency which necessitates a recourse to empirical experience; this is what will truly prevent the psychological regression from ever uniting with phenomenological progression."[13] Philosophically this is the basis of the tension and ambiguity which are inherent in all the writings of the non-Christian existentialists.

The application of phenomenology may best be seen, in so far as the non-Christian existentialists are concerned, in Sartre's *Being and Nothingness*. The opening sentence of this work reveals Sartre's close affiliation to the empirical tradition and is a key to the existential philosophy that he presents in later pages. "Modern thought has realized considerable progress in reducing the existent to the series of appearances that manifest it." No longer does Kant's distinction of noumenal and phenomenal worlds stand. Things are replaced by totalities of appearances and the essence of the real world is appearance. That which does not appear is nothing, and therefore "the phenomenon can be studied and described as such, because it is absolutely indicative of itself."[14]

[12]Sartre, *Esquisse d'une théorie*, p. 49.
[13]*Ibid.*, p. 52.
[14]J.-P. Sartre, *L'Etre et le Néant*, p. 12 .

Sartre goes on to ask if there is a phenomenon of being and he feels that this is manifest to all in emotional experiences, especially those of boredom and nausea. Ontology will be the description of the phenomena of being as they are manifest without intermediary.

Is the phenomenon of being identical to the being of phenomena? Being cannot be regarded as the quality or the meaning of an object; rather it is simply the condition of all appearance. The being of phenomena can never be reduced to the phenomenon of being because each and every experience whether of emotion or of something else always requires the prior condition of the transphenomenality of being. Nevertheless, the phenomenon is as it appears.

Does this reduce Sartre's system to that of Berkeley's *esse est percipi*? Sartre feels that this aphorism is based on a naïve idea of perception. It was not till Husserl analysed the *cogito* of Descartes that it was realized that perception is seeing and feeling as well as knowing. The being of knowledge cannot be dependent on knowledge itself; for this would make the act of perceiving dependent on being perceived and then nothing and no one could exist. Consequently, both the act of perceiving and the act of being perceived are based on something transphenomenal.

Sartre discovers two phases of consciousness. The first is that of reflection, of rational thinking and of knowledge in which the self examines itself and objects about it in a detached way. The second phase of consciousness is that of pre-reflective awareness which includes immediate sense experience and emotion. It is this pre-reflective level which constitutes the very being of the subject. Here is the being preceding perception. For the seventeenth-century rationalists, the absolute was the object of knowledge, but for Sartre the absolute is not a logical construction on the field of knowledge but the subject of the most concrete of experiences, not relative to the experience because it is the experience. Because of the identity, on this level, of appearance and existence, pre-reflective consciousness may be considered as the absolute. Sartre believes that he has escaped idealism by a being which escapes knowledge and which, at the same time, is necessarily precedent to any act of knowing. The being of being perceived cannot be reduced to that of perceiving any more than a table can be reduced to a collection of images.

Husserl has pointed out the fault of Descartes who began by dichotomizing being into the two levels of mind and body. Sartre affirms that being must always be taken as a totality. The dualism of Descartes is not to be found in being itself, but it is really a psychological dualism which Sartre rediscovers in the two levels of consciousness.

Sartre turns the ontological proof into reverse. To say that consciousness is consciousness of something signifies that there is no being for consciousness outside of the need to give meaning to one's sense impressions and feelings in a world in which one participates. This is not to imply for the being of consciousness the existence of objective and spatial phenomena; rather the being of consciousness only implies, in its being, a being which is non-conscious and transphenomenal. "Consciousness is a being whose existence presents essence and, inversely, it is consciousness of a being whose essence implies existence, that is, whose appearance requires that it be. Being is everywhere."[15] The being of the world is implied by consciousness of phenomena, not as noumenal but as transphenomenal. The transphenomenal being, or the something of which one is conscious, is called by Sartre "l'être en soi" and the consciousness which is conscious of something is called by Sartre "l'être pour soi."

"L'être en soi" simply is what it is. It is not necessary because nothing determines it, nor is it possible because nothing precedes it. Although it is contingent and should have causes, for Sartre "l'être en soi" has no cause. It is simply there with no reason for it. On the other hand, the "pour soi" really is not. It is to be in the future. Whereas the "en soi" is a complete self-identity, an object, the "pour soi" is synthetic—always becoming.

However, since the distinction of "l'être en soi" and "l'être pour soi" is a psychological one, it may really be reduced to a subject-object unity in the consciousness of the individual human being. Being is then a synthetic totality and consciousness and phenomenon are the two moments of being.

[15]*Ibid.*, p. 29.

Gabriel Marcel also follows a phenomenological method, but it is a method distinct from that of Sartre and Merleau-Ponty. Sartre and Merleau-Ponty seek by their method for the unity of the rational and empirical traditions in the self-conscious subject, whereas Marcel seeks to transcend both by a further study of being itself. Sartre and his followers refute idealism because of its basis upon a non-real, subjective, conceptual field and they seek constant verification of principles on the unified existential field of phenomenology. However, this existential field is taken for granted and their main contribution is the discovery of new and valid ways to search for essence, along with the recognition that this essence of an existence in space and time is always in a process of becoming and must constantly be related to the existential level for verification. However, the mystery of existence itself, and its relation to being, they do not consider.

For Marcel, on the other hand, it is this existential field which precedes all conscious awareness that is the centre of his study. Merleau-Ponty quotes Fink's expression of astonishment as the initial stage to knowledge in meeting the existential world of experience: Marcel's astonishment turns inwards in wonder at the possibility of his own existence and at his separation by consciousness from the existential field.[16]

In contrast to Sartre and his followers who limit the field of study to the existential field of phenomena, Marcel refuses to narrow his method, and indeed, he regards such a limitation as prejudicial to the discovery of truth.[17] He feels that the philosopher should pursue the light of truth as freely as possible, probing experiences and ideas and intuitions as they arrive. Consequently, he pursues no systematic method. (This lack of system is clearly seen in his philosophical diaries—the *Metaphysical Journal*, and *Being and Having*.) His probings often follow one another without any logical connections, and frequently in the probings questions are left open for possible further investigation. Nevertheless, in comparison with Sartre and his followers, Marcel reveals some striking similarities in the experiences which are probed.

[16]See G. Marcel, *Du refus à l'invocation*, p. 88.
[17]G. Marcel, *The Mystery of Being*, Part I, p. 15.

As Sartre in his earlier writings on the imagination sought to clarify the distinction between being and being true in modern thought, Marcel begins with an investigation into truth. Some say that truth has to do with judgments, but in the case of sensations or feelings, they are what they are and escape the judgment of true or false. The reality of a thing is always to be distinguished from the way in which men's minds comprehend the truth of this reality. By a comparison of connoisseur and non-connoisseur, Marcel demonstrates that one's reality does not depend on the truths that one recognizes. Furthermore, one can have a grasp of the truth even though one's reality may be lacking in some degree, for example, because of deafness or blindness. Marcel too recognizes the confusion of the notion of "fact" in modern empirical science. There is no such thing as an external fact; the fact is given its power by the understanding mind. Marcel affirms that the great function of the work of art is to make clear the unity of these facts within the interior life. A tension exists within the self between the self who determines the facts and the self whom the facts determine. The inner self faces the temptation to arrange facts as it would wish to have them rather than in the light of truth.

What is this light of truth and how is it related to a love for truth? For the scientist, the love for truth can be reduced "to a passionate interest in research as such, and also, as a rather more remote consideration, an unbounded confidence in the social utility of research."[18] Yet, as Josiah Royce has pointed out, those engaged in the search for truth are bound in a community which is beyond any individual. It is treason against this community for the scientist to recant any of his conclusions, either for fear or for self-interest. This level of community where, for example, scientists from every part of the world find a common loyalty, and where a mutual interchange is possible, cannot be treated objectively and yet it is precisely on this level that Marcel believes the search for truth must begin. It is clear that Marcel's interest is centred on a level that transcends the purely rational or the purely empirical approaches to truth as well as the psychological subject-object being of Sartre.

[18]*Ibid.*, p. 72.

Marcel begins a search into the nature of reflection and affirms that it is a personal act inextricably linked with living personal experience.[19] Bergson's philosophy contrasted reflection with life, but Marcel opposes any interpretation of life as pure "élan vital" or spontaneity. This biological approach may serve for animals, but something more needs to be said about human life of which reflection is an essential part. "The more we grasp the notion of experience in its proper complexity . . . the better we shall understand how experience cannot fail to transform itself into reflection, and we shall even have the right to say that the more richly it is experience, the more, also, it is reflection."[20] Possibly as a pointed contrast to Bergson's system of *Creative Evolution*, Marcel calls his approach "creative fidelity" and in *Existentialisme Chrétien: Gabriel Marcel* (p. 7), Gilson notes the importance of this distinction.

Marcel distinguishes between a primary and a secondary reflection. Whereas primary reflection tends to break down the unity of experience through analysis, secondary reflection seeks to restore it through the very reality of the self. This leads to a reflection on the nature of the self which surpasses any categories of one's being. These categories are perhaps best exemplified by the questions in the many printed forms and applications that modern society requires the individual to answer. It is through a refusal to regard oneself as a number or as just another person completing a form that one comes to realize one's uniqueness and also the individuality of other persons. Marcel points out that by the type of solipsistic idealism (that is seen in Sartre's writings) it is impossible to comprehend the fact of one's own existence and the ontological relation of that fact to the existence of other persons.[21] The self in its particularity must be examined, not as an object of a particular study, but in the intimacy of one's subjectivity.

The difficulty is that in questioning one's own existence, one is apt to regard the self that exists as some object, as a "that." The self cannot be taken out of its situation and from its act of existing. Sartre seems to substitute emotion or feeling or sense experience

[19]*Ibid.*, p. 77–79.
[20]*Ibid.*, p. 83.
[21]Marcel, *The Mystery of Being*, Part I, p. 86.

for existence and Marcel recognizes that this act of feeling or seeing is only the *cogito* of Descartes in disguise. The *sum*, the act of my existing, lies at a level beyond consciousness and one begins to see this in emphasizing the *ex*, the "standing out from," in existence. By primary reflection, one tends to separate one's body from the self as an object, as one among many bodies. Secondary or recuperative reflection refuses to accept this separation.

Traditional logic inevitably treats the human body and soul as predicates, as things which make up the human being. Descartes divided human being into a body-soul dualism and thereby really made it impossible to use the phrase "my body" with any meaning. In answer to Sartre, who regards the body as an object, Marcel affirms that, "far from transcending experience, he has not yet reached the stage of grappling with it.[22] Marcel insists that his own effort to give full meaning to the phrase "my body" is a true phenomenological method. "We are accepting our everyday experience and asking ourselves what implications we can draw from it."[23] Marcel believes that in Bergson's philosophy there is a tendency to regard the body as an instrument. Yet an instrument is defined as "an artificial means of extending, developing, or reinforcing a pre-existing power which must be possessed by anyone who wants to make use of the instrument."[24] My body as my body cannot be so detached from the self. "I am my body"[25] in so far as my body cannot be regarded as a mere material object. It is of this secondary reflection which Marcel pursues towards the notion of the incarnation of the self that Jean Hippolite writes in contrasting Bergson and Marcel. He states that Marcel leads us into a mystery at the threshold of which we are led to a reflection on reflection.[26] Gilson also writes of Marcel's method: "Instead of beginning from a *cogito*—that is to say from a thought which, because it is presented as subject, as distinct from any object, will never succeed in joining with it, it [Marcel's thought] begins from the intimacy of the self,

22*Ibid*, p. 94.
23*Ibid.*, p. 94.
24*Ibid.*, p. 99.
25*Ibid.*, p. 100.
26J. Hippolite, "Du Bergsonisme à l'existentialisme," *Mercure de France*, July, 1949, p. 411.

understood as anterior to the self as an object of thought, and which precisely because it is not the self as object of thought whose openness would be interposed between itself and the other, communicates with these depths of being in which and by which we are."[27]

While Sartre's study of being and nothingness is based on an examination of the *cogito* (reflective and pre-reflective), Marcel in his book *Position et approches concrètes du mystère ontologique* affirms that the *cogito* concerns only the epistemological subject as the organ of objective knowledge, and it inevitably leads to a dualism (clearly seen in the title of Sartre's major work *Being and Nothingness*). It should also be added that, because of Sartre's preoccupation with the *cogito*, his ontology is restricted to pure psychology. On the other hand, Marcel affirms that "to present the ontological problem is to question oneself both on the totality of being and on oneself as totality" (p. 55).

The notion of incarnation at which Marcel has arrived has developed through his metaphysical diaries to the assertion that "we cannot really separate—(1) Existence. (2) Consciousness of self as existing. (3) Consciousness of self as bound to a body, as incarnate."[28] He writes: "Incarnation—the central 'given' of metaphysic."[29] It is by this "given" that Marcel cuts through and transcends the French non-Christian existentialists, and, by doing so, he reveals a more devout phenomenology than those who claim to be more rigid phenomenologists.

Because his method seems very different from that of Husserl, it is important to note why Marcel calls his method phenomenology at all. His main reason seems to be to make clear the non-psychological character of his study . "I reply that the non-psychological character of such an enquiry as this must be emphasized as strongly as possible; for it really concerns the content of the thoughts which it is trying to bring out, so that they may expand in the light of reflection."[30] Again he writes: "The point we are discussing now lies at the very heart of the world of every day, the world of daily experience with its dangers, its anxieties, and

[27]*Existentialisme chrétien: Gabriel Marcel*, p. 5.
[28]G. Marcel, *Being and Having*, p. 10.
[29]*Ibid.*, p. 11.
[30]*Ibid.*, p. 158.

its techniques. At the heart of experience, but also at the heart of the unintelligible."[31] Through his "Phenomenology of Having," Marcel finds an irreducible of "my body" and he affirms that to conceive of an irreducible is also to conceive of a Beyond.

Marcel notes that, in many cases of having in which we become more and more attached to the object that we have, we become servants of the possession, for example, farmer to farm, gardener to garden, violinist to violin. In these cases, having becomes sublimated into being. This is true in human creativity where the quality of possessor and possessed is lost in a living reality. Here Marcel distinguishes between the ideologist and the artist or thinker. Whereas the ideologist has tyrannically enslaved himself to a set of his own ideas, the thinker "lives in a continual state of creativity and the whole of his thought is always called in question from one minute to the next."[32]

It is on the level of love that the tension of the self and the other, the tension of having, is transcended completely and this Marcel calls the "essential ontological datum." "I think, and will say so by the way, that the science of ontology will not get out of the scholastic rut until it takes full cognisance of the fact that love comes first."[33] It is true that the body can be regarded as an object for the self and it is necessary at times for it to be regarded as such. By making the body an object, an intelligible setting is provided by which scientific thought and communication are possible for the mind. However, before any body is regarded objectively, it is important to have an ontological view of the reality of intimate unity in being. In contrast to Marcel's view of the personal intimacy of the individual with his body, Sartre, in his short story *Intimacy*, presents Lulu and her friends as stock characters, obvious in every thought and every deed. He presents intimacy to deny it, as he does with the virtue of love itself.

Sartre, in his *The Emotions: Outline of a Theory*, asserts that it is in emotion that the self (that is, consciousness in a state of pre-reflective awareness) participates in being and that, when

31*Ibid.*, p. 164. In a passage concerning "having my body."
32*Ibid.*, p. 166.
33*Ibid.*, p. 167.

thought begins, the self introduces nothingness into its being. In a chapter on "Feeling as a Mode of Participation," in *The Mystery of Being*, Part I, Marcel affirms that it is on the level of feeling that I realize my body as my body. However, for Marcel, feeling, in contrast to emotion in Sartre, is more of a mystical assurance. On the level of emotion, according to Sartre, the mind is not conscious of being conscious, whereas, for Marcel on the level of feeling, there is a mystical realization wherein the mind is conscious of being conscious of the total reality of the self as incarnate.

On the level of primary reflection, sensation is regarded as a stimulus sent from some outside source, in space and time, and intercepted by a subject. Yet the difficulty is to see how this mechanical action is translated into consciousness; for it is only on the act of sensing that the phenomenological method can bear. The question of the object in itself that is sensed is an ontological one passing beyond the limits of phenomenology. However, by secondary reflection which is contemplation, sensation cannot be conceived "on the analogy of a transmission and reception of a message." Every such analogy presupposes the existence of sensation as the use of an instrument presupposes the existence of my body. In considering my body, or feeling which cannot be detached from my body, we reach a "non-mediatizible immediate"—"the very root of our existence,"[34] and it is through this discovery that Marcel sees that feeling and sensation must be interpreted in a new light as a non-instrumentalist language. This existential immediate of my existence transcends any thought content and Marcel suggests that it is best expressed by some exclamation such as "O," "Ah," "Ugh." The answer to the ontological question of the object in itself is mystical participation which surpasses any explanation in objective terms.

As an example of non-objective participation, Marcel cites the example of persons "melted into a single love" in adoration to God where neither time nor space nor numbers participating make any difference to the reality of the participation. Yet participation emerges from an idea, however indistinct it may be (in the example, it was the idea of God), and Marcel goes on to question if a sub-

[34]Marcel, *The Mystery of Being*, Part I, p. 109.

merged participation is possible, signified by the existence of feeling.

For Sartre, the visible shape of the participation is all in all, but Marcel seeks by contemplation an inner reshaping. It is by this inner reshaping that the individual's will to participate in a dangerous task without hope for reward can be understood. This feeling of the will to participate can only be made intellectually articulate with great difficulty. Such is the attachment of the peasant to the soil or the sailor to the sea. Marcel believes that much metaphysical importance should be placed on the French word *chez* (for which there is no English equivalent). To receive *chez soi* becomes active participation as the guest is given a hearty welcome.

Marcel goes on to distinguish between the activity of the scientist and that of the artist. By reconstructing material conditions, the scientist seeks to show how the universe runs perfectly smoothly by itself without the need for an intruding creative power.[35] For the artist, what is important is not the development of phenomena by laws, but participation; in so far as he is interested in the laws of phenomena he misses this participation. A distinction is made between the scientist, who is a spectator, and the artist, who is a participant.

The spectator doubtless has emotions similar to those who are really committed to some action, but these emotions have no practical outlet; for they exist only in a make-believe world. Contemplation is regarded by some as a means of remaining aloof from a difficult situation in order that the self may be just a spectator. However, Marcel is emphatic that the contemplative is the true participant, and in sharp contrast to the mere spectator. Though Marcel was not active in the French Resistance movement, yet he affirms that by contemplation he was more truly working for the spirit of France than those who took an active part. In any case, he is sharply critical of those who remained aloof from the tragedy of the French defeat. "The contemplative is certainly somebody essentially different from the sort of spectator to whom a war, from a safe distance, is a stimulating spectacle."[36]

---

[35]*Ibid.*, p. 121. Marcel calls this playing the drama of Genesis over again in the laboratory.
[36]*Ibid.*, p. 122.

The modern stage and screen provide an interesting basis of comparison between feeling as mystical contemplation as in Marcel and feeling as mere emotion as in Sartre and his followers. For Sartre and Merleau-Ponty, the pre-cognitive level of emotion is the existential field which the artist seeks to express. Therefore, for them, art is purely emotional. In an article on "Le Cinéma et la nouvelle psychologie" in *Sens et non-sens* (pp. 97f.), Merleau-Ponty writes that the significance of the art of the screen is that by the rapid succession of immediate sense impressions in each section of film, the spectator is roused pre-consciously to share in the emotions of the characters in the film. Therefore, the screen is one of the best ways to bring people to an awareness of the true level of being. On the other hand, Marcel affirms that the screen presents people with a shallow and make-believe world and, because of this, it has hindered many people from understanding the real nature of contemplation.

Marcel believes that the rediscovery of contemplation may be the most important element in all of his philosophical writings. He feels that the lack of contemplation has led to the great evils of our time. "It may be that the discovery of this connection between the presence of evil and the absence of contemplation will turn out to be one of the most important results of this volume and its successor."[37]

In *Existence and Analogy* (p. 57), E. L. Mascall writes that "if Gilson's interpretation is correct, St. Thomas' existentialism is shown in his theory of perception no less than in his ontology." It would seem well, therefore, to relate certain aspects of St. Thomas's theory of perception, as interpreted by Gilson and Mascall,[38] to the phenomenology of Sartre and his followers and also to that of Gabriel Marcel.

In the first place, St. Thomas, like the phenomenologists, says that it is through the senses that we gain knowledge of the external world. "Nihil in intellectu quod non prius in sensu." Marcel, more in the Platonic tradition, regards sense perception taken in its broadest sense, as a spark to lead one to the light of truth, but for St. Thomas there is a knowledge of a real object through sense

---

[37]*Ibid.*, pp. 122–3.
[38]Mascall, *Existence and Analogy*, pp. 53 f.

perception itself. However, contrary to Sartre and his followers, St. Thomas does not say that an intelligible object can be inferred or constructed only out of sense data. The sensible species is not the "objectum quod" but the "objectum quo"; for it is the instrument by which the intellect grasps the extrasubjective being. Whereas the phenomenology of Sartre and his followers makes an abstraction of the perceptive act by separating the act of sensation and the act of intellection, St. Thomas affirms that there is only one act of perception in which sense and intellection are "intricately combined." Whereas sensation has as its object the particular as the "objectum quo" and not the "objectum quod," the intellect, though it penetrates to the actual existent knows it not as a particular but as a universal form of a specific essence. Existence then is a mystery (as is recognized by Sartre and Merleau-Ponty and Marcel). "The sense can receive particulars but cannot know them; while the intellect can know but can only know universals."[39] The essentialist Cartesian Thomists, by stressing the intellect alone and by equating knowledge with clear and distinct ideas, have wrongly interpreted St. Thomas.

Husserl sought to build knowledge upon a study of the object as such, as distinct from Kant's interest in the knowing subject. Gilson affirms that the problem of human knowledge must be approached through a study of both knowing subject and known object. "It is man himself who knows the particular things from the fact that he thinks about what he perceives."[40] Yet how is it possible for the human mind to know that particulars exist? Kant regarded that question as unanswerable and said that we could not know existence, only phenomena. Sartre and his followers ignore the real question of existence and influenced by Kantian subjectivity, they develop a psychological study of human consciousness. Mascall, in refuting Tennant, affirms that a psychological study of the human mind may be helpful, but it cannot deal with the ontological question of the existing of things. "We may agree in principle with Dr. Tennant that the deliverance of psychic immediacy need to be checked by psychological reflection and discrimination, but we must

[39]*Ibid.*, p. 54.
[40]*Ibid.*, p. 54, quoted from Gilson's *Réalisme thomiste et critique de la connaissance*, p. 186.

insist that this discrimination must be applied not merely to the mechanism of perception, which (through its expression in terms of the functioning of the sense-organs, nerves etc.) itself involves an assumption of the real existence of finite beings, but, also and primarily, to the object of perception, in order that it may be plainly understood what is the ontological status of the objects perceived."[41]

In a doctrine in which singulars exist, there can be no existential index other than sensation. " 'In some way man conceives the singular and perceives the universal'; and this is directly connected with the fact that the proper object of the human intellect, as the intellect of a being in which soul and body together make up a unity, is not being in general but the being of sensible things."[42] With sensation as the index, the problem of hallucination becomes great. (That is the central problem of Sartre's work on the imagination—*L'Imagination*.)

Sensation indicates the particularity of the thing perceived and its existence, but the degree of truth in perception depends on the proper functioning of the mechanism of sensation. Thus the truth of perception is to be tested not by analysis of the object (as in Husserl) but by an examination of the sense organs. In Mascall's example, if a man persists in saying he sees pink snakes with green spots, we are not content to ask him to more carefully examine the snakes, but we ourselves examine the man. We seek to find how error arises and how it is to be corrected, rather than where it occurs.

The senses indicate both the particularity and the existence of things. Sartre, accepting this assertion, believes that the mind must transcend the phenomena to imagine an infinite series of phenomena in order that a universal concept of the object or essence may be grasped. Therefore, his phenomenology is a nominalism, as he himself affirms in his Introduction to *Being and Nothingness*. However, for St. Thomas, the intellect plays an active part in perception both in abstracting the universal form from the sensible species and in affirming its embodiment in the existing extrasubjective being. It is the whole man who performs the act of perception by his sense and intellect.

The intellect itself appears to have two functions, conceptualiz-

[41]E. L. Mascall, *He Who Is*, p. 94.
[42]Mascall, *Existence and Analogy*, p. 55.

ing the universal and judging actual existing in the particular. But again no separation is implied and the intellect in its two functions unites with the senses in the one perceptive act.

As we have seen, truth for Sartre is the meaning which the individual consciousness makes of its own immediate sense experience and emotions. For Marcel, vitally concerned with moral aspects of reality, truth is a light or an appeal by which the individual can escape the isolation of his own consciousness into a fellowship in being itself. St. Thomas has defined truth as "the adequation of the intellect and the thing." This has been interpreted in an idealist, Cartesian way by many French Thomists, but Gilson affirms that it should be interpreted in a realist meaning in accordance with the assertions of St. Thomas. "To give this formula its full realist meaning we must rise above the plane on which the thing is reduced to an essence which in turn is reduced to the quiddity expressed by the definition. All the noetic of St. Thomas invites us to take this step, and he has even gone so far as to state it in so many words, although it was doubtless self-evident to him: it is not the essence but the act of existing of a thing that is the ultimate foundation of anything true that we know about it. . . . Veritas fundatur in esse rei magis quam in ipsa quidditate."[43]

The general conclusions that have been reached in considering the philosophical methods of the existentialists may be summarized as follows:

1. Husserl sought for a logical basis for all science by bracketing the question of existence and by concentrating on the *cogitans.*

2. Heidegger, adopting Husserl's philosophy as a method, seeks for the being lying beyond human consciousness.

3. Sartre and his followers, influenced more by Husserl, limit the existential field to that of which the subject is aware in sense experience.

4. Marcel, in a phenomenological method which he formed at a date prior even to Husserl's writings, is more in line with Heidegger's approach. He affirms that the existential field of sense experience can only be truly meaningful in relation to that part of being which escapes sense experience.

[43]*Ibid.,* p. 57, quoted from Gilson's *Réalisme thomiste,* p. 224.

5. St. Thomas and his existentialist interpreters affirm that the existential field of sense experience can be known in the unified perceptive act of the subject, but they go on to emphasize that this kind of knowledge of reality is not the only kind of knowledge of what is.

Finally, it would be interesting to consider what similarities, if any, exist between the approach of Gabriel Marcel and the more recent writings of Gilson. In an interview on January 13, 1953, Marcel claimed that the similarities with Gilson's approach are only in language. On the other hand, Gilson in an article in *La Vie Intellectuelle* of June, 1945, writing on "Le Thomisme et les philosophies existentielles," says (p. 148): "Between the Thomist ontology of which I have just recalled the initial theses and that of Gabriel Marcel, there is much more in common than the word 'existence.'" He recalls that in 1940, after he had delivered a series of public lectures on St. Thomas at Harvard, the philosopher W. E. Hocking shook him by the hand and said, "Eh, bien! et Gabriel Marcel?" Gilson suggests that after reading Marcel one might say, "Eh, bien! et saint Thomas d' Aquin?"

Chapter Five

EXISTING AND THE INTELLECT

Professor H. J. Paton, in his *In Defence of Reason*, concludes his chapter on "Existentialism as an Attitude to Life" by saying, "So far as I can see, existentialism is not a theory to argue about, but rather an attitude to decide about—either for or against—unless indeed we decide to ignore it altogether" (p. 214). Whether this is true or not, it is important to see that the main purpose of all existentialists is to restore realism to philosophy. If philosophy is only a theory, then it is restricted to an idealism in which the idea is the only reality. On the other hand, if the psychological interests of the non-Christian existentialists reveal their approach to philosophy as pure attitude, the attitude nevertheless is based on an immediate contact with reality by phenomenology in which, through sense experience and emotion, one realizes an immediate participation with the world that exists outside the mind. The conditions for this existentialist aim to restore realism to philosophy may be clarified through a consideration of subject and object.

In Descartes, the concept was not real in itself. Through God's mediation it was assured that this concept was a true concept of the object existing in space and time. Because God was beyond space and time, the concept of God could be most clear and distinct and, therefore, knowledge of God was surer than knowledge of anything else. The sense image was overlooked. The proofs for the existence of God were taken to provide a sure knowledge of God's essence and this had a strong influence on Thomists who read Descartes' philosophy into St. Thomas Aquinas. For Descartes, the subject was the knowing subject and the object was an existing thing, but this object could be known only through the concept in the mind of the thinking subject. Also, the Cartesian dualism divided the subject into mind and body—the mind being the subjective part of the subject and the body being the objective part of the subject.

The empiricists, on the other hand, though maintaining Descartes' distinction of knowing subject and object as an existing thing, affirmed that this object was not known by concept but by image in immediate sense experience. Since God cannot be experienced in immediate sense experience, many empiricists concluded that God could not be known and some concluded that God did not even exist. The concept was regarded as equivalent to the image and some later scientific empiricists went on to treat the image as a concept, giving it universal validity, as a knowledge of the existing object.

With Kant, a confusion arose between subject and object, because he made the object not a thing but phenomena. There was no knowledge of an existing object because that remained unknown; there was only knowledge of ideas and phenomena. The subject was the Ego that transcended the objects or ideas in the mind and made them knowledgeable by a universal process of thought. For Kant, as for the empiricists, a rational metaphysic was impossible.

In Hegel, and the neo-Hegelians, the problem of subject and object became more confused than ever. The subject was treated as consciousness and the object was purely an idea. Therefore, knowledge was only consciousness.

In both the rational and the scientific empirical traditions, the object came to be regarded as a rational structure in the mind, not as the object of knowledge existing outside of the mind. Furthermore, as seen in Bergson, the subject's awareness was divided into subjective and objective impressions—the subjective being the vital and emotional, and the objective being the concept. Following along Bergson's thought, the word "subjective" was taken to refer to sense experience and "objective" was taken to mean the rational concept.

Faced with this confusion, the existentialists seek to shed some light on subject, object, concept and image, and to clarify of what knowledge is. In this they seek to return to the world as it exists and not as someone thinks or feels it might be. In other words, they recognize the real world as it exists in space and time and distinguish it from the rational, empirical or emotional response which human beings make to this world. When we commonly say that we are going to be objective in our research, it means that our research is to bear on a concrete object existing outside of the mind. As subjects, thinking persons, we seek to gain a true adequation, as far as possible, within our own minds, of objects existing outside our minds. A further difficulty, which complicates the problem, is that existing human beings are themselves participating in reality and are unable to completely withdraw in order to reflect on reality as a whole. Also, as the existentialists are well aware, the essence of finite human beings is in a constant state of becoming until the moment of death when they cease to exist on this earth. Man is confronted with severe limitations in his search for truth.

One immediate and obvious way to gain some measure of truth is through sense experience and, as we have seen, all the existentialists base their search for knowledge on sensation because through sensation one is given an immediate awareness of the existence and particular characteristics of an object in space and time. However, knowledge by sensation is only a knowledge of the moment and the problem is to see if a true concept of the object can be grasped in the mind which will be a knowledge of some more lasting truth. This would be gained by reason. A further question would be whether it is possible to gain knowledge of anything which is not sensed.

As we have seen, the reaction of the existentialists against idealism and essentialism has been strong and they have been particularly critical of the assumption that the world can be objectified and categorized into a set of universal facts. At the same time, by various uses of phenomenology, they recognize an underlying unity in all experience and feel that the abstraction of one thing, one object, from the field of experience or being for the purposes of analytic study destroys to a degree the picture of reality. In other words, the subject-object relationship is always an artificial one.

Gilson affirms the merit of the existentialists in noting that the non-problematizable cannot be objectified, but he asks if the radical opposition, in Sartre's thought, between existential subject and object is not itself an objectivization.[1] Metaphysics in its truest sense has sought to problematize the non-problematizable because the concepts which derive from the mystery of being cannot be truly separated from it. Kierkegaard was correct in protesting so strongly against the tendency to reduce religion to mere objective knowledge, but though he saw that the person who thinks exists, he was guilty of abstraction himself in failing to note that the person who exists thinks.[2]

If we objectify existence, does that destroy it? Gilson says "no." The object is not opposed to the subject but includes it necessarily. For a doctrine that presents existence at the root of being, there are no pure objects—only subject-objects. When I say "I"—I am subject. When I say "you," you are subject. Gilson writes: "I do not then think of myself as an act of existing in connection with pure objects, that is to say with objects that are existentially neutral; I think of myself as the "I" that I am in connection with the "I"'s that are the others, an "I" that I myself am able to express for them, if they themselves are incapable of saying it; in short, I think of myself as an act of existing in connection with other acts of existing. The object has no other content than the subject which it signifies, but it is for us the only possible way of signifying it."[3]

Gilson states that one must move from phenomenology to ontology, from existing to being,[4] from subject to object. If this passage is impossible, then all ontology of existence is impossible. The distinction between essence and existence is no less artificial and

[1]E. Gilson, "Le Thomisme et les philosophies existentielles," *La Vie Intellectuelle*, June, 1945.
[2]See E. Gilson, *Being and Some Philosophers*, chap. IV.
[3]Gilson, "Le Thomisme et les philosophies existentielles," p. 154.
[4]For example, R. Troisfontaines' work on Marcel entitled *De l'existence à l'être*.

abstract than that between subject and object. Neither existence nor essence is a thing. A thing is a subject apprehended as an object which is neither essence nor existence, but the actualization of one by the other. To actualize an essence is to realize the content of a static definition, but finite existence is never completely actualized and, therefore, it is never completely possible to actualize an essence of a finite existent. Man in general is a rational animal, but man in particular is not a rational animal; he becomes it. Because he is it, he can become it.

The chief interest of Sartre and Merleau-Ponty is the fleeting nature of a reality experienced with the senses. In the face of idealism, this is an important contribution to realism. However, Gilson sees the danger in their treatment of consciousness in making its existence the sub-product of a thing, which exists but which has no essence as yet: "See for example, the whole introduction to *Being and Nothingness* of J.-P. Sartre where existence appears as a malady of being."[5]

For Sartre the function of reason is to question being. But before the question is asked concerning the connection of man to the world, the existence of both the questioner and of the questioned is presupposed. The reply comes as being unveils itself and in this reply, there is always a possibility of affirmation or negation. Thus the questioner is in a state of non-determination, not knowing if the response is affirmative or negative. The question brings together, first, the non-being of knowledge in the man, and secondly, the possibility of non-being in the being that is questioned. The third aspect of non-being Sartre finds in limitation of imaginary possibilities by the discovery of truth. These three aspects of non-being are involved in every metaphysical question. Non-being circumscribes the response to any question because for Sartre being will be discovered on the basis of what is not. Sartre writes as if nothing were something when he talks of being being that, and outside of that there is nothing. Yet he recognizes that the idea of nothingness arises in the mind and is sustained in existence by mental activity. Nothingness is incapable of existing by itself, but non-beings are discovered only after being presented by the reason as possibilities.

[5]"Le Thomisme et les philosophies existentielles," footnote, p. 154.

Sartre compares this being of non-being with destruction because destruction assumes the discovery of a being that is fragile (that has the possibility of non-being.) As non-being comes to the world by human reason, so does destruction, because the individual limitation is the condition of fragility. It is man who makes cities destructible precisely because he presents them as fragile, and of worth because he takes for their care a number of protective measures. In spite of these measures a volcano can destroy these human constructions. Thus Sartre concludes that destruction leads to the same end as interrogation.

For Hegel, being and non-being were purely logical distinctions and, therefore, were revealed in every object. But Sartre points out that in being there is no other determination but to be identical with itself whereas nothingness is parasitic on being and this is what he means when he says that nothingness haunts being. "Non-being is found only on the surface of being."[6]

However, Sartre reveals that his approach to nothingness is purely psychological in a consideration of "Phenomenological Conception of Nothingness," where he writes that there exist numerous attitudes of the "human reality" which imply a "comprehension" of nothingness: hate, defence, regret, etc.[7] The human mind cannot change things but only its attitude to things.

Descartes questioned the *cogito* in its functional aspect, but in his desire to pass from the study of the mind to science itself he has fallen into the error of substantialism. Husserl dwelt so furtively on the level of functional description of consciousness that Sartre believes he should be called a phenomenalist rather than a phenomenologist. Heidegger, seeking to avoid this phenomenalism of description which leads to the isolation of essences, has refused the *cogito* as the starting-point. (His approach is quite similar to that of Marcel.) However, Sartre believes that the ecstatic character of human reality falls back into an "en soi" if it does not surge from an awareness of ex-isting. He writes: "To speak truly, one must begin with the *cogito*, but one can say of it that it leads to everything provided that one proceeds from it."[8]

[6]J.-P. Sartre, *L'Etre et le Néant*, p. 52.
[7]*Ibid.*, p. 53.
[8]*Ibid.*, p. 116.

In contrast to Marcel's treatment of body as the incarnation of the self, Sartre regards one's body, as distinct from the consciousness, as the part of the self that is known by another. All that I can know of another is his body, not his consciousness, because all that can be seen is the body. What Sartre is really saying is a point on which all existentialists would agree. It is namely that as long as a human being is regarded as a mere object, and not as a person, he cannot be truly and fairly known. Maritain says that whether a person treated as object is condemned or, more rarely, honoured, he still is unjustly known.[9] In any case, to see one's self as others see it always involves shame for Sartre.

Sartre feels that Kant with universal subjective laws has little room for persons. The subject for Kant is only the essence of persons in common and the problem of the other is overlooked. Sartre believes that one must accept a solipsistic position in order to preserve the uniqueness and dignity of the human individual because he feels that the only logical alternatives to solipsism are idealism or materialism. As long as the true essence of the human being is his isolated consciousness, then he can never be determined by the observations or thoughts of other people. Philosophical and political systems will have no real effect upon him.

Merleau-Ponty believes that the greatest contribution of phenomenology has been to act as a check upon extreme idealism and extreme materialism. Reason, though limited by experience of the existing world, still has an important function. "There is rationality, that is to say: the perspectives are checked, the perceptions are confirmed, a meaning appears."[10] However, reason cannot be presented in isolation in the sense of Absolute Spirit or as a law inherent in the world.

The phenomenological world is not the world of being but the existing world of sense experience whose essence is becoming in space and time. Meaning is found in this world by a rational comparison of subjective experiences of past and present and also by intersubjective comparison. Therefore, the study of being for the phenomenologist does not involve an explanation of a pre-

[9]J. Maritain, *Court traité de l'existence et de l'existant*, p. 126.
[10]M. Merleau-Ponty, *Phénoménologie de la perception*, p. xv.

established being but the discovery of the basis of being and the realization of a truth, just as an artist realizes a truth. The world and reason are not problems which demand in the absolute idealist or materialist sense an ultimate solution. "The world and reason are not a problem; let us say, if you wish, that they are mysteries, but this mystery defines them, there is no question of dispelling it by any solution. It precedes solutions."[11]

Philosophy then is life which is described as well by historical narrative as by a rational treatise. Life may include moments of reflection, but it equally includes decisions in which we involve ourselves. The truths of life's activities are not verified by reason but in the practice of human existence. However, the various fields of knowledge are based on certain rational presuppositions for purposes of communication. Philosophy in principle should be deprived of these presuppositions, yet since it is in the world and in history, it has recourse to them. Because of this, philosophy must constantly question itself and its presuppositions on its path to reveal "the mystery of the world and the mystery of reason."[12]

Like Sartre and Merleau-Ponty, Gabriel Marcel seeks a mediating position between the extremes of rationalism and empiricism, and of idealism and materialism. Furthermore, as Merleau-Ponty affirms that philosophy must always be growing and that the philosopher must constantly question his presuppositions, Marcel affirms that the philosopher must always proceed as a *Homo viator*. Since the essence of human existence is always in a process of becoming, the individual philosopher's quest for truth cannot be expressed in terms of "isms." Even philosophers of the concrete in previous ages have tended to become formalized and devitalized and Marcel seeks to avoid anything which is called Marcelism.[18] For Marcel the "Je suis" infinitely transcends the "je pense," and when priority is given to the "je pense" (as in Descartes) it is always degraded to thought in general.[14]

Since the act of existence precedes the act of thought, thought itself is a mystery "since the characteristic of thought is to appre-

11*Ibid.*, p. xvi.
12*Ibid.*, p. xvi.
18G. Marcel, *The Mystery of Being*, Part I, p. 3.
14G. Marcel, *Du refus à l'invocation*, p. 87.

hend every objective representation, every figuration of itself, every symbolization as inadequate."[15] Many metaphysical problems such as those of evil or of freedom have been presented as degraded mysteries by idealist philosophy and Marcel makes a fundamental distinction between mystery and problem, as Merleau-Ponty also has done. "Distinguish between the Mysterious and the Problematic. A problem is something which confronts me. It is before me in its entirety. A mystery, on the other hand, is something in which I find myself caught up, and whose essence is therefore not to be before me in its entirety. It is as though in this province the distinction between in me and before me loses its meaning. . . . The Mysterious and Ontological are identical."[16]

Gilson also stresses the mystery in the pure act of Being in the writing of St. Thomas Aquinas and he is very critical of the traditional Dominican interpreters of St. Thomas who tend to ignore the element of mystery and treat Being purely as a rational problem. He writes: "It is true that the 'I,' which cannot be thought without being objectified, nor be objectified without being destroyed, is presented to us as a sort of mystery. But is it not with respect to St. Thomas that Father Garrigou-Lagrange spoke not long ago of the 'mystery of being,' and this mystery of being itself is it not first, even if those who speak of it forget it, that of the act of being?"[17]

Though Sartre and Merleau-Ponty recognize an element of mystery when they say that existence precedes essence, they really have not escaped the level of the problematic. Marcel would recognize the validity of the conclusions of Sartre and Merleau-Ponty in so far as they are on the level of the problematic. The philosopher must begin philosophizing from his own experience in his own situation and can, therefore, gain no rational picture of being as such; for the world is and can be only the world of his own experience. There is no justification for universalizing the process of the human intellect and Kant and Descartes may both be criticized for approaching the human mind anthropologically. The individual may reason out his own scheme of his world according to his experience, but because each individual is in a different situation, the

[15]*Ibid.*, p. 95.
[16]G. Marcel, *Being and Having*, p. 100–1.
[17]"Le Thomisme et les philosophies existentielles," p. 149.

system of each individual necessarily clashes with the worlds of other individuals. However, Marcel is more interested in the level of mystery wherein the individual is able to transcend all conceptual objectivity.

This appeal to mystery involves an inevitable ambiguity, because a mystery cannot be known by the mind, nor can it be verified by sense experience and it is through the light of mystery alone that true meaning can be brought to the realms of mind and sensation. By revelation, the world does not appear to be rational, but reasonable. Marcel writes in *Du refus à l'invocation* (p. 109):

As for the ambiguity of the word mystery, I will answer only this: just as it seems embarrassing for the spirit to admit that the mysteries of faith superimpose themselves upon a world which can be completely problematized, and in consequence robbed of ontological density, upon a world which reason would pierce as a light plays through a crystal block, in the same way it seems to me not absolutely rational perhaps, but reasonable to think that this world is rooted in being, and therefore transcends in every way localized problems, of which the solution, itself localized, permits the insertion of technique into things.

To think or rather to assert the metaproblematical is to assert it as indubitably real, as a thing of which I cannot doubt without falling into contradiction. This idea is certainty; it is the assurance of itself. It is something other and something more than the idea. It cannot be a content of thought for this is only found in experience and the metaproblematical transcends all experience, free and really detached. In recollection alone is this detachment accomplished. "I am convinced that no ontology—that is to say no apprehension of ontological mystery in whatever degree is possible except to a being who is capable of recollecting himself and of thus proving that he is not a living creature pure and simple, a creature, that is to say, which is at the mercy of its life and without a hold upon it."[18] Recollection is to recollect the self as a unity but also in relaxation and abandon. In recollection, the self withdraws from its own life and thereby introduces a gap between its being and its life.

Marcel distinguishes this recollection from the *für sich sein* of the German idealists. To withdraw into oneself is not to be for oneself or to mirror oneself in the intelligible unity of subject and object.

18G. Marcel, *Position et approches concrètes du mystère ontologique*, p. 63.

In I Corinthians 6:19, St. Paul says "Ye are not your own," and in withdrawal in recollection this statement receives concrete and ontological significance. Rather than speak of intuition, Marcel believes it would be better to speak of an assurance which underlies the entire development of thought, even of discursive thought. This can only be approached by "un mouvement de conversion" which is a secondary reflection wherein he asks how and from what starting-point he proceeded in initial reflection which postulated the ontological without knowing it. This secondary reflection is "recueillement" in the measure in which recollection can be self-conscious.

Marcel's approach to the ontological basis which underlies any development of thought can be clearly seen in his consideration of the proofs for the existence of God. He begins his consideration in *Being and Having* when he recognizes the facts that the proofs have not been universally convincing. "How can we explain their partial ineffectiveness? The arguments presuppose that we have already grounded ourselves on God, and what they are really doing is to bring to the level of discursive thought an act of a wholly different kind. These, I believe, are not ways, but blind ways, as one can have blind windows."[19]

In a "Meditation on the Idea of the Proof of the Existence of God," in *Du refus à l'invocation* (pp. 226f.) Marcel asks what it is to prove. To prove is always to prove to someone, who is either myself or another. In doing so, I, in proving, assume a field of apperception which is common to myself and the other and yet in proving to another I assume an advanced or dominant position in this field. The one who proves seeks to enlighten the field for another. It is from this phenomenological level that the valid proof begins. Therefore, the act of proving always assumes a claim of the prover, not of pride that he has knowledge which the other does not have, but of an ontological unity that cannot fail to be seen by a certain degree of inner concentration.

Yet so often the prover appears like a hypnotist or a juggler. When the proof fails, many who listen to it say that it failed because they felt it rested on a sophism to be unmasked once and for all; the prover says the proof met with an ill will, a will not favourably

[19]Marcel, *Being and Having*, p. 98.

disposed towards it in the first place. Marcel believes that the first attitude is untenable for the very fact that many great minds (both neo-Thomists and others) are content with the proofs. No one can say in the face of these persons that he is in a more advanced position. Rather should one not look for something essential which those who offer the proofs omit? The second attitude is not sound either. "When I incriminate the ill will of the other, I must ask myself in reflection if his attitude does not appear to me as such because it is contrary to my will, my will to convince him, to subdue him."[20] Even if there were ill will in the other, it is important not to deplore it, but to understand it and it may even be possible by sympathy to see that what one at first took to be an ill will may not be an ill will at all.

Again, Marcel suggests that the appearance of ill will may be a refusal of the end of the proof—that is, the existence of God Himself. This refusal may be made as a result of experience: the individual sees the existence of suffering and evil as incompatible with the existence of God; or in the name of freedom: the individual feels that he would be degraded if God existed. "This is extremely important and, in reality, expresses this singular fact that what the demonstrator presents as perfection is interpreted by his contradictor as a hindrance to the expansion of his own being, which is more or less implicitly deified, or as the negation of the Sovereign Good."[21] These arguments form the basis of most of the reasons given by the non-Christian existentialists for the non-existence of God.

It would seem then, according to Marcel, that proof is only useful for the person who is really in no need of it. On the other hand, for the person whom one desires to convince, it will appear only as a verbal game or as an appeal to principle. Therefore, Marcel concludes, that, rather than being a substitute for belief, the proof presupposes it and serves only as a reassurance to the believer who feels a dichotomy between his faith and his reason.

The proof requires a certain communication between me and the other on a concrete level. The error of idealist philosophies (and also of the current essentialist interpretation of St. Thomas)[22] has

20Marcel, *Du refus à l'invocation*, p. 230.
21*Ibid.*, p. 231.
22Marcel writes: "which is undoubtedly not real Thomism, but which is the usual interpretation of it" (*Du refus à l'invocation*, p. 232).

been to assume an abstract notion of natural man as a transhistorical invariant, through which rational communication was guaranteed and Marcel believes that the greatest danger in this notion of natural man is that, though its original meaning is based on belief in God, its present meaning is so often taken in opposition to any supernatural truth. Furthermore, because man is always in history, and therefore always becoming, apologetics based on a rational theology has been relatively ineffective. Finally, it is because the unity of man is broken, and because his world is broken, in our contemporary tragic world, that the irrefutable rational proofs are unconvincing.[23] Marcel seeks to find how the certitude of his faith can be imparted to another within the vital, dramatic situation in which he finds himself involved.

When one is faced with an unbeliever, there is a great temptation to judge his attitudes as implying bad faith or bad will, but Marcel believes that one must seek to understand him from his own point of view. The reality of faith does not rest on a sense of its validity or in its practical efficacy; for it cannot be boasted of as a great possession or it is destroyed. The believer must see his own inadequacy in relation to his faith; that is, see the unbelief that remains in himself in the light of his belief. It is as a result of this insight that a communication can be realized between the believer and the unbeliever.

On the level of faith, which is reached by reflection, the distinction of the ideal and the real lose their objective significance. The reflection, "I believe in Thou, my only refuge,"[24] unites traditional philosophy with the dialectic of affirmation in Marcel's unique use of the ontological proof. By this reflection the objective level of problem is transcended in mystery. The reality is given to me as I give myself to it, and as I centre myself upon it, I truly become a subject. Marcel concludes that the grave error of idealism has been in not seeing that to be a subject is not a fact nor a point of departure, but a conquest and a goal.[25]

---

[23]It is interesting to relate this statement of Marcel to that of Mascall in *He Who Is* (p. 80) in which he affirms that the unnatural condition of modern living makes it difficult for people to see the necessity of the existence of God.
[24]Marcel, *Du refus à l'invocation*, p. 235.
[25]*Ibid.*, p. 236.

Jacques Maritain writes, towards the conclusion of his *Existence and the Existent* (*Court traité de l'existence et de l'existant*): "We have seen how the existentialism of Thomas Aquinas differs from modern existentialism, both because it is rational in type and because, being founded upon the intuitiveness of senses and the intellect, it associates and identifies, being and intelligibility at every point."[26] Descartes made philosophy totally rationalist and separated it from mystery. But, Maritain continues, "St. Thomas reconciles intellect and mystery at the core of being, at the core of existence."[27] One of the most interesting and fruitful discussions of the relation of the act of existing to the intellect is presented by Thomistic existentialists.

The Thomistic existentialists strongly oppose a proof of existence from essence because essences are understood by the mind whereas existing is affirmed by a judgment. Descartes revived the ontological proof for the existence of God and his approach has had a tremendous influence on interpreters of St. Thomas to the present day; so much so that even Jacques Maritain speaks of the concept of existence.[28] In the essentialist interpretation, wherein the form and matter pattern (Aristotelian) of St. Thomas's thought is taken to the exclusion of his distinction of Being and Existing inherited from Hebrew thought, the five proofs of St. Thomas are taken as leading to a clear and distinct knowledge of God's essence as well as His existence. However, the fact remains that, despite these proofs, men simply do not have a clear and distinct idea of what God is like and, furthermore, St. Thomas never believed that men could know God in His essence by their natural reason.

Gilson and Mascall believe that St. Thomas's Five "Proofs" were intended to point out five characteristics of finite beings which demonstrate that no finite being is able to account for its own existing but necessarily receives it from a being whose existing is not received. "The Five Ways are therefore not as much five different methods of manifesting the radical dependence of finite

---

[26]J. Maritain, *Existence and the Existent*, p. 147.
[27]*Ibid.*
[28]*Ibid.*, p. 32.

being upon God, of declaring, in Dom Pontifex's phrase, that the very essence of finite being is to be effect-implying-cause."[29] The scientific method seeks by infinite regress of causes to explain the individual act of existing. By his first three ways—that from motion, that from efficient causation and that of necessity— St. Thomas points out the impossibility of making this infinite regress of essentially subordinated causes because such a search would lead no nearer to the solution of the problem. Rather, such a search leads to an unmoved mover, a first cause, a necessary being who initiates the process of change in nature. Though St. Thomas himself does affirm that God Himself is outside of this series with a radically different nature from that of the finite beings in the series, he fails in the formulation of the proofs to show that despite the causation of one finite being on another, God's causality bears through time on every finite being in its process of change. E. L. Mascall has pointed out that in his thought as a whole St. Thomas certainly found God's causality in every event and indeed St. Thomas regarded this to be of supreme importance.[30]

Mascall points out, in *Existence and Analogy*,[31] that St. Thomas' treatment of the Fourth Proof (on degrees of perfection) demonstrates that he did not intend an ontological proof of God's existence; it makes clear that all the proofs were not intended as five different proofs of God but as five demonstrations of a finite existent's inability to account for its own existence. "In the last resort St. Thomas has only one datum for an argument for the existence of God, namely the existence of beings whose existence is not necessitated by their essence; that is, beings in which essence and existence are really distinct. The Five Ways are not so much

[29]E. L. Mascall, *Existence and Analogy*, p. 71.
[30]*Ibid.*, pp. 75–7. Though of great importance for St. Thomas, in the light of modern thought, the proof from infinite regress would bear little weight. The biological approach of Bergson to philosophy would regard causation as abstraction. Change is rooted in the vital existent. Sartre and his followers, influenced by Bergson would regard this proof and any positivistic scientific search for cause in infinite regress as pure abstraction, a pure nothingness produced by the free consciousness. (See Mascall, *He Who Is*, p. 42).
[31]*Ibid.*, pp. 77 f. This interpretation is based on the fact that in the Fourth Way, St. Thomas makes no effort to pursue an infinite regress of the causes of perfection but rather implies that the fact that limited beings exist "declares their immediate dependence upon a being that is absolutely and infinitely perfect."

syllogistic proofs that finite being is of this type, as discussions of finite being which may well help us to apprehend that it is. . . . The existence of being in which essence and existence are really distinct does not logically imply the existence of a being in which essence and existence are really identical" (p. 78). Mascall disagrees with Scholastics who base the passage from finite to infinite on the principle of contradiction. Rather the passage from finite to infinite depends on a grasp of the ontological reality by which finite existents exist. Therefore, we will not grasp God in His full essence (as Descartes has declared) but as the agent by which finite beings exist. The object of the cognitive act is finite being, demonstrating at every moment its dependence on a Creator.

Mascall believes that the Fifth Way, the argument from finality, demonstrates that to exist is an activity in itself—to be tending to an end—and is not a static demonstration of certain characteristics. In this way, the act of existing for St. Thomas is distinguished from Sartre's consideration of existence. For Sartre, the existence of the "en soi" is to be what it is and there is no process of becoming in it at all. On the other hand, for the "pour soi," whose existence is recognized as distinct from its essence, existence is nothingness unless the "pour soi" is authentic—projecting itself into the future. Thus, in *Existence and Analogy* (p. 43), E. L. Mascall writes: "To exist is to do something, not in the sense of Sartrians, according to whom you cannot exist unless you are doing something else, but in the sense that existing is the most fundamental thing that you do."

In the same book (pp. 81–2), Mascall wonders what effect these Ways might have upon the logical empirical philosophy of contemporary Britain and he concludes that there can be no possibility of proving the existence of God to adherents of these systems on their own terms. In the same way, we might ask what effect these Ways might have upon contemporary French non-Thomistic existentialism. One difficulty is that the approach of St. Thomas is so closely associated with Aristotelian influence, but Mascall affirms that this Aristotelian influence is not in fact necessary and it clouds the issue. "What then is necessary for a mind if it is to recognize the truth of the Thomistic Ways? What is necessary is the recognition of finite being as being in which there is a real distinction of essence and existence, as something which is there and yet need not be there, as perfect in its degree and yet not self-subsistent perfection, as being whose very limitation declares that whatever it is and has it receives from without, as an effect implying a cause that possesses in its own right all that it communicates" (p. 85).

How would this relate to the approach of Sartre and his followers? As we have seen, Sartre takes the existence of consciousness as given, as abandoned—"as something which is there and yet need not be there." Yet by the distinction of existence and essence, St. Thomas does not mean that a finite existent has no essence. Rather its essence is becoming and, consequently, its essence does not necessitate its existence. However, Sartre abstracts this dependent existence from any essence at all. Because the conscious act of existing can find no reason for its being there, it must go on by acts of volition to create its own essence. The future belongs to the conscious act of existing to create itself and the past is the essence which the conscious act of existing has created for itself. Therefore, if consciousness finds any perfection in the self, it is the perfection that the self has made for itself. Consciousness stands as an independent atom which owes nothing and which is owed nothing. Consciousness, by dwelling on the nothingness in its own state rather than on what it is, preserves its freedom and its independence. The only thing for which it cannot be independent is its own act of existing which, it recognizes, is not caused by itself but which it accepts as a mystery. However, the very use of the word "mystery" for Sartre suggests a barrier and a refusal to go any further on that line of thought.[32] Furthermore, this refusal is inherent in the whole system because only that which is seen in sense experience can be said to be. Consequently, God, who is outside of sense experience, is automatically excluded.[33] In the

[32]Gabriel Marcel in his *Homo viator* (p. 255) emphasizes this refusal of Sartre in excluding any possibility of the reality of the supernatural.

[33]E. L. Mascall writes in condemnation of the limitation of the logical empiricists to sense experience. The same may be applied to the empiricism of the non-Christian existentialists. "If a man persists in limiting his gaze to the phenomenal surface of reality there is nothing that can be done about it on the purely human level, except to treat him kindly and to point out to him as

name of the freedom of the will the self can create itself, and the intellect is limited to its only function, sorting out sense images and giving meaning to them. Thus Mascall is led to write: "It would perhaps be too narrow a definition to say that the specific differentia of Thomist existentialism is its intellectualism, as contrasted with the voluntarism of both non-Christian existentialists like Sartre and non-Thomist Christian existentialists like Kierkegaard; rather it would, I think, be true to say that in St. Thomas both the rational and the volitional elements receive their proper recognition."[34]

On the other hand, the writings of Gabriel Marcel do not seem so far removed from the philosophy of St. Thomas as interpreted existentially. A sentence of Mascall in *Existence and Analogy* (p. 85) suggests very well that one may reach the same position as that to which St. Thomas's Five Ways lead by contemplation of any finite being. "There are still people in whom this grasp of finite being in its dependence can be induced by the study of St. Thomas' Five Ways, but for most of us I think it comes more easily by quietly contemplating any finite being, however humble, in the attitude of wonder."

Marcel has been criticized for not putting sufficient emphasis upon reason. Jeremiah Newman writes, in an article on the "Ethics of Existentialism": "In point of fact, the absence of a sound view of the concept is the feeble point in the philosophy of Marcel. It is exposed to the danger of a false mysticism."[35] For this reason, Jacques Maritain feels that the writings of Marcel can add nothing to Thomistic thought but only run parallel to it. In regard to Marcel's philosophy, he writes:

I do not believe that it can ever develop into a metaphysic properly so called, any more than any other philosophy which refuses to admit the intellectual intuition of being. It cannot father a metaphysics that is comprehensive, articulated, founded upon reason, and capable of exercising the functions of wisdom as well as of knowledge. For the

gently as possible that by playing for safety in this way he is desperately impoverishing his experience. In our time this sort of metaphysical myopia has become a habit and almost a disease. In the last resort it can be cast out only by prayer and fasting." (*Existence and Analogy*, p. 90).

[34]*Ibid.*, p. 64.
[35]*Irish Ecclesiastical Record*, Fifth Series, vol. LXXVII, 1952, p. 430.

same reason, I do not believe that in the evolution of philosophical thought, it will ever succeed in becoming more than a side issue, nor will it successfully resist the historic impetus which at the present time gives to atheistic existentialism (and will in the future give to new systems issuing in like fashion out of the central positions of the long tradition that goes back to Descartes) an ephemeral but vast power over men's minds.[36]

On the other hand, though Marcel's thought, not being rational, may be regarded only as a passing phase in the history of human thought, it must also be remembered that the writings of St. Thomas though rational, must constantly be reinterpreted in the light of contemporary thought if they are to be meaningful. Furthermore, unless a satisfactory distinction is made in the functions of the active intellect, the danger is that the rational existentialism of St. Thomas will fall back into the ontologism of Descartes.

E. L. Mascall has made the difficulty clear in *Existence and Analogy* (pp. 86 f.) Though the notions of substance and causality have reference to a real world of our sense experience, the difficulty is to see whether these notions can apply to God who transcends sense experience. If God were merely like any finite being, then any finite being would be as effective as God and there would be no need to prove His existence. On the other hand, if God is totally transcendent, then any statements we make about Him would be meaningless or paradoxical. Such is the approach of Kierkegaard and Barth who affirm an absolute qualitative difference between God and man. The choice would seem to be God either unnecessary or unthinkable. This is the dilemma of asserting that man is able to conceive a being and an activity which are unthinkable. However, what the cosmological approach claims is that only God exists self-existingly and that He causes the existing of finite beings.

An important truth which all existentialists emphasize is that the act of existing cannot be contained in a concept. As we have seen in Thomist epistemology, existing is affirmed in a judgment. When it is said that God exists, God is not defined by a concept but by affirming His mode of existence, which is "self-existingly." God is given to us in our concept of finite being which cannot be

---

[36]Maritain, *Existence and the Existent*, pp. 135–6.

the cause of its own existing. This affirmation of God's existing is unique because God Himself, if He exists, is unique; but the Way itself has provided us with no concept of God's essence but only the judgment of His self-existing.

As a result of the affirmation that God exists, the world becomes reasonable and Sartre accuses theists of creating God in the mind in order that the meaningless world may be made meaningful. However, the Way has led to the affirmation of God as self-existing. Then, as Mascall writes: "The ultimate problem is seen to be not whether God exists but why a self-existent God should create anything outside Himself. This is the final mystery, and by the nature of the case it is one to which God alone can know the answer."[37] Thus the affirmation of God's self-existing does not lead one back into an essentialist, idealist position. The finite mind discovers a reasonableness but not an absolute rational order.

Mascall affirms that this process of thought leading to the affirmation of God's existence is not to be called an argument, or a logical deduction, but an apprehension of finite beings as effect manifesting a transcendent cause. He quotes E. I. Watkin's *Philosophy of Form*: "The existence of God is not demonstrated, as a demonstration is usually understood, namely as a process of cogent but non-intuitive reasoning. It is monstrated to contemplative intellection."[38] Nevertheless, Mascall sees three uses of argumentation in the approach. First, it can put men into the frame of mind prepared for the apprehension of finite dependence on God; secondly, it can convince us that the apprehension, when made, is not an illusion; thirdly, it can elucidate the nature and the content of the apprehension as far as possible.

Let us summarize the relation between the act of existing and the intellect in the existentialist writings.

1. For Descartes and the essentialist Thomists, reason provides the truest and most perfect picture of God and the existing world. The more clear and rational the picture in the mind, the more certain is the correspondence to the object existing outside the mind.

---

[37]Mascall, *Existence and Analogy*, p. 89.
[38]*Ibid.*, p. 90. Quotation from E. I. Watkin, *Philosophy of Form*, p. 291.

2. Sartre and his followers affirm that reason is only a product of the mind and that there is no justification for affirming that a rational concept corresponds to an existing object outside of the mind. The only way the self can gain knowledge of existing things is by sense experience. These existing things simply are and because they simply are, they appear to the self as void of meaning. The self must use reason to impose meaning upon the existing world, but the self can only impose a meaning from its own point of view. Therefore, there is no justification for saying that another person will necessarily impose the same meaning and, in fact, different people usually impose different meanings on the world of their experience. A common rational meaning may arise only by chance or by common agreement.

3. Gabriel Marcel affirms that any rational meaning is necessarily untrue to the real meaning of the existing world. A common meaning for the world of being can only be attained through communion in being which is reached through contemplation and mystical participation. In the light of this communion, the world may appear to be reasonable but not rational.

4. The existentialist interpreters of St. Thomas affirm that the rational intellect can identify itself with the universal characteristics of the objects of sense experience, but existing necessarily escapes the reason. On the other hand, any rational knowledge of God's essence which is beyond sense experience is impossible. The self can know God's existence as a self-existing being only by deducing the dependent, finite existence of itself and of all things that it experiences by the senses. The five *Ways* of St. Thomas were intended not to prove anything about God's nature but rather they were designed to demonstrate the dependent existence of all creatures. Also, one may come to an awareness of his dependent existence by contemplation as well as by an act of intellect.

Chapter Six

THE ONTOLOGICAL NEED

In his Introduction to *L'Etre et l'essence*, Professor Gilson seeks to shed light on some of the ambiguities that have developed concerning the word "being." The French word "être" is used both as a verb and as a noun. As a verb it signifies that a thing "is" and, as a noun, it signifies one of the things which one says they are. If *x* is a being (un *être*), it does not follow that *x* is, because *x* may be a real or only a possible being. For the sake of clarity, therefore, in order to say in French that a being is, one says that it exists. In English, the verb "to be" is used so frequently as a copula that, again, for the sake of clarity, the verb "to exist" is used. "Therefore, in both languages, when you wish to say of any thing that it 'is,' the verb 'to be' tends to be translated by another verb—the verb 'to exist'."[1]

The verb "to exist" is derived from the Latin "existere" which is used most frequently in traditional and scholastic Latin in association with verbs "to appear," or "to go out from," and therefore it suggests less the fact of being than a connection to some origin. Thomist existentialists in using the verb "to exist" put the emphasis on the fact of being whereas contemporay existentialists, in using

[1]E. Gilson, *L'Etre et l'essence*, p. 13. The Introduction to the French original is not found in the English version *Being and Some Philosophers*.

the same verb, put the emphasis on the "appearing" and the "going out from." Thus Thomist existentialists speak of God's existence, whereas contemporary existentialists tend to say that if God is, God does not exist. God does not appear and God has no origin.

However, in the eyes of contemporary existentialists, the verb "to exist" does apply well to human beings although, again, a certain ambiguity is involved. It may refer to a "standing out" from the Being from which the human existence originates in a creator to creature relationship, or it may refer to an alienation from God and from other human beings. Thus existence with respect to human beings implies a feeling of creatureliness and alienation, and it is when the human being is aware of his creatureliness and alienation that he can become aware not only of what he desires to become but also of what he should and could become.

Sartre defines the human being as one who is aware of a lack in his being,[2] and a predominant theme in Sartre's writings is of the awareness of the self as existing without any reason for it. Accompanying the sense of deficiency there is an awareness of being somehow cut off from other existing things. Thus, in self-consciousness, the self is aware not only of what is lacking to the self as such but also of what is lacking to the self in its relation to other existing things. The self-conscious self discovers itself to be in a state of tension arising from what it is, what it may become, and what other things are. This is the tension between existence and being. The human existence for Sartre is parasitic on being. Merleau-Ponty writes of this in *Sens et non-sens* (p. 144): "*Being and Nothingness* shows at first that the subject is freedom, absence and negativity and that in this sense, nothingness is. But that means also that the subject is *only* nothingness, that it has need of being carried into being, that it can be thought of only on the foundation of the world, and finally, that it is nourished by being as the shades in Homer were nourished by the blood of living things."

Characters in Sartre's plays and novels express their alienation as a feeling of resentment not only against the situation in which they find themselves but also against the very fact of what they are in an

2J.-P. Sartre, *L'Etre et le Néant*, p. 60.

existence which they did not choose. It is partially to this feeling of resentment that Sartre's use of scandal and sordidness in his plays and novels may be traced. Marcel remarks on the association of scandal and resentment in a review of two of Sartre's plays— *Men without Shadows* and *The Respectable Prostitute.*

It would indeed be interesting to consider how closely his determination to stir up controversy is related to the mainspring of his thought. I am inclined to believe that this desire is bound up not so much with the ideas actually set forth in his writing as with inner impulses which dominate his whole approach to play-writing and are more in the domain of psycho-analysis than of true philosophy. His two latest plays are definitely based on emotions of resentment, though it is impossible to state the exact object of this resentment; it may be the hierarchy of established, conventional values; or it may be life itself; or on a deeper level the author may be expressing resentment against his own being, the fact that he is the man he is and no other.[3]

What Marcel fails to note in this review is that Sartre's approach to ontology is intricately bound up with psychoanalysis. The tendency to scandal in his writings is closely connected with his desire to bring people to an awareness of their alienation in their existence and of their consequent responsibility.

The psychological character of Sartre's approach to the ontological need may be clearly seen in his examination of the conscious self. Sartre finds conscious awareness to be of two kinds— immediate awareness and reflective awareness—and these two levels of consciousness lead to an ambiguity in his whole system. This ambiguity, deriving from the same source, is revealed in his approach to ontology.

The first kind of awareness is that of immediate sense experience and of emotion. In the act of emotion and desire, the conscious self is most intricately combined with the body. Also in sense experience, one becomes aware of things that exist outside of the mind. We can only have sense experience of material things and, since for Sartre sense experience is the only existential index, then in Sartre's system only material things exist. Here we can see his affinity to dialectical materialism. In affirming that matter is the only thing which is and also in leaving a place for consciousness of this fact

[3]*Theatre Arts,* May, 1947, p. 44.

in the nothingness of the subject, the non-Christian existentialists believe that they are truer interpreters of Marx than are many who call themselves Marxists. This leads Merleau-Ponty to write in *Sens et non-sens* (p. 164): "A living Marxism ought to 'deliver' existentialist research and to integrate it instead of stifling it." Gabriel Marcel, in his essay on "L'Existence et la liberté humaine chez J.-P. Sartre,"[4] notes the reply of Sartre when questioned concerning his materialism (p. 168): "What do you want? In spite of what you say, matter is the only reality that I grasp. Marcel goes on to predict a possible union of the non-Christian existentialists with the Communists if the Communists will accept them.

Matter for Sartre is not the usual physical object which we associate with materialism but it is "nausea," a sliminess, the disgusting and absurd secretions of the human body. Marcel compares Sartre's matter to a lump in a bowl of soup or to "muqueuse sécrétante" (pp. 113 f.). In Sartre's disgusting material world, man is only a by-product. Marcel writes (p. 169): "In Sartre, by the fact that man's belonging to the cosmos is misunderstood or denied, and that we fall thus to a level which is situated thousands of feet below a pantheism whether Stoic or Spinozist, it is completely natural that man tries to prove himself to be more and more as it were waste and as a kind of excremental possibility."

Man, cut off from the material world of being, by the nothingness of self-consciousness, feels a need to achieve his being. This ontological need in respect to matter is expressed in emotion and desire. First, the desire for death by suicide springs from a desire in man to achieve his being as a material thing and to escape the anguish and responsibility of a self-conscious existence. Second is the desire for food and drink. Man constantly needs replenishment by food and drink in order to attain his being. Simone de Beauvoir has one of the characters say in *Le Sang des autres* (p. 126): "There is no better way to attain being than by eating." Thirdly, Sartre has been greatly influenced by Freud and because of this he says that it is in the sexual desire that the ontological need is expressed most strongly. In the sexual act, the self loses it reflec-

⁴G. Marcel, "L'existence et la liberté humaine chez J.-P. Sartre," *Les Grands Appels de l'homme contemporain*, p. 168.

tive consciousness and becomes identified not only with being but also with the being of another person, in a material unity. However, after the self has experienced the sexual act and achieved its onto-logical desire, then it immediately returns to its alienated state of self-consciousness. It is at that moment that the self feels that it has betrayed its dignity as a subject by fulfilling such a material need through the loss of its reflective consciousness. Furthermore, it is only for the moment that the self is united to the other in a physical union and then the two people fall back into isolation. In Simone de Beauvoir's novel *Le Sang des autres* after the sexual act, "Helen felt suddenly intimidated; he no longer belonged to her; he was there before her, he was judging her" (p. 79). In Sartre's novel *The Reprieve*, Ivich feels resentment in the fact that she has betrayed herself in the sexual act and that she has been afterwards betrayed.

Even the desire for sex is resented as a determining factor for the subject. Though E. L. Allen notes in *Existentialism from Within* (p. 61) that Sartre differs from Freud in that Sartre denies that the self is controlled by sub-conscious forces; yet, in the *Age of Reason*, Sartre seems to regard the fact that man is deter-mined by a sexual desire to be degrading for the free subject. One of the characters, Boris, thinks: "'I loathe making love. No—to be honest, that isn't what I loathe most, it's the entanglement of it all, the sense of domination; and besides, what's the point of choos-ing a girl friend, it would be just the same with anyone, it's physio-logical.' And he repeated with disgust 'physiological'. . . . 'A monk, that's what I'll be when I've left Lola.' "[5]

In her large two-volume work, *The Second Sex*, Simone de Beauvoir strongly opposes the tendency to regard women as inferior to men. The traditional view is that women's bodies are more in-sufficient than men's; therefore, their ontological need expressed in sexual desire is much stronger. The traditional view of marriage has fooled women into thinking that they are better off when they are protected and not forced to accept responsibility, but in reality women have become enslaved creatures of man's desire. It is not possible to eliminate sexual and emotional enjoyments, but Simone

[5]J.-P. Sartre, The Age of Reason, p. 43.

de Beauvoir wishes to stress the importance of a rational agreement between men and women in the equal partnership of marriage. She affirms that, biologically and otherwise, women are the equals of men and she cites the example of Russia where women are given equal opportunities and responsibilities in all things. Thus, in *The Second Sex,* we may clearly see the empirical and vital ontological need for the material, being checked or matched by the conscious ontological need for the rational ideal.

The subject, being conscious of its desires, feels itself to be inferior to material things which have no desires because they simply are. However, at the same time, the subject feels superior to material things because it has the power of consciousness to impose meaning upon material things and upon itself. Material things without consciousness can give no meaning to themselves and they can have no value because they simply are. Only things which have an awareness of becoming can have an awareness of value and since human beings alone have this awareness, they may regard it as a unique power and dignity.

It is through the concepts created by the subject that ideals and values are presented which the subject seeks to actualize. The ontological need of the subject realized through concepts and values is expressed by reflective thought and by activity.

It is clear from Merleau-Ponty's remarks in *Sens et non-sens* that he regards Christianity as an ideal system of philosophy which seeks to actualize the ontological need of human consciousness. Speaking of Catholics, he writes (pp. 149–50): "They would like to put mind into things and to make of the human mind a thing." He goes on to accuse Marcel of the very idealism which Marcel refuted in his *Metaphysical Journal* and thereby Merleau-Ponty demonstrates a lack of understanding of Christianity and of Christian existentialism.

However, because the self finds ideals and values which it must act upon to realize itself in the future, then the self must be minus these values in the present. Thus, the self in the present finds itself to be evil in that it thinks of so many ideals and values which it could and should realize. The living self finds itself in a constant dilemma in its ontological need to actualize the ideal and it is this dilemma of which, Sartre feels, Baudelaire was most conscious. "Thus did Baudelaire try once more to remove the contradiction between his choice of existing and his choice of being: this person that the mirrors reflect, it is his existence in the act of being, his being in the act of existing."[6]

The highest ideal or value that the conscious self can have is that the conscious self will become the basis of its own being by the consciousness that it has of itself. This ideal Sartre calls God. Thus, for Sartre, the greatest ontological need for man is the need to be God. God, the supreme end and value of human transcendence (consciousness), represents the ultimate limit beginning from which man is made to proclaim what he is. "To be man, is to try to be God; or if one prefers, man is fundamentally a desire to be God."[7]

This does not mean that all men may be defined as essentially a desire to be God because this desire always springs from an existing individual as a particular invention of his own ends. Also this does not deny human freedom since the only being who can be free is the one who sees negation in his being. It is in choosing the unattainable ideal of being God that the individual can be most aware of what he is not and, consequently, of his freedom.

The self may realize his desire to be God, to a degree, in his power over material objects. As the self slides on ice or through water, it is the master who does not have to raise his voice to be obeyed. Sliding on snow is less perfect because it leaves a trace and thereby the self is compromised. However, Sartre believes that outdoor sports can have a tremendous psychological effect since a participant appears to himself as conqueror of enormous masses of air, earth and water.

God asserts his power over things by creating them, but if the self is unable to gain power over a certain object, then it can seek to destroy it because to destroy an object is to gain as much power over it as to create it. "Destruction—perhaps more finally than creation—realizes appropriation, because the destroyed object is no longer there to reveal itself to be impenetrable."[8] Generosity

---

[6]J.-P. Sartre, *Baudelaire*, p. 180.
[7]Sartre, *L'Etre et le Néant*, p. 652.
[8]*Ibid.*, p. 683.

is a primitive form of destruction because in giving away an object one destroys all the power that, through sentiment or association, it has over one. Furthermore, the act of giving is the act of enslaving the one who receives the gift because he will have to keep it. Another common form of destruction is smoking. The solid tobacco turning into smoke is a symbol of the subject's destruction of the entire world.

By the appropriation of material objects, the self seeks to satisfy its ontological need. There is no desire to be without having and no desire to have without being. "Thus my freedom is a choice to be God and all my acts, all my schemes translate the choice and reflect it in thousands of ways, because there is an infinity of ways to be and an infinity of ways of having."[9]

However, all of these projects of the conscious self to achieve its ideals are doomed to failure by the very fact that these ideals have no existence. They spring from the nothingness of the conscious self. The only thing the self can do is to act with an unfounded hope of actualizing these ideals.

The supreme ideal of God which the self seeks above all to become is seen to be contradictory. God stands for the satisfaction both of the ontological need with respect to the empirical, vital desire in the material realm, and of the ontological need with respect to the conceptual conscious desire in the ideals of the conscious self. Yet this implies a contradiction in a being which is (pure matter) and which is not (pure concept) at the same time. Thus, it is impossible according to Sartre for men to satisfy their ontological need to the full. "All human reality is a passion because of the fact that it schemes to lose itself in order to create being and in order to constitute at the same time the thing in itself which escapes contingency in being its own basis, the *Ens causa sui* that the religions call God. Thus, the passion of man is the reverse of that of Christ, because man loses himself as man in order that God may be born. But the idea of God is contradictory and we lose ourselves in vain; man is an unnecessary passion."[10]

Absolute idealism or Christianity (as the non-Christian existen-

[9]*Ibid.*, p. 689.
[10]*Ibid.*, p. 708.

tialists interpret it), and absolute materialism, or Communism, are contradictory. The contradiction between the two is seen to spring from man himself in his ontological need both for a conceptual ideal and for material being. The horror of human existence is seen in this dilemma; man's two basic needs cannot be satisfied. "The ugly or the horrible is the fundamental discord of the interior and of the exterior. Mind appearing in things is scandalous among them and inversely, things in their brute existence are scandalous for mind."[11] The focal point must be on the consciousness of the existing individual which cannot escape from its situation either through mind or through body.

Gabriel Marcel begins his essay on the *Position et approches concrètes du mystère ontologique* with a consideration of the man who has lost his sense of the ontological. So many people in this century seem to be merely a collection of functions. As we have seen, Sartre has been greatly influenced by Marxism and Freudianism in his materialist sense of the ontological, but Marcel believes that both of these reduce man to a collection of vital functions. Furthermore, Sartre also finds the ontological ideal through reason, but Marcel believes that this purely rational approach has reduced man to a collection of social functions. Sartre affirms that the human reality is always acting at being some function such as that of a waiter or of a father and that this is the essence of bad faith because man can never actually be the function but only act at being it. His ontological need from the view of reflective consciousness is to be the function.

One day Marcel went down to the Paris underground, down to the platform where crowds wait for the trains which rush out of the tunnel, stop momentarily and then roar off to the next destination. Marcel handed his ticket to be punched by the official standing there—a man who stands in the same place for eight hours a day, year in and year out, and Marcel wonders what the inward reality is of that man when all inside and out seems to ally him with his function.

Man allots so many hours for each function. Even sleep becomes a function which must be discharged so that the other functions

[11]M. Merleau-Ponty, *Sens et non-sens*, pp. 86–7.

may be exercised in their turn. All life in this century seems to move by a schedule or routine. It is true that certain disorderly elements such as sickness or accidents break in on the smooth working of the system, but then the hospital becomes a repair shop. As for death, it becomes, objectively and functionally, the scrapping of what has ceased to be of use and must be written off as a total loss. "There is scarcely need to insist on the impression of suffocating sadness, which is released from a world so centred on function."[12] It is sufficient to recall the dreary image of the retired official or of those urban Sundays when the passers-by look like people who have retired from life. In this age, the man who has retired seems to receive a mocking and sinister tolerance.

Besides the sadness felt by the one who observes life as it passes by, there is the dull, intolerable uneasiness of the participant who is reduced to living as though he were, in fact, submerged by his functions. It seems that life goes on like some appalling mistake caused by a misinterpretation implanted in defenceless minds by an increasingly inhuman social order and an equally inhuman philosophy. Life in a world centred on function is liable to despair because, in reality, this world is empty, it rings hollow. Marcel writes: "In such a world, ontological exigence, the exigence of being, is weakened in the precise measure on the one hand in which the personality is broken up, and on the other hand, when the category of everything natural triumphs and when, consequently, what we must call perhaps the powers of wonder are stunted."[13] The world of our time seems to be so full of problems and yet there seems to be no room for the mysteries of life.

Marcel sets out to try to find what this ontological need of man really is. His method of finding being is to say that being is what withstands an exhaustive analysis of human experiences which aims to reduce them step by step to elements increasingly devoid of intrinsic or significant value.

There are two classes of philosophy which refuse to endorse the ontological need. The first is agnosticism which is purely negative—an intellectual policy of not raising the question. The second is

<hr>

[12]G. Marcel, *Position et approches concrètes du mystère ontologique*, p. 48.
[13]*Ibid.*, pp. 50–1.

idealism which claims to be positive and wipes out ontology as an outworn dogma. Marcel feels that this idealism tends to an unconscious relativism or else towards a monism which, ignoring both the personal and the tragic in every way, denies the transcendent, seeking to reduce it to its caricatured expressions which distort its essential character. Both of these philosophies ignore *presence* in stressing verification. *Presence* is an inward realization of personal union through love which infinitely transcends all possible verification because it exists in an immediacy beyond all conceivable mediation.

Sartre has based his ontological need in the different levels of consciousness, and because of this, it is best expressed by desire. It is for this very reason that Marcel refuses to base his ontological need in consciousness. The ontological need is not a desire or a vague aspiration but a deep-rooted urge which comes as an appeal. Marcel suggests that to call this a "need" is in some ways unsatisfactory because it may suggest more what is *wanted* than what is *demanded*.[14] For Sartre what is important is *his* being, while on the other hand, what is important for Marcel is his *being*.

Marcel rejects the Cartesian dualism of mind and body because the ontological study must deal with Being as a totality. Marcel sees himself to be the scene of the inquiry rather than its subject, and this leads him to assume a form of participation which has the reality of the subject. This participation is beyond all problems in the *metaproblematical*. This is the level where being is prior to knowledge and knowledge is seen to be contingent to a participation in being for which no epistomology can account because it continually presupposes it. It is here that the distinction that Sartre makes between what is in the self and what is only before the self breaks down. The obliteration of this distinction is best seen in love.

A meeting with a person walking along the street may have a lasting effect upon your life. This arouses a problem in the mind as to how it could ever have happened as it did. The scientific mind may presume to say that it is this thing or that event which has determined the meeting, but such an explanation is a trans-

[14]G. Marcel, *The Mystery of Being*, Part II, p. 37.

gression of the validity of reason. One here faces a mystery—a reality beyond the problematical. To say it is a lucky chance is an empty formula.

To assert the metaproblematical is to assert it as indubitably real, as a thing which I cannot doubt without falling into contradiction. It is something other and something more than the idea.

Each person becomes the centre of a sort of mental space arranged in concentric zones of decreasing interest and participation. But this pattern may be upset by meeting a stranger. What seemed near becomes remote and what seemed distant seems to be close. The experience almost leaves us with an anguish and a sadness. Yet Marcel feels that this experience is beneficial; for it shows us in a flash all that is contingent and artificial in the crystallized pattern we form in our lives.

Some people give the feeling of presence and others do not, no matter how much good will there may be. The distinction between presence and absence is not at all the same as that between attention and distraction. The most attentive person may not be able to make room for other people in himself. There is a way of listening which is giving yourself and another way which is refusing yourself. For one, I am a presence—for the other, an object. Unavailability is rooted in a measure of alienation and the moment another person is thought of as just another case, then the self feels nothing, even though it may want to and also may see every reason for doing so. "But the characteristic of a soul which is present or available is precisely not to think in terms of cases; there are no cases for it."[15]

To be incapable of presence is to be encumbered with one's own self. Marcel, of course, does not oppose preoccupation with one's own being, but he does oppose a manner of preoccupation which concentrates on the self to the exclusion of other beings. Sartre and his followers are those who have clearly shunned presence and, therefore, it has no reality in their experience.

The soul which is at the disposal of others is consecrated and inwardly dedicated. It is protected against suicide and despair which are interrelated and alike. The best use it can make of its

[15]Marcel, *Position et approches concrètes*, p. 84.

freedom is to realize that it does not belong to itself; for this is the starting point of activity and creativeness.

Some philosophies which profess to supply all the answers are dogmatic, and other philosophies say that all the difficulties are mysteries. Marcel follows the line of Plato (whom Marcel believes has seen with incomparable clarity), and of St. Augustine and of St. Thomas who say that the way to philosophy is discoverable by love, to which it is alone visible. Marcel's idea of presence is best understood in the Holy Eucharist and through creative fidelity to the Church although he affirms that Christianity is not necessary for the experiencing of presence. Marcel says that he experienced presence twenty years before considering conversion to Catholicism.

Presence, an immediate intimacy, is born in the I-Thou relationship of sympathetic contact, which, in a mysterious way, breaks the isolation of the individual. The final impulse in the progress of existence carries the self to the very threshold of Being—into the presence of God. Interwoven with this as with all preceding forms of mystical communion are the theological virtues of Faith, Hope and Charity. These three virtues are closely related. The presence which is revealed in Hope is no presence if the self is not in a relation of Love to it, and it is Faith that supports the delicate web of this relation.

How is this ontological need to be expressed? For Sartre, the ontological need is expressed either by self-annihilation in which the self seeks to identify itself with pure matter or else by extreme egocentrism in which the self seeks to increase its power by destroying other things and by enslaving other people.

For Marcel, the ontological need is best expressed in prayer. The incarnation and participation which characterize existence are transformed step by step into an invocation and an appeal. The judgment implied in "thou" is already an appeal to a being with whom we are united by a spiritual presence; the judgment in "we" is a sublimation of it at a higher level at which we arrive by invocation and prayer. Thus, in the end we reach God, understood as an absolute "Thou" which is different from the empirical "thou" in not being convertible to a "him."

Marcel asks what it is "that allows us to say that one prayer is more authentically prayer than another?"[16] Certainly it is not a formal validity. Marcel believes that prayer on behalf of another is purer than prayer for oneself because this prayer for another presupposes "the active recognition, in and through God, of the bond which constitutes all real love."[17] The spirit of prayer is not to be one of total submission if this implies that the self becomes resigned to all the evils and illnesses of the world. Rather the spirit of prayer must adjust itself to the demands of reason in any given situation. The doctor who prays before an operation does not regard God as the cause of the illness which he must cure nor is his prayer to be regarded as a cause which will effect a definite cure for his patient. The relation of prayer to the world of daily experience is a mystery which precludes pride and despair. In any case, prayer is only possible when the self seeks not isolation but intersubjectivity or a communion with his fellow beings.

Consequently, the ontological need is also expressed in giving and receiving. As we have seen, to give something, in Sartre's thought, is to destroy it and to receive something is to be enslaved by it. Yet Marcel affirms that when you give something, you embody something of yourself in it. If my intention becomes personal and finds a means of revealing itself in the object I purchase, then it becomes possible to speak of a transmutation. The object changes from being a mere thing on a shop-counter to become a gift from me to some particular person. The being of it for another is not the objective quality of the thing but the genuine communication of myself. The gift is not just one more thing added to his possessions—it exists as a testimony of friendship and love.

When a child brings three bedraggled dandelions to you, he expects you to admire them, awaiting a recognition of the value of the gift. If you lose them, or put them down carelessly, you are guilty of a sin against love. The transmutation of a thing in becoming a gift has its continuation in an accretion of being in the one who receives. One is at liberty to refuse the gift by refusing recognition and response. There may be some ungrateful natures who are

[16]Marcel, *The Mystery of Being*, Part II, p. 96.
[17]*Ibid.*, p. 98.

deprived of the gift of responding as some are incapable of faith and trust. In Sartre's world, where the individual is totally isolated, man appears as a victim of a cosmic catastrophe, flung into an alien universe to which he is bound by nothing.

So often Christians, in opposition to atheists, tend to regard grace as a causal force which moves as any natural phenomenon, and in this way, they destroy what they are trying to prove. It is for this reason that Marcel talks of grace as the supreme gift of all. Generosity is not the cause but rather the soul of the gift and it is through an awareness of the gift that one can see the generosity and whence it springs. Through an awareness of the source of generosity, one becomes aware of the metaphysical light which reveals the fact of life and in particular of one's own life as a gift.[18] It is at this point that grace, freedom and truth are seen to meet unless the self denies the light in favour of a game of self-destruction.

E. L. Mascall affirms that the more we see the work of God in His creatures, the more we shall understand about God because every creature depends on God for its total being. He quotes, in *Existence and Analogy* (p. 141), a remark of Osuna that "the greater a creature is, the more it has need of God." If God can be most deeply concerned about the condition of His creatures and yet remain untouched in His nature by human suffering, then we can begin to get a vision of the glory and the joy open to men who attain to their being in God. If God's nature were affected intrinsically by the sufferings and miseries of the world, then the need for being by the man who experiences these sufferings would be reduced. Mascall writes: "It follows that God's unruffled beatitude is not something in which he luxuriates in self-centred detachment; it is something which he intends to confer on us."[19] It is only through divine impassibility that a salvation truly worthy of the name is conceivable.

Nowhere is Sartre's deviation from a truly existential philosophy more evident than in his treatment of the ontological need. In Sartre's terms, if a subject tends to being, it must tend to become

[18]*Ibid.*, p. 122.
[19]E. L. Mascall, *Existence and Analogy*, p. 143.

a purely material object. If a subject tends to God, or to be God, then it is tending to its own non-being because it is seeking to actualize a product of its own mind which is nothing. This is to assume that a creature left to itself continues to exist in its nothingness. This is pure abstraction.

On the other hand, Mascall affirms that God does not leave creatures to themselves and that creatures are what they are as objects of God's creative act. He quotes a passage from Father Sertillanges' *L'Idée de création* to the effect that creatures cannot tend to nothingness because nothingness, which is not, cannot be the object of a tendency. Rather creatures tend to being and the perfection of their being. But this tendency comes from God who grants being to creatures. If a creature tends to non-being (as Sartre does), it is not because of his being but because of a deficiency in his being.[20] Nevertheless, the fact that creatures exist and that they continue to exist does not rest upon a prior choice of the individual as to whether he will exist or not exist because existing precedes any such possible choice. Rather the act of existing of a creature is in constant dependence upon God's power who wills that the creature should exist and should continue to exist. If "to be or not to be" is the question, it is a question whose answer lies not in man's mind but in God's will.

Now we may ask what relation there may be between the approach to the ontological need in Gabriel Marcel and in St. Thomas and his existentialist interpreters.

As we have seen, Gabriel Marcel affirms that the ontological need of man is best seen in presence, a personal "I-Thou" relationship. E. L. Mascall notes that Martin Buber and his followers have attacked Catholic theism for ignoring such a personal relationship and for regarding men as "passive and inactive objects in which the possibility of any direct responsible confrontation of human persons

---

[20]As we have seen, Sartre defines consciousness as the deficiency in the subject's being and it is through this deficiency that the subject tends to be God, to achieve its non-being which is only its idea of perfection. Here as in many other places, Sartre's thought is seen to be parasitic on much Thomistic thought, though of course he adjusts the terms to his own choice and omits the fundamental question of Being. I think that a strong case could be built up to show that one of Sartre's greatest desires is to show the impossibility of a valid psychology of religion in an essentialist Cartesian Thomistic system.

with a personal God is to all intents and purposes absent."[21] Such a criticism is perfectly valid against an essentialist Cartesian Thomism, but it is invalid against an existentialist Thomism. This does not mean that the existentialist Thomists would go as far as some who propound the "I-Thou" relationship and say that all relationships are personal. Nevertheless for every creature "in existing is not just passive, but it is performing, on its own level of being, an activity —the activity of existing—which, on a vastly higher level and in the analogical mode proper to rational beings composed of soul and body, we too perform."[22] As Marcel has strongly criticized man's misuse of material things in this century, so does Mascall affirm that such an exploitation derives from a refusal to admit that all creatures share in a common dignity as creatures of God. A proper regard for sub-human creatures will lead one to the personal "I-Thou" relationship with fellow humans and with God. Mascall writes:

> *Esse* is *esse a Deo* but it is also *esse ad Deum*, for the final end of every creature, the purpose for which it exists, is to glorify God, by manifesting in its operations, in *actu secundo*, the nature which it possesses in *actu primo* as the sheer gift of God. Subrational beings glorify God involuntarily and necessarily, and this is something not to be despised; but rational beings have the even greater privilege of glorifying him by the free and loving offering of their service. This is an offering that they are free to make or withhold; therein lie both the greatness and the wretchedness of man.[23]

However, Mascall affirms that man is made not only to serve God but to be united with Him. Yet a creature by itself cannot attain to union with its self-existing Creator and that is why a distinction is made between nature and supernature. Gabriel Marcel also affirms the value of such a distinction at the conclusion of his essay *Position et approches concrètes du mystère ontologiques* and in the concluding paragraph of *The Mystery of Being*, his Gifford Lectures. This does not mean that supernature is added in an extrinsic relation to nature. Rather by supernature the powers of nature are "released, enhanced and vivified."[24] The

[21]Mascall, *Existence and Analogy*, p. 182.
[22]*Ibid.*, p. 183.
[23]*Ibid.*, p. 184.
[24]*Ibid.*, p. 185.

natural order in itself is found to be incomplete and relative and, contrary to the essentialist belief, it cannot be explained in itself. Only in relation to God can the world be understood and thus there is felt the ontological need in the minds of conscious creatures to move into closer and fuller association with the one who made them. Gabriel Marcel writes: "It seems to me that if one investigates the Christian's fundamental notion of created nature, one is led to recognize at the basis of nature and of a reason which is ordered for it, a principle of radical inadequation to itself which is as the anxious anticipation of another order."[25] E. L. Mascall writes: "The dim and conditional yearning for union with God which is so striking a feature of human religion shows that in man the essential incompleteness and insufficiency of created being has at last reached a conscious awareness". . . . "Natural theology, by its very essence, cannot be a neatly rounded whole, for finite being, which is its subject-matter, is not a neatly rounded whole."[26]

Thus the human creature, aware of his dependence upon a self-existing Being, moves into a new knowledge of and union with his Creator through the grace and truth revealed to him by Christ and His Church. Therefore, for the existentialist interpreters of St. Thomas, the ontological need is best expressed in the fellowship of the Christian Church.

Let us summarize the existential approach to the ontological need.

1. Sartre in the ambiguity of his system finds an ontological need on both material and ideal realms. The material need which truly leads to being which exists, because it can be seen, is best expressed in suicide, in eating and drinking, and by sex. On the other hand, the ideal need in which man seeks a greater dignity through his nothingness is best expressed in man's desire to be God, by destruction and by enslavement of others. Yet these needs work against each other and the existing consciousness is left alone in the anguish of its dilemma.

2. Gabriel Marcel sees so many people in this scientific age whose ontological need has been stifled. He seeks to reveal this

[25]Marcel, *Position et approches concrètes*, pp. 90–1.
[26]Mascall, *Existence and Analogy*, p. 186.

need not in desire but in the need of man's whole being where he finds presence, a personal union with other beings. Thereby man escapes the isolation of his own existence. This ontological need for personal communion with other creatures and with God is best expressed in prayer and in generosity where grace is found to be the greatest gift of all.

3. E. L. Mascall and the existentialist interpreters of St. Thomas affirm that the more the creature realizes its dependence on God, the more it realizes a need of Him, and the more it realizes the glory of God's nature. Contrary to Cartesian Thomism, Mascall affirms that creatures are not mere passive objects but that all creatures participate in their own way in acknowledging God's glory. Like Marcel, he affirms that human beings do this in a personal way.

4. Finally, both Marcel and the existentialist interpreters of St. Thomas affirm that natural theology ends with a feeling of yearning for a greater knowledge of the Creator, which is only satisfied by Divine Revelation. This ontological need for a knowledge and power beyond the natural sphere is best expressed in the fellowship of the Christian Church.

Chapter Seven

THE PHILOSOPHERS' ABSOLUTE

SELDOM in the history of thought have men made such absolute declarations of an atheist position as those made by the French-non-Christian existentialists. Nietzsche declared that "God is dead" and a whole philosophy has been built up contingent upon that. Sartre writes in *Existentialism and Humanism* (p. 56): "Existentialism is nothing else but an attempt to draw the full conclusions from a consistently atheistic position."

The basic proposition is that the world is absurd because the atheist existentialists can see no sense in it.[1] This discovery of the world's absurdity results partly from their method because Sartre affirms that only that which is seen in immediate sense experience exists. Furthermore, since sense impressions vary from instant to instant, they bring no meaning in themselves; the "pour soi" or the individual consciousness forms the patterns and creates the possible conceptual meanings. Sartre concludes that, since the individual mind has to create its own meaning for its immediate sense impressions, then the world that exists, being only that which can be seen,

---

[1]The absurdity of the world, it should be stressed, is a basic proposition, not a conclusion. Sometimes in their writings, for example, Sartre's *The Wall*, or Camus' *Cross Purpose*, they seem to be trying so hard to demonstrate the absurdity that they fail to be convincing.

is absurd. Consciousness imposes its own meaning upon the existing world. However, the meaning which comes from the nothingness of consciousness is nothing. Only things which can be seen, not ideas, exist.

Consciousness may create meaning for things which can be seen and also meanings which do not apply to things which can be seen. Such are the concepts of value and of God. The word "God" may be very meaningful for a person but, in Sartre's terms, He cannot exist because He cannot be seen. He is pure nothingness. Therefore, when Sartre speaks of God, he must necessarily speak of Him in idealist essentialist and not existentialist terms, except in so far as he validly affirms that the absolute of Descartes and his rationalist successors was a pure creation of the mind which could have no existential validity. In other words, he has limited himself to a certain way of knowledge and refuses to recognize any other possible path. He has prejudiced himself against possible religious truth. This fact, combined with the overwhelming disorder of modern Europe, leads the atheist existentialists to substantiate their atheistic position in an absurd existence.

In his conception of being, Sartre distinguishes between the "pour soi" and the "en soi." "En soi" is self-contained being, or thing, and "pour soi" is conscious being, or man. A conscious being is always able to transcend itself by its consciousness and to seek new possibilities for itself by creating ideas and by directing its physical acts. Man is always seeking complete realization of his being. He yearns to experience the complete satisfaction of his own being in complete totality when he can be conscious of the fulfilment of all his hopes and dreams; he yearns for the identification of the 'pour soi" and "en soi." This totality of being is designated by the word "God." But it is impossible to achieve this end. For one reason, the ambition itself is a contradiction. In seeking to become God, man is aiming at a contradiction.

What is contradictory about God? If God is a supreme being, He must include all being. He must be the supreme "en soi." If He is the foundation of things, He must be a knowing being; then He would have to be the supreme "pour soi." But the nature of the "pour soi" is non-being. God then must be the non-being of Himself as "pour soi"; therefore, He must not be what He is. The idea of God is a contradiction in terms.

The "en soi" is all possibility, but it is the "pour soi" by imagination which introduces negation or lack into the world. However, only in a human world can there be lack. The French word "manque" (lack) is ambiguous and Sartre, in finding in the world only a God who is lacking, uses the word "lack" with three different meanings. First, in his treatment of the Philosophers' Absolute, God's lack is equivalent to His non-existence since He is, in this case, only a product of human consciousness. Secondly, in Sartre's criticism of God as presented by Christians, God's lack is not in existence but in essence because He does not ensure the triumph of goodness or destroy those who blaspheme. Thirdly, God's lack is Sartre's lack in so far as his desire to be God cannot be satisfied. This tripartite lack is the Trinity of Sartre's world.

Because there can be no possible synthesis of "pour soi" and "en soi," Sartre believes that he has proved a twofold lack, namely, the non-existence of God and the inability of human beings to achieve their highest ideal. He writes in *Being and Nothingness* (*L'Etre et le Néant*, p. 133):

When this totality whose being and absolute absence is hypostatized as a transcendence beyond the world, by an ulterior movement of meditation, it takes the name of God. And is not God at the same time a being who is what he is in so far as he is all positivity and the basis of the world—and at the same time a being who is not what he is and who is what he is not, in so far as he is a self-conscious and necessary basis of himself? The human reality suffers in its being because it arises from being as perpetually haunted by a totality which cannot be, since it could not become an "en soi" without destroying itself as "pour soi." It is then by nature unhappy consciousness, without possible transcendence from the state of unhappiness.

However, in the denial of God through the "pour soi–en soi" contradiction, it is important to note that Sartre proves nothing about God's existence, but rather he clearly demonstrates four other important truths.

1. Human beings may desire to be God.

2. Human beings are always becoming and live in a state of incompleteness.

3. If God exists, He is not a human being.

4. If God exists, He is more than an idea in the mind.

Descartes' ontological proof for the existence of God rests on the fact that man has a sense of perfection though perfection is lacking in the self; Sartre believes that he has shown the impossibility of Descartes' proof by his presentation of the "pour soi–en soi" contradiction. However, though Sartre criticizes Descartes for his anthropomorphic tendencies, yet in his criticism he remains guilty of anthropomorphism himself, applying human psychology to a divine nature.

A second proof of the non-existence of God arises for Sartre out of the problem of the other. Descartes sought refuge in God to ensure the correctness of the ideas in his mind with regard to the physical world; Leibniz sought God as a negation of the complete uniqueness and isolation of the individual consciousness. Leibniz, accepting the God of Descartes, endeavours to show how the monadistic world is pre-ordered at creation as the best of all possible worlds. However, Sartre demonstrates that, if the God of Leibniz has the single essential function of pre-establishing a harmony at creation, then the freedom of the individual is really a sham. God is really unnecessary; for one might just as easily begin with the assumption that everything including human beings runs by a predetermined principle. This is the assumption of the rationalist theistic systems of Spinoza and Hegel and the atheist systems of the eighteenth and nineteenth centuries.[2]

However, to adopt atheism for the reason that, if there is a God, He would determine Sartre in some way and invade his privacy, is not so much a denial of God's existence as a revolt against any being who determines Sartre's nature. If freedom is the key to Sartre's philosophy, then it is in his avowed atheism that he feels his greatest freedom, not in proving God's non-existence but in revolting against an essentialist God whose essence involves His existence and who governs His creatures by the necessary laws of His nature.

Furthermore, this God against which Sartre revolts is not the Christian Creator, but, as he points out himself, the God of Descartes, Leibniz and Hegel, ordered by the human mind's conception

2J.-P. Sartre, *Existentialism and Humanism*, p. 27.

of perfection. It may be that we are all completely determined, but it is only God who is able to see the complete plan of the universe. If we are completely determined, it would be impossible for a human being to have the freedom to stand aside to see the plan of determination. Nevertheless, a true element of freedom, as Spinoza has clearly seen, comes through a recognition of the laws which partly determine our existence.

Sartre conceives of God as the artisan who gives form to the matter of his craftsmanship, much like the Prime Mover of Aristotle. But the Christian Creator gives not only form but existence to His creatures and, therefore, the analogy of the artisan is always inadequate in presenting the Christian doctrine of God. Kant has shown that a creature is to a certain point determined by necessary laws, but also, in so far as it exists as a thing in itself, it has a measure of freedom. This freedom is centred in the acceptance or refusal of the divine imperative. As Sartre has pointed out, the created product becomes an object for the artisan and, in its separate existence, it may enjoy a certain measure of freedom and privacy. It is this measure of freedom that Sartre cherishes.

Leibniz's doctrine of creation and Sartre's creation by the artisan are not the same as the Christian doctrine of creation. For the Christian, it is a miracle that he was created, but it is equally a miracle that he continues to exist. God did not create the world and leave it, but goes on creating and sustaining it, working through the free souls of men. Gabriel Marcel appropriately uses the analogy of music in which the various parts flow in harmony or discord in relation to the basic theme.

A third approach to the question of God is made by Sartre through a discussion of being perceived by another. As exemplified by many of his novels, this discussion, which is clearly related to Berkeley's conception of God, seems to have a great appeal for Sartre.[3] The basic way to knowledge, for Sartre, is by sense experience. However, since the self cannot see itself, it cannot know itself, except as seen by another. However, as the self is looked at by another, a new dimension is added to the situation which escapes the self and, in some ways, makes it vulnerable. The other person

[3]Note particularly Daniel's conversion in *The Reprieve*, pp. 122-3, 363.

has opinions about the self which the self cannot know and the other person looks at the self from an angle which it is impossible for the self to share. Indeed, anything which escapes me in my situation is the manifestation of another entering my situation. For example, I draw a small table toward me gently in order to bring a fragile vase on the table within my reach. But this movement makes a bronze statuette fall which breaks the vase. There is nothing here that I could not have foreseen if I had been more attentive; there is nothing that escapes me by principle. However, if another person enters the situation, a new dimension is introduced that I did not want. I am no longer master of it. Carried to the extreme, this is what Gide calls "le part du diable" and it is also the unforeseen that the art of Kafka tries to describe. For Kafka it is the divine for whom the human act is truly constituted. But Sartre sees that God is here only the idea of the other pushed to the limit.

When another person looks at me, I know I am in space and time and this produces in me feelings of fear (a feeling of being in danger in the face of the freedom of the other), shame (a feeling of being finally what I am), and slavery (a feeling of alienation from all my possibilities). Shame is the feeling of original guilt, not because I have committed any sin, but simply because I have fallen into the world and I have need of the mediation of another to see myself as I really am. "Shame before God is the recognition of my objectivity before a subject which can never become object. At the same time I realize my objectivity in the absolute, and I hypostatize it. The position of God is accompanied by a reification of my objectivity; rather I posit my being-object-for-God as more real than my 'pour soi'; I exist alienated and I make myself learn from my exterior what I ought to be. That is the origin of fear before God."[4]

The self, feeling a sense of shame before the absolute subject, may come to resent this subject and seek to treat the absolute subject as an object in order that the self may gain some power over the one who controls him so absolutely. This effort to make the absolute subject an object is black magic. The aim is to make God suffer, to irritate Him by turning to evil on purpose in order to preserve the privacy and self-respect of the "pour soi." It is clear

---

[4]J.-P. Sartre, *L'Etre et le Néant*, p. 350.

that Sartre himself, especially in his play *Lucifer and the Lord*, is practising black magic because that is the only way that he can protect himself and his freedom in case the God of Berkeley does exist, a God who would try to make him a determined, physical object by looking at him.

Yet Sartre points out that this God who regards him cannot but be a contradiction; therefore His existence is impossible. However, even if this God of Berkeley does exist who looks at him as an object and treats his being as an "en soi," by the very fact that he can think that God is looking at him, there is an act of perceiving within him that escapes God's gaze. It is this nothingness at the heart of his existence that ensures for Sartre his freedom. Kierkegaard has said that the essence of man is sin; for that is the only thing that separates him from God. For Sartre, freedom in self-consciousness is the equivalent of sin; for its essence is in a rejection of God. It is the one thing that ensures for Sartre that God will not enslave him and regard him as any other purely physical object.

Is this to assume the existence of a God whose existence Sartre himself has so vehemently denied? Perhaps so, but that is the very thing that Sartre does in dealing with the question of God. To say "no," he must have something to deny. It is clear that what Sartre is really talking about is not being or existence, which he has already assumed, but a psychology of religion. He is not on a metaphysical level but on a practical level in which he aptly demonstrates the disastrous reaction that may occur in the human soul as a result of a false conception of God.

To say that God can see me only as an object is to apply the phenomenological method anthropomorphically to God. This is an invalid application of phenomenology since God is beyond our sense experience. Furthermore, to deny the existence of a God who is total being and who is also aware of His total being is to apply a human psychology to a divine nature unjustifiably. Doubtless Sartre is here endeavouring to reveal the contradiction in Hegel's dialectically ordered Trinity.

The fourth approach by Sartre to the question of God is made through a desire for community. Often God is said to unite people, to bridge the gap between self and others. However, this is only an unrealizable ideal because it is impossible by one's very nature to overcome the contingency of one's relationships with other people. Of course, the ideal, the motive and the end of love is this value of unity. However, in love, one person makes another an absolute reference around which everything else is purely relative. The person loved is even treated as the absolute source of values. In other words, when one person loves another, it is to make him a God.

To wish to be loved, then, is to wish to be God in order that the self may gain power over other people and other things. To wish to be loved is to wish to have one's ego supremely exalted. But if this is true, then the relationship between lovers cannot be regarded as just one example of love-in-the-world, but rather it must be seen as some absolute. Lovers must say that they were made for each other, and, at this point, God is introduced as a means of expressing the passage to the absolute. In fact, says Sartre, God is not necessary; what the loved one needs is for the lover to make of him an absolute choice. The loved one's existence then feels justified.

Obviously this is a complete degradation of the ontological view of love. In the first place, love is represented as a means to enslave people and to gain power over the world. Any love that the loved one has is no more than a sham, a mask for the seducer. If the loved one is a human being, his desire to be loved can be no more than the will to power. If God seeks the love of people, Sartre feels that He can be no more than a seducer, who wants people to love Him in order that He may gain power over them. Therefore, for Sartre, to love God would be to freely deny freedom and to enslave oneself to an autocratic power. However, Kierkegaard has already pointed out, in his *Diary of the Seducer*, that a human being who seeks love may be a seducer, but the greatest paradox is that God who first loved us is not a seducer. The First Epistle of St. John in many places answers the atheism of the non-Christian existentialists and in 4:10, 11 the writer gives the Christian answer to Sartre's reasoning: "Herein is love, not that we loved God but that He loved us and sent His Son to be the propitiation for our sins. Beloved, if God so loved us, we ought also to love one another." In the metaphysical order, we love one another because God loved us.

Sartre, emphasizing the epistemological and psychological level, says that when men love they seek justification for their love in the absolute—God. By explaining the psychological origin of the faith of some people, Sartre feels he has explained God away. Yet to explain the psychological origin of religion is to say nothing about God whatsoever, let alone deny His existence. This is the same fallacy that Freud commits when he says that men turn to God to replace their earthly father. Therefore, Freud, like Sartre, falsely concludes that God is an illusion.

A fifth approach to the question of God is made through the desire for a possible concept of humanity. If two people act together or if a third person watches the two, they are regarded as either "we" or "us." This implies that there can exist a projection, abstract and unrealizeable, of the "pour soi" towards an absolute totalization of itself and all others. The recovery of human totality is impossible without the existence of a third, distinct by principle from humanity, through the eyes of which all humanity is object. It is a third in connection with all possible groups, and in no case can enter into community with a human group; therefore, it is a third to which no one else can be a third. This concept is the same as that of the regarding being who can never be regarded, namely God. Thus God is characterized by radical absence or transcendence.[5]

Sartre here presents a truth that Christians have declared already. It is only through God that the natural law, a universal picture of humanity, can be gained. In the face of so much chaos in the world, this cannot be emphasized too greatly. However, Sartre, excluding the existence of any concept, opposes even more strongly this concept of God because, if such a God existed, He would determine Sartre's freedom by giving him a human nature. Sartre says that any sense of human order comes only when I and others create an order and agree to it, a statement which reflects his views on responsibility in politics.

In this approach, Sartre emphasizes the total otherness of God. This is in the tradition of Kierkegaard, and Karl Barth, but they say that God is totally other because the human creature is sinful. Although he professes to be opposed to logical systems of thought,

[5]*Ibid.*, p. 495.

Sartre appears to be strongly influenced by them; for his views of God demand either total immanence or absolute transcendence. He reflects much of the spirit of eighteenth-century deism.[6] E. L. Mascall writes in *He Who Is* (p. 126): "The God of Deism oscillates between a genuine transcendence and a spurious immanence; but he is far from being the God of Christian theism." Because of his deistic approach, Sartre is never able to enter into a full understanding of the Christian conception of God who is both immanent and transcendent. Mascall writes (p. 129):

The God of traditional Christian theism is both transcendent and immanent. He is transcendent because, as we have maintained in a previous chapter, "a first cause who was himself in even the very least degree involved in the mutability, contingency or insufficiency of the universe would provide no more in the way of an explanation of the existence of the universe than it could provide itself; such a God would provide a foundation neither for himself nor for anything else." He is immanent because unless every finite being was sustained at its ontological root by his incessant creative action—unless, to use the scholastic terms, he was in it by "essence, presence and power"—it would collapse into non-existence through sheer insufficiency; it would in Julian of Norwich's phrase, "fall to naught for littleness." And both the terms "transcendent" and "immanent" are relative to the created world; God is transcendent to it and immanent in it. Furthermore, they are intimately related to each other, for they both arise out of the fact that the world is God's creation.

A sixth approach is made by Sartre to the question of God through a discussion of morality in freedom. For some people, suffering is being; for they cannot see themselves in a better state. But when one can imagine a better state for oneself, one acts with the intention of achieving that state. The state of things cannot motivate an act because an act is a projection of the "pour soi" to what it is not and what is cannot determine, in itself, what is not. Therefore, the indispensable condition of all action is the freedom of the acting being. Some people try to explain freedom by laws and rules, but laws and rules necessarily destroy what freedom is. The reason

[6]To show the deistic approach to God in the writings of Merleau-Ponty, J. M. LeBlond writes in an article on "Atheistic Humanism at the Collège de France" (*Etudes*, March, 1953, p. 338), "This God, a projection of man himself, is certainly impossible. However it is not God."

for our acts is in ourselves; we act as we are and our acts contribute to make us what we are. Human reality is free in the exact measure in which it has to be its own nothingness. Sartre would say that Kant's moral governor, God, is only presented to justify his moral acts.[7]

It is important to recognize individual freedom and responsibility in making moral choices. However, because we are free, we must be free to accept guidance to make the best choice, and especially God's guidance. If we declare that the reasons for a moral choice are always our own, we are limiting our freedom and becoming slaves to ourselves. Sartre has been so concerned not to become a slave to God that he has become a slave to himself as he strives himself to be God. This leads him not to contentment but to solitude and anguish. This is demonstrated in *The Flies* when Orestes says to Jupiter: "Be careful; you have just avowed your weakness. I do not hate you. What are you to me? We'll slip against each other without touching, as two ships. You are a God and I am free: we are likewise alone and our anguish is similar."[8]

Beigbeder, taking *The Flies* as an example, shows, in *L'Homme Sartre*, that by human freedom God for Sartre is reduced to nothing. "It is human freedom which makes God pass away into nothingness. From the moment that Orestes has recognized the fact of his freedom, Jupiter no longer exists in the words of the theatre. There is no need for a creator, there is no creation, the creature creates itself, rather: it is itself." (P. 28.)

All the proofs that Sartre gives to deny the existence of God fail to do this and Sartre recognizes that his aim is not actually to disprove God's existence but to make man aware of his own existence. He writes: "Existentialism is not atheist in the sense that it would exhaust itself in demonstrations of the non-existence of God. It declares rather that even if God existed that would make no difference from its point of view. Not that we believe God does exist, but we think that the real problem is not that of His existence; what man needs is to find himself again and to understand that

[7]Sartre, *L'Etre et le Néant*, p. 516.
[8]J.-P. Sartre, *Les Mouches*, p. 135.

nothing can save him from himself, not even a valid proof of the existence of God."[9]

Despite all his efforts to disprove God's existence in *Being and Nothingness*, Sartre believes that God's existence cannot be proved either way. Pascal felt the same way, but he felt it was better to take a chance on God's existence, with a hope for infinite reward. Sartre feels that it is better for man not to take the chance but to face up to himself. Beigbeder, in *L'Homme Sartre*, attempts to present Sartre's thought in this way (p. 27): "I really wish that one could demonstrate that God is not, but one will never demonstrate that he is. I defy you to know anything of it. No faculty permits me to attain it or to infer it. Kant, after having shown the impossibility of acceding to a superior noumenon, re-establishes it as a postulate. What necessity is there, at least in being circumvented by pseudo-moral reasons? It is wiser to follow Lucretius and to deny with him this God who is never seen in his heaven."

Sartre's declarations of atheism are certainly obvious and yet they are so stressed that one comes to doubt if Sartre is actually an atheist. At times in his writings, he gives the impression of a baby crying in order to draw attention to itself—to tempt God to become angry and really come forth and show Himself. At other times, he gives the impression of one who desires to come close to God the easy way—to be an associate of God. He will not lower himself to come the usual way through the Church; perhaps he feels that as a sophisticate he has a better chance and will gain more respect from God by coming in his own way. At times he reminds one of a civilian visitor on a Navy Ship who escapes the disciplinary procedure and who may have a chance to "hob-nob" with the Captain whereas the rating comes strictly under the ship's discipline and will seldom see the Captain, and probably never have the opportunity to "hob-nob" with him.

It has been suggested that Sartre might become a Christian and this certainly is not beyond the range of possibility. Yet despite frequent contact with Christians he still declares himself to be as strong an atheist as ever. Even when Georges Bataille, a close

[9] Sartre, *Existentialism and Humanism*, p. 56.

associate of his, turned to mysticism, it had no effect on Sartre's declared position, despite his keen preoccupation with religious concepts. Even some priests have expressed admiration for religious sentiments in Sartre's writing.[10]

A philosophical position which grew in close association with Sartre is that of Albert Camus—*The Rebel*. His preoccupation was not with atheism but with an anti-theism, indeed, an anti-anything that seeks to dominate man in his situation.[11]

Like Sartre, Camus, in *The Myth of Sisyphus*, begins with the assumption that the situation into which man is born is absurd and full of despair. Man's responsibility is to put meaning and happiness into the world. If a God made a world such as ours, He is not to be obeyed but to be resisted at every turn. This God cannot but be evil and man must fight for goodness and rationality in the world. That is his destiny. Therefore, Camus sets himself up as a champion like Prometheus to seek to release man from his burdens. This attitude is exemplified in his novel *The Plague*.

Camus' whole argument centres on the very ancient theme that if God is all-powerful, He cannot be good, or if He is good, He cannot be all-powerful. If He were good, He would alleviate misery and absurdity in the world, if He could. But if He wants to help but is not able to do so, then He needs the help of men. In any case, the responsibilities fall upon men who cannot honestly avoid them. Camus suggests that despite an unjust creation and a threatened punishment in hell, God is not to be dreaded as much as the cruel conquerors of this age. God may punish in hell, but the conquerors seek to dominate by restricting the freedom of man and that is worse.[12]

For Camus, the idea of God becomes the denial of human reason, justice and freedom. Gabriel Marcel asks: "Why does the man not

[10]M. Beigbeder, *L'Homme Sartre*, p. 33.

[11]Camus' obvious anti-theism was one of the reasons for the break between him and Sartre. In a review of Camus' *The Rebel* in *Les Temps Modernes* (May, 1952, p. 2085), F. Jeanson accused Camus of anti-theism as well as severely criticizing his book. "Camus is most certainly not an atheist: he is a passive antitheist." Camus wrote to Sartre complaining of this review of his book but Sartre replied supporting Jeanson. A rift resulted in a friendship which had lasted throughout the war. Gabriel Marcel also affirms Camus' refusal of salvation in *Homo Viator*, pp. 278 f.

[12]See A Camus, *L'Etat de siège*, p. 223.

want to reach the affirmation of God which awaits him at the end of the journey? It may be because the affirmation seems to him incompatible with the fundamental data of experience, with the existence, for example, of suffering and all the forms which evil takes. A man like Albert Camus, for instance, cannot see how a God worthy of that name can tolerate the sufferings of children."[13]

Primarily, the non-Christian existentialists react against the philosophers' God who is a necessary being whose essence involves His existence, and who consequently must act as an autocrat to His creation if He is to act at all. As a result, there is a strong prophetic element in their writings, implying that, if they are to accept God, He must be a more perfect being than the perfect absolute of the philosophers.

E. L. Mascall clearly points out that God revealed in Christ is not the philosophers' absolute. In chapter IV of *He Who Is*, he has carefully noted objections to the first formulation of the ontological proof by St. Anselm who defined God as "that than which nothing greater can be conceived." He notes St. Thomas's criticism of St. Anselm's argument because of its failure to recognize the fact that, though a God with a nature as defined by St. Anselm must be thought of as existing, that does not say that this God exists. Rather God is the self-existing Being whom I find by reason of the dependent and finite existing of myself and of all creatures. In chapter II of *Existence and Analogy*, Mascall goes on to show the similar weakness of the ontological argument as presented in its later form by Descartes, Leibniz and Spinoza.

If God is perfection, then perfection is not to be discovered in an idea, or a definition, nor is it to be discovered as an object of a desire, but rather perfection is seen in the pure act of Being. It is sometimes said rather disparagingly that a thing barely exists, and yet to exist is the most perfect thing that any being can do. So often philosophers, in seeking to find an absolute, have overlooked the act of existing or taken it for granted, and the result has been purely a creation of the mind. Sartre has shown the fallacies of philosophers in their creation of an absolute and yet he can approach God in no other way, by the very terms of his philosophical method.

[13]G. Marcel, *The Mystery of Being*, Part II, p. 175.

In an article in *Being and Having* entitled "Some Remarks on the Irreligion of To-day," Gabriel Marcel seeks to point out essential weaknesses in modern thought which tend to destroy man's religious faith. In the first place, he considers rationalism or the philosophy of the Enlightenment as exemplified by Brunschvicg. Though rationalism tends to reduce man to being just another atom in the universe, God is also reduced to merely an abstract ideal. Furthermore, though man seems to be reduced in one sense, he exalts himself by an undue pride through his science in affirming that, in the modern age, man can understand the world as never before. "To Saint Augustine, Saint Thomas and Saint Bonaventure, God is the center and God alone. But to-day it is the human mind, dehumanised, stripped of all power, all presence, and all existence and then put in God's place to act as His substitute."[14] Marcel emphasizes that the basis of such a rationalist approach to the world is a pride which escapes the living, historical and concrete realities of the world.

Modern rationalism would not be any great stumbling block to religious belief if it did not have the powerful ally of applied science. It is in the distinction between idealism and applied science that the difference between the approaches of Sartre and Camus to God can be made clearer. Though the idealist approach implies a pride, the measure of pride is not as great as that of the narrow scientist. Marcel writes of the distinction: "Man is treated now not as Mind but as technical power, and appears as the sole citadel of orderly arrangement in a world which is unworthy of him; a world which has not deserved him, and has to all appearance produced him quite haphazard—or rather, he has wrenched himself out of it by a violent act of emancipation. That is the full meaning of the Prometheus myth."[15]

Marcel finds a second weakness in modern thought in the scientific attitude to man which seems to invade man's whole being and leave untouched only the human feelings for pleasure or pain. By applied science, man seeks a firm hold upon himself. Pure religion, as Marcel affirms, is the exact contrary: "No gesture is more signifi-

---

[14]G. Marcel, *Being and Having*, p. 184.
[15]*Ibid.*, p. 187. It is the Prometheus myth that Camus adopts as his own.

cant than the joined hands of the believer, mutely witnessing that nothing can be done and nothing changed and that he comes simply to give himself up."[16] This attitude of prayer is not a passive state but an activity distinct from that of the technician. Kant's division of reason into theoretical and practical seemed to leave no place for the contemplative virtues and this division has had a tremendous influence in modern philosophy, especially in the writings of Sartre and his followers, who also allow no place for contemplation. It is by a reliance on the unfounded postulates of one's own mind that an act of worship may be regarded as completely divorced from reality. However, Marcel believes that if we go behind these postulates, "it is possible for us to recover the basic idea of sacred knowledge: and this alone can restore its reality to contemplation."[17]

A third weakness in modern thought comes with a love for life, for the Vital, seen in the philosophies of Bergson and Gide. There is an inherent ambiguity as to whether the concern is with "my life" or with life in general. To live by life in general is to revert to rationalism and to live by a vital approach to life is to be a slave of desire. "A man who really lived by it would be destined, is destined, and will be destined to the worst of spiritual catastrophes."[18]

Marcel affirms that salvation can only be found when the self makes a distinction between his being and his life. The distinction implies both that my life has been given to me and that meaning comes to my life by the fact that my being is somehow at stake. Christianity stands or falls by this truth to which it bears witness, but this truth can only realize its full power as Christians work to clear away the rubble of so much in modern thought about man and his being.

It is important not to underestimate the work that Sartre has done in clearing away so many of the false conceptions of God in modern idealism. He has truly pointed out that the God presented in Descartes, Leibniz, Berkeley and Hegel is unworthy of the name since He is purely a creation of the mind.

If one can move from Sartre's clearing of the rubble into Marcel's thought, it will be possible to see how Sartre has been limited in his

[16]*Ibid.*, p. 190.
[17]*Ibid.*, p. 192.
[18]*Ibid.*, p. 199.

terms by the very idealistic and empirical tendencies against which he reacts. In Marcel, we see the reintroduction of the third dimension, contemplation, which has been lost since the beginning of modern philosophy. By contemplation, a new vision is opened into the reality of God. Finally, if one moves from Marcel to St. Thomas and his existentialist interpreters, a solid intellectual basis is found in which modern knowledge may be given its true setting in relation to the supreme existential fact of the self-existing Being who creates and sustains in existing everything and everyone that is. This God is both immanent in a world which He creates and preserves and transcendent to it in His self-existing.

Let us summarize the approach of the French existentialists to the philosophers' absolute.

1. All deny the validity of arguments by philosophers to prove an absolute being whose essence involves His existence.

2. Sartre by means of psychology demonstrates that the absolute is merely a product of wishful thinking. However, after exposing philosophers' arguments for the absolute, he affirms that the existence of God cannot be proved either way. His basic assumption is that there is no God and the world is absurd.

3. Marcel exposes the philosophers' absolute by showing that thinking which leads to such an absolute has led to most of the contemporary irreligious tendencies.

4. Mascall and the existentialist interpreters of St. Thomas expose the philosophers' absolute by showing the fallacies of the ontological argument for the existence of God as presented by St. Anselm and by Descartes and idealist philosophers who have followed him. Those who pursue the ontological argument seek perfection in an absolute creation of the mind, but perfection can only be found in the act of existing and absolutely in the pure act of Being.

Chapter Eight

VALUES

A COMPARISON of values[1] in the writings of Christian and non-Christian French existentialists must necessarily be inadequate because Sartre's expected work on ethics has not yet been published. However, in Sartre's own writings and in those of Simone de Beauvoir, a great deal of the ethical approach of the non-Christian existentialists has been revealed.

The recognition of any permanent ethical values presents a peculiar difficulty for non-Christian existentialists. As we have seen, the two instruments of truth which Sartre recognizes are reason and immediate sense experience. Immediate sense experience provides the existential index and, because of this, it enjoys a slight superiority over reason. A completely rational essence is a static, universal essence which is not in keeping with the historical character of all things that exist in space and time. Therefore, there is great difficulty for Sartre in presenting a system of values which, if presented as absolute, would destroy the historical character of the human situation. Camus notes this difficulty in *The Rebel* when he writes: "Atheist existentialism has at least the will to create a

[1]Part of this chapter has already been published as an article in the *Anglican Theological Review*, April, 1956, under the title "Freedom and Being Free."

morality. One must wait for this moral system. But the true difficulty will be to create it without reintroducing into historic existence
a value that is foreign to history."[2]

For a stone or for a table, there is no need of values because they
simply are. Yet man is aware of a nothingness in his own being and
also of his becoming. It is the mind of man, according to Sartre, that
introduces nothingness into the world and it is the mind that projects the self into the future to imagine what the self will become.
Consequently, it is also the mind of the individual which creates
values for himself as he imagines himself as he ought to be. Thus,
for Sartre, values are a product of the nothingness of the human
existence and there is no value that can have ontological validity
unless chosen by a human consciousness. Simone de Beauvoir
writes in *Pyrrhus et Cinéas*: "Without me, no values exist that are
completely made and whose hierarchy is imposed upon my
decisions" (p. 91).

A value has no existence in itself, according to Sartre, yet any
value receives actuality in the person who acts upon it, having first
created it by his choice. What the non-Christian existentialists call
the "authentic man" is a man who must choose. Even a refusal to
choose is in reality a choice. Furthermore, since each man realizes
himself to be a subject among other subjects, each choice must be
taken in responsibility not only to the individual self but also to all
men. However, the great difficulty in choosing is to choose the good
and not the bad and man's existence is constantly coloured by
anguish because it is hard for man to know whether he is choosing
the good or the bad, even though each man decides for himself
what is good and bad. Sartre writes in *Existentialism and Humanism*: "To choose between this or that is at the same time to affirm
the value of that which is chosen; for we are unable ever to choose
to worse. What we choose is always the better; and nothing can be
better for us unless it is better for all" (p. 29). A worker may
have the choice of joining a Christian or a communist union. If he
chooses the Christian, according to Sartre, he is choosing the good
that resignation is "the attitude that best becomes a man" since
Sartre believes that, for the Christian, man's kingdom is not upon

[2]A. Camus, *L'Homme révolté*, p. 305 n.

this earth. Therefore, to choose the Christian union is to choose resignation not only as a value for the individual worker but as a value for all men.

Sartre's approach to values is almost the same as Kant's approach to the categorical imperative. The difference, of course, is that whereas for Kant the categorical imperative was the result of a universal mental process which, though used by the individual, was valid for all men, Sartre believes that the minds of people are separated by existence and there is no guarantee of any universal mental process. Nevertheless "one ought always to ask oneself what would happen if everyone did as one is doing."[3] Furthermore, in making such a choice, one is never sure of all the circumstances of the choice or of its consequences. Sartre refers to the anguish of Abraham in the angel's command to him to sacrifice his son Isaac. Kierkegaard has considered this in his book *Fear and Trembling* and regards Abraham's choice as the supreme choice or "leap into existence." Yet Sartre points out that there was no certainty in making the choice since Abraham could not be absolutely sure if it was the angel who was calling him, nor if he was the Abraham who was called. There is no absolute value and there is no proof for the self that it is choosing according to a certain value.

Gabriel Marcel affirms that, when the universal realm of being is ignored, then ethical values are reduced to pure subjectivity and in Sartre they are reduced even further to choice in its most gratuitous form. Though Sartre affirms that one should act for the freedom of all men, yet his very approach opens the way for any sort of abuse, as the teen-age existentialists of Paris have shown. The total disregard for values held sacred by past ages will lead people to think of all conduct usually called virtuous as pharisaical, without at the same time distinguishing "between prejudice and the free adoption of loose conduct."[4]

Kantian ethics had the great merit of asserting that persons should be treated as ends, and Marcel affirms that the great success that Kant's writings enjoyed in the nineteenth century was due to a "mental climate soaked in the Christian spirit."[5] The fault of

[3]J.-P. Sartre, *Existentialism and Humanism*, pp. 30–1.
[4]G. Marcel, *The Mystery of Being*, Part II, p. 92.
[5]*Ibid.*, p. 93.

Kantian ethics was to assume the existential perspective and to treat morals on a purely abstract level. According to Marcel, "the qualities proper to the affirmations of the moral conscience and the way in which they should actually be considered, cannot be taken as being independent of the concrete context which is their setting."[6]

Furthermore, science cannot help in the realization of values, nor can popular polls. So often people feel justified in pursuing a certain type of conduct because many other people are found to do the same thing. Marcel sees a danger that the"technocratic craze will gradually succeed in drowning every feeling for values, and this is precisely because they are eternal, and a man who lived two thousand years ago was at bottom no better and no worse off, than we are, for knowing what is or is not right."[7] At the present time, man may regress in morals to the level of pre-Christian thought which was a preparation "not only for welcoming Revelation, but even for the acceptance of any moral evidence."[8] The recognition of values is intimately associated with the life of worship —"worthship"—which is best expressed in prayer and service. It is here that the worldly and vulgar value of efficiency is transcended in a reverence not only for other persons (including young children and the aged) but primarily for Being itself. It is on this level that the false unity in identity of modern science (assumed in Communism and in Sartre's humanism) is replaced by a unity in value, which is to be recognized in true affection, in fellowship and in love.

Though at the conclusion of Existentialism and Humanism (p. 56), Sartre says that it makes no difference if God exists or does not exist, yet he says in the middle of this essay (pp. 32–3) that he is seeking to draw the consequences of the fact that God does not exist. Furthermore, he suggests that, if God did exist, he would be the reality of certain values rationally determined. Sartre deplores those who seek to "suppress God at the least possible expense" (p. 33). They deny God's existence but affirm the values traditionally embodied in a God determined by human reason. He sum-

[6]Ibid., p. 93–4.
[7]Ibid., p. 99.
[8]Ibid., p. 100.

marizes their attitude (p. 33): "It must be considered obligatory *a priori* to be honest, not to lie, not to beat one's wife, to bring up children and so forth; so we are going to do a little work on this subject, which will enable us to show that these values exist all the same, inscribed in an intelligible heaven although, of course, there is no God." In opposition to this attitude, Sartre affirms that, because God does not exist, there is no good *a priori*. There are no values or commands than can legitimize human behaviour and man is left alone without justification or excuse.

However, it is at the moment when Sartre concludes that there are no absolute values that he discovers one—freedom. Since man is not rationally determined, he is *freedom*. "We have neither behind us, nor before us in a luminous realm of values, any means of justification or excuse. We are left alone, without excuse. That is what I mean when I say that man is condemned to be free. Condemned, because he did not create himself, yet is nevertheless at liberty, and from the moment that he is thrown into this world he is responsible for everything he does."[9] The young man who came to Sartre for advice whether he should stay with his mother or join the Free French forces could not be helped by any abstract ethical formulae, nor did he have any instinct to guide him. Feeling is formed in immediate participation and therefore it cannot be a guide to action. "I can neither seek within myself for an authentic impulse to action, nor can I expect from some ethic, formulae that will enable me to act."[10] Sartre advised the young man who came to him to invent his own morality because he believes that, in concrete circumstances, the one absolute value of freedom can have no other end but itself and any man who realizes how abandoned a creature he is can will nothing else than freedom as the basis of all his values.

This freedom must be willed by the separated consciousness, and not in community, because the individual initially finds himself isolated. However as soon as he chooses freedom, the individual also, is obliged by his very choice of this value to choose the freedom of others.

[9]Sartre, *Existentialism and Humanism*, p. 34.
[10]*Ibid.*, p. 37.

In an article on "La Liberté cartésienne,"[11] Sartre reveals his debt to Descartes in establishing his approach to freedom. By his doubt, Descartes recognized that truth required the acceptance by the individual mind before it could really be regarded as truth. In that sense, truth is human. Consequently, the human mind is always free to avoid searching for truth, to affirm that truth is untruth or to affirm that an untruth is truth. Sartre notes that for Descartes God was the author of truth and therefore the individual could not invent the truth but only say "no" to it. That for Sartre is the only freedom allowed to the Christian.

It is this negative aspect of freedom which is most important for Sartre. It is when *The Chips are Down*, when the self feels itself to be most determined, most oppressed, that the self in self-consciousness is aware of its freedom. There is always a measure of freedom in the self-conscious subject who is always able to say or think "no." In the moment of greatest oppression, the issue is then made most plain because the self is then aware of its own consciousness which belongs to the self and to no one else. If the self is destroyed, self-consciousness is also destroyed and therefore it can never be ruled by anyone but the living self. During the war, at the time of the German occupation of France, when every activity was watched by the Germans, it was then that Sartre felt most free. "Never have we been more free than under the German occupation. We had lost all our rights and that of speaking first; we were insulted to our faces every day and we had to be silent; they deported us 'en masse,' as workers, as Jews, as political prisoners. Everywhere, on the walls, in the newspapers, on the screen, we recognized this impure and dull look that our oppressors wished to give us of ourselves. Because of all that we were 'free.' "[12] In Sartre's play *Men without Shadows*, it is freedom in negation that the men who refuse to talk under torture seek to preserve. In this case, freedom is preserved in the face of physical compulsion. However, Sartre regards all necessity as a form of physical compulsion. Therefore, it is probably in his atheism that he experiences his greatest freedom. Since Sartre regards God as the neces-

[11]Sartre, *Situations*, I, pp. 314 f.
[12]J.-P. Sartre, "La République du silence," *Eternelle Revue*, I; quoted in R. Campbell, *Jean-Paul Sartre ou une littérature philosophique*, p. 223.

sary being of Descartes and of the essentialist Cartesian Thomists, he sees that such a God determines everything that is. Therefore, in *The Flies*, Orestes revolts against his parents and the rulers of the state, but perhaps his strongest revolt is against Jupiter. Though Sartre denies God's existence, it is in the act of denying God's existence that he realizes his own abandonment and consequent freedom.

In his consideration of freedom in Descartes, Sartre sees that in the Cartesian system God Himself is the only one who is really free. God as the *causa sui* is able to determine His own nature as well as that of His creation. He notes that Descartes, like Goethe, would not say "in the beginning was the word" but "in the beginning was the act."[13] God first existed and then He created His own nature by His will. God willed the truth. But then Sartre asks, if God does not exist, is not man free to create his own nature and his own truth? Here we find the possibility of Sartre's positive freedom which is associated with his humanism. Though the self is doomed for life to be oppressed in some way or other, yet in resisting certain oppressors the self may realize a companionship with others who are resisting the same thing. This aspect of positive freedom developed from Sartre's association with the Resistance movement during the German occupation of France. "Each one of them (The Resisters) freely and irretrievably undertook to be himself against the oppressors and in choosing himself in his freedom, he chose the freedom of all."[14] By an imaginary projection into the future, the self visualizes the end for which it is acting. This projection is produced by the free consciousness of the self and, in imagination, the self is free to set a goal and the self immediately defines itself in a new freedom in choosing a new goal for itself. As long as the self is living, it freely projects itself into the future. At death, the self becomes itself and then it is nothing.

It is important to note that, when Sartre speaks of freedom or of any other value, he deals with them abstractly, as ideas in the mind of the existing person. Because of this, all values such as

13Sartre, *Situations*, I, p. 333.
14Sartre, "La République du silence," quoted in Campbell, *Jean-Paul Sartre*, p. 223.

love, joy, hope and justice are artificial values to be artificially imposed upon the existing world. Any attempt to impose these values is really done in "mauvaise foi." Since, for Sartre, negative freedom is the only value that has ontological validity, then only the negation of value can have existence in desire, isolation, hate, masochism, indifference and sadism.[15] Therefore, when a person seeks freedom or any other value (except negative freedom to which man is condemned), he is attempting the impossible task of actualizing an abstract ideal. In contrast to this, Gabriel Marcel does not ask the question "What is freedom?" but rather "What is a free man?"[16] It is by the variation in the question asked that one can see the distinction between the ideal, psychological approach of Sartre and the ontological approach of Gabriel Marcel.

Marcel accuses Sartre of degrading freedom by making it too easy.[17] In his statement that "man is condemned to be free," however, Sartre refers to the freedom in negation which is not a value chosen for a man's good but an affirmation of the isolation of the human consciousness which is characteristic of the deficiency in the human being. Marcel notes that Sartre is twisting words by turning this privation in the human being into the value of freedom.[18]

Marcel distinguishes the ego or the individual from the person. The person is characterized by commitment with responsibility for what is done and what is said. Effective commitment is an act of freedom, but Marcel does not regard freedom as irresponsible or as total. Personal freedom is a freedom orientated to others and to God; it is founded in and orientated to Being. For Marcel, personal commitment, community and Being go together and must be apprehended together. In contrast to this, Sartre seems much more materialistic, his writings showing a marked influence of the French Enlightenment.

From the intensity of the inner life, Marcel turns to the purity of the spiritual life. He is not one condemned to freedom, but

---

[15]J.-P. Sartre, L'Etre et le Néant, pp. 430 f.
[16]G. Marcel, Les Hommes contre l'humain, pp. 17 f.
[17]G. Marcel, "L'Existence et la liberté humaine chez J.-P. Sartre," Les Grands Appels de l'homme contemporain, pp. 164–5.
[18]Ibid., p. 155.

one who yearns to become a truly free person. Thus Paul Ricœur distinguishes Marcel's approach to freedom from that of Sartre. "When all the other existentialisms emphasize the power of existing by freedom, one is struck with the care which arouses G. Marcel not to confine himself in the avarice of the 'I-myself'; what interests G. Marcel is not the moment of self-assertion of freedom but the moment of participation."[19] Marcel's thought is full of the virtues by which one participates in the world of Being.

For Sartre, the only transcendence available to the self is self-consciousness. Therefore, those people who break down under torture, and express their secret thoughts, have betrayed themselves and destroyed their freedom. On the other hand, Marcel holds to a transcendence beyond the self as such, in the order of spirit and grace, by which the self can repudiate any deeds or words into which the self may be forced by an external worldly force.

Marcel affirms that there is only value when there has been a previous devaluation and the task of the philosopher of value is to try to express what has been lost in the human soul. In the past, he feels that the philosophy of values has failed in trying to recover in words what has really been lost in human souls.[20] Values must be apprehended ontologically not conceptually.

While both Sartre and Marcel believe in creativity in value, there is a great difference between their beliefs. In Sartre, the free man, that is the self-conscious man, the man who is lacking in his being, creates his own values out of his own nothingness. Because he is nothing, the free man can create himself by his own acts of self-assertion. Marcel also affirms that the self must be a creator and, as a creator, it is free. "It is as creator, however humble the level may be where this creation is accomplished, that a man, whoever he may be, can recognize that he is free."[21] However, for Marcel, man as creator is intricately combined with the man of fidelity. Marcel's consideration of "creative fidelity" (by which phrase he has described his whole approach to philosophy) stands out in contrast to Sartre's consideration of creativity and sincerity.

---

[19]Paul Ricœur, *Gabriel Marcel et Karl Jaspers*, p. 26.
[20]Marcel, *Les Hommes contre l'humain*, p. 96.
[21]*Ibid.*, p. 24.

In his consideration of what he calls "mauvaise foi," Sartre points out the impossibility of a man being sincere. If a person is sincere, then he confesses and lives by what he has been in the past. However, if he lives sincerely by his past, the man is refusing to acknowledge what he would like to become in the future by creating himself. Thus he is not really sincere. On the other hand, if a man acknowledges himself to be creative, to be his projects, then he is really only acting at being something which he is in fact not. Thus, since man's being is characterized by non-being, sincerity is impossible. However, as Marcel notes, if sincerity is itself bad faith, then bad faith loses its meaning since it only has meaning in opposition to sincerity.[22] If one recognizes what he has been in the past, it is only then that he can sincerely seek to improve his life. Sartre himself, despite his declaration of sincerity as "mauvaise foi," seems to seek sincerity as one of the greatest virtues for the existing individual.

Sartre's discussion of sincerity reflects Kant's discussion of the antinomies. The only way Sartre can realize a value is to conceptualize it, but by being conceptualized it becomes ambiguous in respect to the human situation. Marcel notes the similarities of Sartre's approach to that of André Gide. He calls Sartre, "un Gide aggravé,"[23] and affirms that sincerity is not to be treated as an idea in itself but rather it must be understood on an ontological basis by which one seeks transcendence in being. Only as values are ontologically based can they really be values. Marcel sees a great fault in much of modern thought in separating man from life. That is basically Sartre's fault in discussing the impossibility of sincerity which, if it were true, would destroy all possibility of validity in his philosophical writings. Values are not to be treated purely objectively since they exist in and out of the self and it is into a world of value that the self is born.

Marcel repudiates Sartre's individual choice of value and regards it as a basic sign of the insufficiency in his ontology. Values that have ontological validity are precisely what cannot be chosen by the self. "It is only too clear that a system of measures is essentially

[22]Marcel, "L'Existence et la liberté," p. 141.
[23]*Ibid.*, p. 142.

relative since it is the object of an initial choice. But contrary to what Sartre has imagined, for example—and that is, without doubt, one of the most serious errors of his philosophy and one with the most weighty consequences—what we call value is essentially something that does not allow itself to be chosen."[24]

Yet if, as Marcel declares, values are not to be chosen, how is creativity possible? Sartre reflects much of Bergson's thought in his notion of creativity. For Bergson, the essential character of creativity lies in its inventiveness—its spontaneous innovation. But Marcel wonders whether by limiting our attention to this aspect of creation we lose sight of its ultimate significance, which is its deep-rootedness in being. Bergson interprets faith as routine—an arbitrary safeguard against the power of renewal which is the spirit itself. But faithfulness is in reality the exact opposite of inert conformism. It is the ontological recognition of something permanent, referring to a presence within and before us which can be ignored and forgotten in a betrayal of oneself. This is to be distinguished from loyalty because, in being loyal to a principle, you may betray yourself. In *Du refus à l'invocation* (p. 200), Marcel distinguishes between constancy and fidelity. Though constancy is not an evil in itself, yet it falls short of fidelity since constancy suggests a more formal character which distorts the aspect of being itself. Frequently there are experiences of fidelity in relation to another person. However, the danger is that fidelity in this case may turn to an idea of the person and not to the person that exists.

In an interesting article in *Sens et non-sens* (pp. 351f.) entitled "Foi et bonne foi," Merleau-Ponty criticizes the kind of sincerity which is associated with a faith in an objective, rational reality. This, he believes, is the faith of Christians and Communists. He himself seems to pursue a new kind of sincerity which he calls "bonne foi," in affirming that the conscious self should face the fact that the pattern of reality is neither rationally ordered nor rationally certain.

However, Marcel meets any such criticism of faith by stating that the more consciousness is rooted not in ideas but in the Being

[24]Marcel, *Les Hommes contre l'humain*, p. 128.

of God Himself, the more one's lack of fidelity will appear as a deficiency in the self. By this "absolute recourse," the self in humility contracts for an infinite credit in Being itself, and it is at this point that Hope is found. Furthermore, it is only through this absolute fidelity, or faith, that fidelity on the human level is given a firm basis.[25]

It is at this point that the great difference in respect to values may be seen between Sartre and Marcel. For Sartre, the basis of all value is the nothingness in man's being, which is his self-consciousness or his freedom. Marcel, in his article concerning "L'Existence et la liberté humaine chez J-P. Sartre," quotes Sartre's *Being and Nothingness.* "My freedom is the unique basis of value, and nothing, absolutely nothing, justifies me in adopting such a value or such and such a scale of values. In so much as I am the being by whom the values exist, I am unjustifiable. And my freedom is aghast at being the basis without basis of values."[26] In contrast to this, Marcel writes: "I seem not to be choosing my values but to be recognizing them."[27] If a man chooses his values, as in Sartre, then he is building his future upon his own nothingness and the future can only be nothingness. If values are recognized, not chosen, then the self, aware of its deficiencies, has recourse to a reality which can create the self into something far beyond the powers of the isolated consciousness. Thus, Marcel affirms that, if creative fidelity is conceivable, it is because fidelity is ontological in its principle, because it prolongs presence which itself corresponds to a certain kind of hold which being has upon us.[28]

When a human being is presented to the self as a presence, he cannot be treated as an object. There arises a relationship which in a sense surpasses mere awareness; he is not only before but also within. This intimacy is higher and more assured, the more it is grounded in total spiritual availability or love.

[25]G. Marcel, *Du refus à l'invocation*, pp. 217–8.
[26]Sartre, *L'Etre et le Néant*, p. 76; quoted by G. Marcel in "L'Existence et la liberté," pp. 165–6.
[27]*Ibid.*, p. 166.
[28]G. Marcel, *Position et approches concrètes du mystère ontologique*, p. 79.

For Sartre, the reaction to being observed by another is first fear, then pride or shame, and the sense of shame is bound up with the sense of falling into the world. Love is of no help. For Sartre, love is purely negative; the aim of love is to appropriate the will of another, not for power but for absolute value in the eyes of the beloved. Instead of feeling that my existence is superfluous, the self which is loved, can feel itself upheld and willed. The essence of the joy of love is to feel the self to be justified. However, the one who is loved does not wish to love; yet he wants the other person to love him. But to want the other person to love him is in fact Sartre's definition of love. Therefore, Sartre finds love to be rooted in destruction because it involves the treatment of a person as a subject who wants to be an object or of a person as an object who wants to be a subject.

For Sartre, any act of a subject may be determined in two aspects—the objective which involves a rational motive and the subjective which involves the movement of desire, emotion or passion which drives the subject to action. But essentially both are involved in the surging forth of the consciousness towards its possibilities to form the single act. With this in mind, Simone de Beauvoir, in *L'Existentialisme et la sagesse des nations* (pp. 17 f.), writes that all love may be judged in terms either of sensuality or of rational motive. Because of this, she feels that the Church has mistrusted all man-woman relationships as evil and that is why she believes that marriage (always resulting in faithlessness or betrayal) has been an object of humour since the Middle Ages. She feels that, even if lovers appear to remain faithful, they are in reality only victims of routine.

In contrast to this view, Marcel says that in love the distinction between "l'en moi" and "le devant moi" disappears, on the level of the metaproblematic or mystery.[29] In love, the mystery of the incarnation of the self in soul and body is expressed. The one who really loves has an assurance that any attempts to explain love away objectively by a study of desire or of rational motive will inevitably fail because in fact these objective studies do not deal

[29]Marcel, *Position et approches concrètes*, pp. 59 f.

with love at all. For love, there can be no objective criteria; its value is best attested perhaps in association with the ontology of fidelity.

Where there is fidelity and love, there is also hope. Contrary to what Spinoza said, fear, according to Marcel, should be correlated to desire not hope. Negative hope is defeatism. In hope the self feels that at the heart of every being, beyond all data, there is a mysterious principle, which cannot but will what it wills if what it wills deserves to be willed and is willed by the whole being. Marcel affirms that this hope is at the centre of the ontological mystery.[30] To hope against hope that a person whom I love will recover from a disease which is said to be incurable is to say: "It is impossible that I should be alone in willing this cure; for reality cannot be hostile to what I feel to be so good." Some say that in the immense majority of cases hope for recovery is an illusion, but it is the essence of hope to exclude the consideration of cases and hope rises, transcending the level of all empirical proof, to the plane of salvation. "I do not wish: I affirm; it is what I will call the prophetic resonance of true hope."[31]

Marcel affirms that hope and despair are inseparable and here it should be noted that Sartre says much the same thing in his *Existentialism and Humanism*. Marcel believes that at the root of despair, "there is nothing in reality which permits me to open a credit; no guarantee for it. It is a declaration of absolute insolvency."[32] For Sartre, despair means that "there is no God and no prevenient design which can adapt the world and its possibilities to my will."[33] The only certainty that one can have for Sartre is the certainty of one's own will. All else remains in the realm of possibility or probability. Yet Sartre believes that at the moment that this is understood, a measure of hope is possible because then the free self realizes that in whatever way it acts, it contributes to bringing meaning into the world.

However, Sartre regards hope as correlative to rational order. Consequently, he regards Christian hope as resignation to a pre-

[30]*Ibid.*, p. 69.
[31]*Ibid.*, p. 69.
[32]*Ibid.*, p. 68.
[33]Sartre, *Existentialism and Humanism*, p. 39.

established order of things. No doubt he derives this view from the approach of essentialist Cartesian Thomists. In the concluding page of *Existentialism and Humanism*, he equates Christian despair with the measure of unbelief in a Christian. This is, of course, true but not as Sartre interprets the terms, because both despair and unbelief in Sartre's interpretation of Christianity imply an inability to see a rational order in the world. Therefore, Sartre concludes his essay by saying that "it is only by self-deception by confusing their own despair with ours that Christians can describe us as without hope."[34] For Sartre, despair is the inability of the self to impose its own meaning on the world and, consequently, hope for him is the possibility of doing so.

Marcel affirms that only a world such as ours which reveals such absolute despair can give rise to an unconquerable hope. Hope is a mystery. When men ignore mysteries or seek to convert hope into a problem, there is no longer hope but wishful thinking, or a desire wrapped in illusory judgments in order to distort an objective reality, which it is interested in disguising from itself. This approach is completely hollow when one is approaching a great inquiry into the value of life. The relation of mystery to problem is the same as that of hope to scientific judgment.

The world of the problematic is a world of fear, desire, function and technics of every sort. Every technique can be made to serve some desire or fear and every desire or fear tends to invent its own technique. On this level, despair consists in the recognition of the ultimate inefficacy of all science, joined to an inability to change to a new ground where all sciences are incompatible with the fundamental nature of being. "Man can do what his techniques can do; but at the same time we ought to recognize that those techniques are revealed to be incapable of saving him from himself."[35]

Yet one of the characteristics of the scientific method is its optimism, animated by certain hope. Marcel asks if this hope can be reconciled with an ontological interpretation of hope. Metaphysically speaking, the only genuine hope is hope in that which

[34]*Ibid.*, p. 56.
[35]Marcel, *Position et approches concrètes*, p. 72.

does not depend on ourselves—hope springing from humanity, not from pride.[36] Since pride consists in drawing one's strength solely from oneself, the proud man cuts himself off from communion with his fellow-men, and therefore from the source of this optimism.

Perhaps the greatest contrast between Christian and non-Christian existentialism may be seen in the contrast between pride and humility. The non-Christian existentialist, relying on his own resources which he feels are alone assured to him, reflects a strong measure of pride. Sartre's recent writings and activities in relation to the Communists show a proud desire to set himself up as a demagogue—the reconciler between East and West.[37] However, in all fairness to the non-Christian existentialists, they generally do not overestimate their own resources upon which they rely and are constantly aware of the contingency of the self.

It is because of their emphasis on contingency that the non-Christian existentialists regard courage as one of the greatest virtues. Marcel notes that courage is perhaps the only bourgeois virtue which they accept.[38] The non-Christian existentialists believe that, especially during the last twenty years, man has attained a degree of boldness and courage which has never been reached before. The saints of the Church and the Communist revolutionaries were not true heroes because they sought assurance that their efforts were already achieved in heaven or in history. The men of the Resistance were because they could not know the outcome of their efforts. "The contemporary hero is not Lucifer, it is not even Prometheus, it is man.[39] Sartre has criticized Camus' Promethean legend wherein everyone and everything is defied. For Camus, any degree of humility is a degree of humiliation. Yet Sartre's great concern for freedom in the individual consciousness suggests, though to a less violent degree than Camus, that any humility in either Christian or Communist is also humiliation.

On the other hand, Marcel affirms that humility is not an act

36*Ibid.*, p. 73.
37In an interview with the author on January 13, 1953, Marcel suggested that Sartre is now a demagogue and no longer a true philosopher.
38Marcel, "L'Existence et la liberté," p. 128.
39M. Merleau-Ponty, *Sens et non-sens*, p. 380.

of self-humiliation but a recognition of our own nothingness. In other words, humility is bound up with the realm of the universal metaphysic of being and any attempt to bind it to a lower rational or empirical level degenerates humility to humiliation and the act of being humble to idolatry. "In so far as there is such a thing as religious masochism, it is always a perversion."[40]

For the Christian, humility, not resignation, is the prerequisite to belief. Humility combined with a measure of diligence and courage are at the gateway to Christian belief, as E. L. Mascall writes in *He Who Is* (p. 77).

The point is that, however clear the truth of the proposition "God exists" may be—and it has been asserted that our recognition of it can be so immediate as perhaps to deserve the name of intuition rather than of argument—unless we have the virtue of humility we shall simply be unable to see the data as they are and so we shall be unable to see God's existence as implied in them. Thus there is a threefold moral activity involved: diligence in investigating the question, humility in recognizing the data and courage in acting upon the conviction when acquired. But it is the second of these that is involved in the actual intellectual acceptance of God's existence, and if it is lacking, we shall simply hide God's evidence from ourselves by putting up a kind of intellectual smoke-screen.

The phrase "intellectual smoke-screen" describes the writings of the non-Christian existentialists in so far as they seek to build up a case for living with a measure of pride, that is to live their own lives as far as possible on their own terms.

A final distinction can be made between the virtue of tolerance of which Marcel writes and the justice of which Albert Camus is the particular exponent. For the non-Christian existentialists, justice is a virtue to be worked for though it may never actually be attained. Justice can never actually be attained because no one but the isolated consciousness can understand what its own motives are. Yet, on the rational level, it is important to make possible the conditions in which conscious men, both free and equal, can be free to exercise their freedom. Simone de Beauvoir affirms in her *Existentialisme et la sagesse des nations* (pp. 157 f.) that the one crime that men should punish is the crime against man which

[40]Marcel, *The Mystery of Being*, Part II, p. 89–90.

seeks to make men something less than men. Thus the need for justice arises when men are aware of injustice. Marcel says much the same with respect to tolerance. However, whereas the non-Christian existentialists treat justice as a rational concept which men seek to actualize in existence, Marcel feels that, if tolerance is treated as an idea, it undergoes a profound alteration.[41] Tolerance is not merely non-prohibition, or submission, but the negation of a negation, as an anti-intolerance. Tolerance is to action what reflection is to thought. "It is then inconceivable without a certain power which sustains it and to which it is as it were attached."[42] Since the power or authority of tolerance is not the individual consciousness, as that of justice is for the non-Christian existentialists, does the practice of tolerance contradict or undermine one's beliefs? To treat belief on this level is to treat it rationally and objectively, not ontologically, and Marcel says that every means used to promote intolerance of another belief in the end compromises and degrades the very belief that one was seeking to preserve and promote. Men are not to be exterminated like rats or mosquitoes for their beliefs, yet, on the social and practical level, Marcel admits that it is almost impossible to be tolerant of men who seem bent on destruction. But here again is the tension evident between the realm of being and the finite realm of space and time, between which men are torn in the period of their earthly existence.

Let us now summarize the existentialist approach to value.

1. Sartre, apart from negative freedom which is the same as self-consciousness, equates value with a rational concept and law. Since these concepts are produced by the human mind and have no existence in themselves, then man must create his own values, imposing them upon a divided world, as he acts. Since men's minds are separated by existence, there is no assurance that other men will choose the same values; yet the individual, as he chooses, must choose as if the value were for all men.

2. Marcel affirms that values do have ontological significance but not as part of any rational structure of reality. Values are not chosen but recognized through contemplation in the mystical participation

---

[41]Marcel, *Du refus à l'invocation*, p. 269 f.
[42]*Ibid.*, p. 271.

of being. These values are best discovered in concrete situations of personal relationship.

3. The values that Sartre chooses may be contrasted to those which Marcel recognizes. Though both use traditional value words such as freedom, faith, love, humility, courage and justice, yet the words for Sartre have a conceptual meaning which he alone gives to them. On the other hand, for Marcel, these words signify the purest activity of Being.

Marcel may be criticized in his approach to values for failing to set any universal standards of morality which can be universally understood. Yet the fact that he uses words to describe values which he has recognized is evidence that he is seeking to expound these values universally. Nevertheless, values which have onto-logical validity can never be adequately explained conceptually, though they can be universally recognized. On the other hand, Sartre uses words to apply to concepts of value and thereby he would imply a universal validity for them. However, since the meaning assigned to these values is based in the isolated conscious-ness of the individual, it is inherently impossible that these values can ever be universally understood or recognized.

Chapter Nine

EXISTING AND RESPONSIBILITY

ALL the existentialists believe that, in this century, the human reality has been degraded more than ever before, and because of this, it has become very difficult for people to see the meaning of human life. The rapid development of techniques has tended to force men to lose their self-respect and become waste-products, despairing of life both intellectually and vitally. In the Nazi concentration camps, not only were the material conditions designed to turn men into beasts, but also the encouragement of suspicion and distrust turned brothers into enemies and devils. Marcel believes that the use of such techniques of degradation is comparable to a spirit of sacrilege wherein a certain joy is found in the risk of overthrowing an established value of which one senses, to some degree, the reality. The will to humiliate a man in such a way that he is not only degraded, but made to feel rotten to the very core, springs from a desire of the persecutor to justify a feeling of superiority. Sartre has ably analysed the psychology of the will to humiliate in *Being and Nothingness*,[1] in his play *Men without Shadows* and in *What is Literature?* where he writes (p. 161): "The supreme irony of torture is that the sufferer, if he breaks down and talks, applies his will as a man to denying that he is a man, makes himself the accomplice of his executioners and, by his

[1] J.-P. Sartre, *L'Etre et le Néant*, p. 447.

own movements, throws himself into abjection. The executioner is aware of this; he watches for this weakness, not only because he will attain the information he desires, but because it will prove to him once again that he is right in using torture and that man is an animal who must be led with a whip."

Marcel points out how closely the use of propaganda is associated with the more monstrous techniques of degradation manifest in this century. As long as one dwells on the utility and goodness of one's cause, then the propaganda or persuasion may be said to be justified but as soon as one begins to point out the material advantages the other would have by joining the cause, then the propaganda becomes illicit. Needless to say, however, it is very difficult to draw an exact line of demarcation between the two. Marcel believes that it is when propaganda is removed from a determined function, to embrace a whole state that it comes closest to the technique of degradation. Not only is there a tendency to look down on people outside the state, but the instigators also assume a superior position to the citizens of their own state by resorting to methods of propaganda. The naïvety of a propagandist who believes that his truth is the whole truth is only conceivable in a complete fanatic. Yet the fanatic is not the best propagandist, and Marcel sees that a certain dichotomy must exist in the minds of propagandists. To effectively combat the other position, they must have some real appreciation of it, in order that they may sense its weaknesses and point them out to people, without suggesting that they are combatting it. Possibly this dichotomy is at the root of the need for periodical purges within totalitarian states; the propagandists themselves have been converted to the other cause. Marcel suggests that the action of grace is nowhere more clearly discernible than in the act by which the free individual decides to interrupt the circuit of prejudice and hatred, of reprisals and counter-reprisals between groups of men.

It is true that the rapid development of modern science has brought man a real power over the material world and, in this, Marcel would see the grandeur of the Promethean claim of Albert Camus.[2] However, Marcel feels that the man who uses the

[2]In his preface to Marcel's *Men against Humanity*, Professor Donald Mac-Kinnon suggests that an interesting comparison could be made between this work and *The Rebel* of Camus.

machine, as distinct from the man who creates it, is strongly tempted to indolence or resentment and envy, or else to a false pride of possession. Furthermore, the overemphasized desire for security leads man to idolize his own scientific creations which seem to give him the greatest measure of certainty. Man seeks for his own self-sufficiency and every activity, even the most personal, is reduced to the coldly calculating level of opinion. Through this, man has lost his sense of belonging, and his belief, and Marcel affirms that "a man who believes in nothing, a man who depends on nothing, is strictly a man without connections. Such a man cannot exist."[3]

Any civilization which seeks to undermine all possibility of contemplation leads to misosophy, not philosophy. Marcel believes that an authentic wisdom will avoid Sartre's dilemma of material "en soi" and the "pour soi" which is in a way only the internal impression of the "en soi." Sartre, in opposing what he calls "l'esprit de sérieux," is opposing wisdom itself.[4]

Any man who refuses to meditate upon the fact that he is created is led either to believe like Sartre that he is only what he makes himself, or else to regard himself as the by-product of an unthinking cosmos. Marcel affirms that the person who denies his created character will go on to assume presumptuously the attributes of the uncreated. 'There exists a clear path which leads from the haunts of the miserable specimens of humanity, that the clientele of Sartre frequent, to the camps of death where the executioners concentrate upon defenceless people."[5] There is also an intimate connection between the cruelty in our world and the unreal notion of the transcendental *ego* found in Kant and Sartre, wherein the subject is really treated as an object, but paradoxically without the determined character by which a real object is defined. It is only in mystery that this sort of a distinction is transcended and the "en moi" and "devant moi" find a real unity.

A philosophy which seeks to limit reason's function is always open to an accusation of fanaticism, and existentialism has been so charged. With this in mind, Marcel prefers to talk of a fanatical consciousness rather than of fanaticism, because the use of "ism"

[3]G. Marcel, *Les Hommes contre l'humain*, p. 51.
[4]*Ibid.*, p. 52.
[5]*Ibid.*, p. 58.

always suggests an illicit transgression of thought from its bounds. He questions just what it is that enables us to say that a certain person is a fanatic. An obsession with an idea does not necessarily make a fanatic, nor does religion. Only when true religion is perverted is there a possibility of a person becoming a religious fanatic.

The man in the mass tends to become a fanatic as he loses consciousness of his own particular substantial reality and of the small concrete group of persons to which he belongs. The press, the radio and the cinema tend to substitute a group of ideas and images for the original reality of the person. Thus propaganda substitutes a superficial reality for the true reality of persons by arousing a fanatical passion in people. "One must certainly add that this passion is at the root of fear, that it implies a feeling of insecurity which is not itself acknowledged and which is expressed in aggressiveness."[6]

By definition, fanaticism is incompatible with a concern for truth. The believer treats doubts as temptations; the fanatic refuses to consider criticisms or to question his position because he relies too much on himself and not on God. For the believer, God is the transcendent Being before whom man can only recognize his nothingness. Therefore, though the believer sees that he is constantly tested, still God cannot be questioned without reducing Him to something He is not. The fanatic substitutes an idol for the true God, and Marcel feels that in the sphere of religion the fanatic is one who accords to mediating powers such as a prophet or the Church a prerogative which is incompatible with the creature considered as a creature. This kind of fanaticism is perhaps illustrated best by the acceptance in modern politics of the works of such fallible creatures as Marx or Hitler as holy books. One of the great values of the true critic (who seems to be dying out in this age) is to check such misconceptions. However, the fanatic seems to give a certain embodiment to a figment of his imagination and seeks to negate any opinion which puts his ideal into question. Marcel notes the radical difference between this embodiment and his own notion of incarnation.[7]

[6]*Ibid.*, p. 106.
[7]*Ibid.*, p. 111.

The Communists have said that Sartre's works are the product of a bourgeois spirit. It is certainly true that Sartre does reflect many middle-class attitudes though Sartre must be particularly sensitive to this criticism since he believes that the bourgeois spirit is one of the greatest signs of man's degradation and humiliation. Sartre's conception of the bourgeois can be seen in his novels. On the one hand the bourgeois spirit is largely determined by the unknown movements of society which surpass the individual and dominate him in his situation. Ivich reflects on this in *The Reprieve* (p. 323): "She passed in review the names of all those sinister powers which control the world—Freemasonry, the Jesuits, the Two Hundred Families, the armament manufacturers, the Gold Lords, the Wall of Silver, the American trusts, International Communism, Klu-Klux-Klan: all of them more or less backing him [Hitler], and very likely yet another secret and formidable association, whose very name was unknown. 'But what can they want?' she asked herself, as two tears of rage coursed down her cheeks. She tried for a moment to guess their reasons, but there was a void within her, and a circlet of metal revolved inside her skull. 'If only I knew where Czechoslovakia was!'" In this passage, Ivich begins to question the movements of society and the meaning of society and this questioning is basic for the "authentic" man or woman. However, the majority of persons are regarded as hypocritical Pharisees who accept the situation into which they are born without question and yet, at the same time, are proud of the shallow goodness in their spirits and their works. They are responsible for nothing. Sartre believes that such people are like children who accept everything that they are told without question although, as Marcel has noted, sometimes it is children and not adults who ask the most fundamental metaphysical questions.

Sartre's first published work, *The Diary of Antoine Roquentin*, was written largely to show the reaction of the young Roquentin against the bourgeois individuals who enter his experience. He outlines the conventional, respectable views of the people whose portraits hang in the art gallery in Bouville. "He had always done his duty, his whole duty, his duty as a son, as a husband, as a father, and as an official. He had also demanded his own rights without timidity: as a child, the right of being well brought-up in a united family, the right of inheriting a spotless name and a prosperous business. As a husband, he demanded the right of being cared for and surrounded with tender affection; as a father the right of being esteemed; as an official the right of being obeyed without a murmur. Because a right is only another aspect of duty."[8] Roquentin finds that no man can truly hide himself in a world of rights and duties, and that those who do are seeking an escape from the vicissitudes of the existing world. "There are those miserable people trying to hide themselves with their idea of right. But what a shabby lie, no one has any rights, they are as completely gratuitous as other men."[9]

The age of reason is the age when the youth surrenders his free life for the respectability of social convention. Mathieu refuses to accept the *Age of Reason* as presented by his brother Jacques, who has become a bourgeois supreme. In his reaction, Mathieu reflects the thought of Sartre himself, as can be seen in Jacques' accusation against Mathieu: "You despise the bourgeois class, and yet you are a bourgeois, son and brother of a bourgeois, and you live like a bourgeois."[10] The discussion between Mathieu and Jacques illustrates the anti-bourgeois spirit arising out of a bourgeois society.

Sartre also classes among the inauthentic people all the foppish, indifferent people who live a life of social form without coming to grips with their own existence. He writes of these people in his *Portrait of the Anti-Semite* (pp. 41–2).

They are not anti-Semites, they are not anything, they are no one, and since, after all, one must appear to be something, they play the part of echo and rumour without thinking of doing evil, without thinking at all, they continue to repeat a few formulae picked up parrot-fashion, which gives them the right of access to certain drawing-rooms. In this way, they discover the delights of idle chatter, and of filling their heads with a huge affirmation, which strikes them as being all the more respectable since it is not their own, but borrowed. In this case anti-Semitism is merely a vindication of their existence, besides, the futility of such people's existence is such that they willingly abandon this particular vindication for any other, provided it is "good form."

[8] J.-P. Sartre, *La Nausée*, p. 112.
[9] *Ibid.*, p. 167.
[10] J.-P. Sartre, *The Age of Reason*, p. 126.

All these inauthentic people are living a lie and Sartre reveals how difficult it is in a bourgeois world not to live a lie or in what he calls "bad faith." The boy in the restaurant tries so hard to be a waiter and yet, by the fact that he is trying to be one, he can never be one. The eloquent speaker plays at being an eloquent speaker because he cannot *be* an eloquent speaker. The pupil at school may play so hard at being attentive that he hears nothing. If Daniel, in *The Roads to Freedom*, says that he is a homosexual, he would be what he says he is, and could be nothing else, which is untrue. Therefore, he is of bad faith. On the other hand, if Daniel says that he is not a homosexual, it would be a sign of bad faith because he has been a homosexual up to the present. Therefore, if Daniel tries to be sincere in either way, he will be of bad faith.

Sartre also considers sadness in this light. To say "I am sad" is to express a mode of being concerning the self. But "to be sad," Sartre asks, is it not to make oneself sad? The fact is that consciousness, affected by sadness, is sad precisely because of that. Marcel strongly attacks the validity of Sartre's position on this point. We may, at appropriate times (for example, when we visit certain friends), seek to assume an air of sadness when in fact, we really feel no genuine sadness. But Marcel affirms that to realize that this display of sadness is a show is also to realize what real sadness is like. "To claim the assimilation of a deep and authentic sadness, an authentic mourning, to a feeling of this kind, is a bad joke."[11]

Sartre concludes that man cannot be validly treated as an object made up of rights and duties. Furthermore, the living man who is always becoming something beyond himself cannot authentically present himself to another as a saved creature who has accomplished his being. In a relationship between two people, one may falsely convince the other of his established superiority. However, the two in the presence of a third may be judged objectively in their relationship and the fraud revealed. That is the message of Sartre's play *In Camera* where he pictures three people in hell. Two are always in the presence of a third and consequently are always revealed

11G. Marcel, "L'Existence et la liberté humaine chez J.-P. Sartre," *Les Grands Appels de l'homme contemporain*, p. 139.

with no hope of escape to hidden consciousness. Robert Campbell in his book, *J.-P. Sartre ou une littérature philosophique*, feels that though Sartre depicts a deserter, a Lesbian who has killed the husband of her friend, and a woman guilty of infanticide, he could in reality have depicted any three people. However, Marcel suggests that Sartre is too clever a dramatist not to have realized that his play would have been unconvincing if he had presented three loving, saintly characters in hell. A spiritual communion is always possible for those who avail themselves of the underlying unity in being itself, but Sartre's characters are essentially characters of refusal.[12]

However, Sartre's attack is directed against a bourgeois morality which seeks salvation by a set of rules and principles. Thus Beigbeder is led to write in *L'Homme Sartre* (p. 71): "The bourgeois wants to believe that there are principles of existence, he strives to possess them and he becomes possessed by them." Perhaps the most valuable contribution of Sartre's writings is to question the established rights and duties of society. Most Christians could agree with many of his criticisms against these rights, which tend to be only human creations distorting the loving grace of God. Sartre, of course, carries his revolt to an extreme, just as Philippe in *The Reprieve* revolts against the army because his father is a general.

For Albert Camus, the complete answer is in revolt. Like Marcel, he is much opposed to the strong tendency in modern society to impose a set of ideas upon other people and, like Marcel, he finds the root of the trouble in the idealist philosophies, beginning with Hegel. The mission of the free man is to revolt against this oppression wherever it is found. "It is better to die standing up than to live kneeling down."[13] In this role of defiance, he reflects the spirit of the French Revolution and indeed the French Revolution is regarded by Camus as the ideal war for grace and justice.[14] The man who lives authentically (according to his conscience) is condemned to live and fight on behalf of other men who cannot live but who suffer in humiliation.

It is interesting to note the similarity of Camus' approach with that of extreme Protestantism. Sartre too in the play, *Lucifer and the*

[12]*Ibid.*, pp. 148–9.
[13]A. Camus, *L'Homme Révolté*, p. 27.
[14]*Ibid.*, p. 143.

Lord, is obviously seeking to copy the atmosphere of Luther's revolt. Simone de Beauvoir in *Pour une morale de l'ambiguité* (p. 185) also expresses sympathy with this Protestant spirit although she feels that modern Protestantism has betrayed its true spirit for a set of objective values and is no longer a religion but a moral system. Camus regards Christ as the supreme man in revolt. He revolted against the God of the Old Testament and He carried this spirit of revolt to the Cross—"My God, my God, why has Thou Forsaken Me?" Camus notes how the Church as an organization has been unfaithful to the witness of Christ and yet he notes how some Christians, in the true Protestant spirit, refuse to abide by the dictates of the organization.

In an address to the House of Dominicans of Latour-Maubourg in 1948, Camus made an appeal to the dictates of their conscience. The danger is that Christians will live but that Christianity itself will die because so many Christians seem to betray their own beliefs by compromise. He expressed violent opposition to a priest who stood up at a Marxist meeting and said that he was anti-clerical. Camus makes an appeal to Christians to join him and other solitary individuals to stand firmly for justice in the world and to encourage and awaken men to face the truth of their existence. "And if you do not help us in this, who else in this world then will help us?"[15]

As we have seen, Sartre classifies Christianity as well as Marxism as abstract systems created by human beings for the purpose of escape from the anguish of responsible existence. Therefore, he classes both Christians and Communists as inauthentic and repudiates them. "It is not a question for us of escaping into the eternal or of abdicating in the face of what the unspeakable M. Zaslovsky calls in Pravda the 'historical process'."[16] In his *Portrait of the Anti-Semite* (p. 75), Sartre shows what he means by an authentic man living by his free choice and he suggests that the Christians and Communists are inauthentic because they do not practice the principles which they have chosen.

[15]A. Camus, *Actuelles-Chroniques*, p. 217.
[16]J.-P. Sartre, *What is Literature?*, p. 165.

If the reader agrees with us that man is "a freedom within a given situation," then he will easily grasp that this freedom may be defined as authentic or as inauthentic according to the choice it makes of itself within the situation whence it arises. Authenticity, it goes without saying, consists in assuming a lucid and true awareness of the situation, in accepting the responsibilities and risks incurred in that situation and in maintaining it in the moment of pride or of humiliation, and sometimes in the moment of abhorrence and hatred. There is no doubt that authenticity requires great courage, and something more than courage. So it is hardly surprising that inauthenticity is the more widespread. Whether it is a question of bourgeois or Christians, the majority are inauthentic, in the sense that they refuse to live fully through their bourgeois or Christian condition, but always conceal certain aspects from themselves. And when the Communists make "the radicalisation of the masses" part of their programme, when Marx points out that the working class must become aware of itself, what does that mean, if not that the worker is also first and foremost inauthentic?

The non-Christian existentialists assert that the believer believes in order to justify his own existence, but the authentic man cannot believe because he has no reason to exist or not to exist. This refusal of justification does not necessarily lead to a pessimism; it does not condemn existence, but declares it unjustified. Therefore, when the authentic man becomes aware of his freedom, it is foolish to ask if he is necessary, or if life is worth living, but rather he asks if he wants to live and under what conditions. If there is no God, man bears the responsibility for the world. "A God can pardon, blot out, compensate; but if God does not exist the faults of man are inexpiable."[17] No one can say whether or not man's existence has any importance: it is up to man to make it important. Responsibility is the key note of authentic existence for Sartre, as H. J. Blackham writes: "They [Sartre and his followers] are acutely aware that only the solitariness of decision discharges the responsibility responsibly."[18]

It must be remembered that Sartre and Camus are writing against a background of French Roman Catholicism dominated

17S. de Beauvoir, *Pour une morale de l'ambiguité*, p. 23.
18H. J. Blackham, *Six Existentialist Thinkers*, p. 155.

in its teaching of doctrine by an essentialist interpretation of St. Thomas Aquinas, according to which, even existence is treated as a concept. Consequently, every obstacle faced becomes a rational problem. There is no recognition of knowledge outside the sphere of reason and the unique existence of the individual comes to be regarded as one of many. Faith is reduced to a set of abstract formulations and God is taken to be comprehended in his essence by the human mind. As a result of this, in preaching to the person who has no faith, the Gospel is presented, in an impersonal way, as a set of statements to be accepted or rejected. The unbeliever, without experience of God, cannot comprehend the meaning of these statements. Kant has shown in his antinomies that the human reason may indeed contradict itself and it is the contradictions of their reasonings that the non-Christian existentialists offer to the rigid essentialist. The discussion moves between the extremes of the absolute transcendence or the total immanence of God.

In France, the Church tends to be symbolized by the church buildings and by the clergy. The high Gothic spires pointing heavenward seem to lead men away from concern with the problems of the world. The priests and nuns, in their black robes, seem to be visitors from another world, cut off from earth and its society. This attitude to the French clergy is suggested in Sartre's *Lucifer and the Lord* and *The Flies* and in *L'Etat de siège* of Camus where the clergy move as dark shadows upon the earthly scene.

The God, symbolized by this, is the God who is absolutely transcendent and who is cold to the suffering and misery of men upon the earth. One of the strongest themes in all the writings of Camus is that, if there is a God, and He allows such horrors in the world, then He must be opposed. Sartre and Camus criticize strongly most Christians who, they feel, resign themselves to the evil in the world. Heinrich prays in *Lucifer and the Lord*: "Lord, you have cursed Cain and the children of Cain: may thy will be done. You have allowed men to have tormented hearts, to have corrupted intentions and you have allowed their actions to decay and smell: may thy will be done. Lord, you have willed that betrayal be my fate upon earth: may thy will be done!"[19] However,

19J.-P. Sartre, *Le Diable et le bon Dieu*, p. 46.

the problem of the existence of evil depends ultimately on a knowledge of God. If there is no absolute good, there can be no question as to why evil is permitted; as Mascall writes in *He Who Is* (p. 183): "If there is no God, then there is no problem of reconciling the existence of pain and sin with his love and his power; and while the atheist may with reason urge against theism that it has set itself a problem which it cannot solve, he has no business to feel evil as constituting a problem for him, except in the purely intellectual sense of causing him to wonder where it came from."

When Camus suffers from hunger or from mental effort, thinking of the problem of evil, he does not rebel because he can see the purpose in this suffering, but he does rebel when he sees the suffering of little children for which he can see no purpose. However, this earthly rebellion suggests that pain itself would be no problem if we were not finite in our knowledge and in our outlook. "If we could see as God sees it would for all we know, be transparently obvious that the sufferings of the present time are not worthy to be compared with the glory that shall be revealed in us, and indeed that the sufferings were instrumental to the glory."[20] Indeed, if anyone should rebel against suffering, it should be Christians because their Saviour had to suffer infinitely on the Cross.

A frequent theme of Christian existentialism, seen in Kierkegaard or Dostoievsky, is that love and joy on this earth can only be experienced through suffering, if at all. Marcel, too, sees that faith in its truest sense often comes through suffering; for it is suffering that makes men go beyond the shallowness of the objective world to face the ontological mystery in life's crucial situations. However, Marcel does not say that the only way to faith is through suffering and he reports that he himself approached his baptism in a spirit of calm, peace and serenity.

At times, the non-Christian existentialists regard God, if He exists, as absolutely transcendent, but at other times, they speak as if He were too immanent either as predestinator or as the weapon of political reactionaries. The doctrine of total predestination results from a belief in the law of God's nature, wherein certain people are chosen by God before birth to be saved and others are

20E. L. Mascall, *He Who Is*, p. 183.

created for damnation. Therefore, in these terms, those in the fellowship of the Church do not need to worry, whereas those outside are left helplessly to their suffering. In Sartre's *Lucifer and the Lord*, Nasty says: "News is never bad for him whom God has chosen."[21] The non-Christian existentialists tend to regard themselves as predestined to damnation because they do not believe that a God worthy of the name has entered their experience.

Closely allied to the preaching of God as the necessary Being who carries out His work in creation as a necessary function is the preaching of a religion of fear. The non-Christian existentialists find a close parallel to the God of fear in the modern totalitarian dictator, who also rules by fear. Camus, in particular, sees a connection between religion and totalitarianism and is very critical of many Christians in Spain who have supported the reactionary forces of France. Father Paneloux preaches to his congregation in Oran who are terrified by the plague which has come. "It was necessary to acknowledge the terrible event because we must choose to hate God or to love Him. And who would dare to choose God's hate."[22] In Sartre's *Lucifer and the Lord*, Goetz proves to himself that God does not exist when Goetz does not suffer but rather prospers after his blasphemy and evil deeds.

In brief, the non-Christians feel that most Christians are inauthentic human beings, either because they support the reactionary political forces which destroy men's freedom, or because they completely resign themselves to the horrors of the world. In any case, the non-Christian existentialists have a strong suspicion that belief in God is a way of avoiding responsibility, and, if this is true, then it also involves the destruction of man's self-respect and dignity.

The authentic man of the non-Christian existentialists must always protest and revolt. For Camus this is all he can do. However, it is interesting to note a development in Sartre's thought through his experience in the Resistance and in the years after the war. He has moved from a completely individualistic position to a consideration of the relation between existentialism and human-

21Sartre, *Le Diable et le bon Dieu*, p. 14.
22A. Camus, *La Peste*, p. 187.

ism, and that was one of the significant points in his dispute with Camus in 1952.

Sartre says that his writings are often criticized for being extremely pessimistic and it is true that, if one faces one's situation honestly, there are strong grounds for pessimism. However, though the authentic man must face his situation, he is also a rational animal and by means of his imagination, he is able to escape momentarily. "It is in the knowledge of the authentic conditions of our life that it is necessary for us to draw strength to live and reasons to act."[23] Though living and facing a tragic situation, the self through its imagination is able to project itself into future possibilities and one possibility that is always present is that the self will find itself in a situation where all men will be working for the common good and the freedom of all. In this sense, Sartrean existentialism can be regarded as a humanism wherein a measure of hope is possible. The authentic man finds himself in the ambiguous position of being alone and yet possibly not always alone. "A morality of ambiguity will be a morality which will refuse to deny *a priori* that separated existing things can, at the same time, be bound together, that their singular freedoms can invent laws which are valid for all."[24] Whereas man in his freedom remains an isolated consciousness, in his responsibility he achieves a unity in making a decision which must be for all men. The choice of the authentic man is not only for himself but for all men. Furthermore, it always involves anguish because there is no possible guarantee for the authentic man that he has made the right choice or the best choice.

One of the outstanding characteristics of the authentic man is that he is a man of action. It is only by acting according to his choice that he can know of the effect of his choice. Yet the self can never achieve a satisfactory justification for its actions. The self is inadequate in the choice it makes and can never achieve the desired perfection. The only principle for the self to follow is "Nothing ventured, nothing gained." The only criterion in ethics is action and involvement (*engagement*).

The authentic man, being a man of action, stands out in marked

---

[23]S. de Beauvoir, *Pour une morale de l'ambiguité*, p. 15.
[24]*Ibid.*, p. 26.

contrast to the contemplative Christian of Christian existentialism. Simone de Beauvoir notes this distinction in her *Pour une morale de l'ambiguité* (p. 108): "One could not justify everything that is in affirming that everything can equally be the object of contemplation, since man never contemplates: he acts."

In the first of his articles in *Sens et non-sens*, Merleau-Ponty presents Cézanne as *the* authentic man. Cézanne realized the ambiguity of his search for truth revolving between ideas and the empirical experience of colour. Furthermore, he saw life as a perpetual development whose value could only be determined by other people who knew him and his paintings.

Sartre has portrayed several "authentic" men in his plays and novels—for example, Roquentin in *The Diary of Antoine Roquentin*, Mathieu in *The Roads to Freedom*, Hugo in *Crime Passionelle* and Goetz in *Lucifer and the Lord*. Perhaps the most "authentic" of all is Orestes in *The Flies*, Sartre's first play. Orestes revolts not only against his parents and Jupiter but against all authority in the name of his own freedom and the freedom of his fellow-men. At the end of the play, Orestes sacrifices himself for his fellow-citizens with the words: "I take all your faults and your remorse upon myself."[25] This sacrifice may be contrasted with Christian sacrifice in worship and love to God. Orestes' sacrifice is that of the anti-Christ hoping to lead men to know themselves and, thereby, to put their trust in their own individuality.

The Flies is given a setting in Argos in Greece and the non-Christian existentialists make frequent references to Greek philosophy and mythology. There are several reasons for this. In a desire to return to ways of thinking uninfluenced by the Christian revelation, which has tended to develop an other-worldly attitude, the non-Christian existentialists seek, through Greek humanism, to encourage a new interest in man's own affairs in his present situation. The Greek way of life seems to suggest a more healthy atmosphere in which all men can rise to an authentic existence.

Gabriel Marcel compares man's situation to that of an actor who has been given his own cues and lines but has not read the play as a whole nor been told what it is about. It is as if a man has been

[25]J.-P. Sartre, *Les Mouches*, p. 144.

put on the stage to improvise by himself; so that he may well doubt the existence of the producer. Life seems to have no point. The authentic man of Sartre, beginning from this position, seeks to confer his own significance upon life. However, Marcel feels that this position is untenable. He writes as one who has come to the Christian faith after a winding and intricate journey and consequently, he feels for those who are still on the road. Yet Marcel cannot say that he is a *convinced* Christian; for the word is too weak and too intellectual. "The freer and more detached parts of me have struggled up into the light, but there is still much of me that lies in shadow, untouched by the almost level rays of the dawning sun."[26] Marcel believes that he cannot be fully enlightened until all of the others are on the road. Therefore, he sets out to reflect and perhaps, by his reflection, to help others. "There is no need for me to say that I chiefly address myself to the less fortunate among you; to those who despair of ever reaching the summit of the mountain, or (what is worse) are persuaded that there is no summit and no ascent, and that the adventure of life is reduced to tramping miserably about in the mists; the process will go on till death, when total extinction will devour or dedicate its incomprehensible vacuity."[27] This is the key to Marcel's philosophical approach which is distinct from that of traditional philosophy. The philosopher's task, according to Marcel, is not to explain the truth, but to lead people to it.

Marcel feels that there are two types of unbelievers—those who think that faith is simply a weakness and a form of credulity and those who think that faith is a boon to the possessor, but this boon is denied to them. There are those who regard faith as a convenient deception "which doesn't deceive me" (here a superiority complex is revealed) and those who regard faith as a pleasant pastime, like music or the arts, and there are those who regard faith as a real communion with a higher reality, but confess that this reality is unfortunately not revealed to them. In this latter case, the non-believer speaks of faith as a blind man would of sight and Marcel feels that there are more people in this state than many

[26]G. Marcel, *Being and Having*, p. 203.
[27]*Ibid.*, p. 204.

imagine. Indeed, Marcel himself was one, who, before his baptism, envied the faith of others which, he felt, was denied to him.

Marcel believes that behind the expression of emancipation of the non-religious man is a feeling of resentment as a "have-not" to a "have." In reality, the militant atheist who claims to be most objective is really dealing purely in the subjective realm since the fact of God's existence is not something that can be disproved; for that would require infinite research which is not possible for the finite mind. "The unbeliever then who is really the same as the absolute pessimist, must not be held up as the defender of objective truth. There is in fact no attitude more subjective, and more insidiously subjective, than his own."[28]

Nor does this approach lead to scepticism. The non-Christian existentialists, dealing in a psychology of religion, equate faith with an attitude of mind. But faith, in its ontological sense involves the whole being of man, as reality enters into him and enfolds him. The unbeliever must say that the believer is practising a humility where he has no right to practise it; and this is, in fact, to evade the terrible realities of life by having recourse to faith. But in situations which engage the whole of the person, no one can put himself in another's place. The more faith is genuinely itself, the more it comes from the whole being and precisely engages the whole being. Marcel points out that many ways of denying faith, including those of the non-Christian existentialists, are formally invalid.

The devout Christian is the one whose life is consecrated to God. The consecration of the non-Christian existentialists is a consecration to an idea, external to life itself. Marcel compares their approach to a man who finds a wallet with a considerable sum of money in it, and, since he cannot find the owner, he wonders what to do with it. He must make a choice. However, Marcel believes that life cannot be compared to the lucky find because "any existence as living being precedes the discovery of myself as a living being."[29] Marcel finds himself diametrically opposed to Sartre's assertion that man is his own maker.

28*Ibid.*, p. 209.
29G. Marcel, *The Mystery of Being*, Part I, p. 174.

The child's desire to attract praise for itself by its deeds is frequently carried into adulthood as a demand for rights. Yet these rights are constantly in danger of being violated or of being overlooked in such a way that the person feels very shy and self-conscious. Marcel gives the example of a young man at his first dance who is "at once pre-occupied with himself to the highest possible degree and hypnotized at the same time to a quite supreme degree by others, by what he imagines other people may think of him."[30] This is very close to what the non-Christian existentialists mean by inter-subjectivity, but it is not Marcel's definition of inter-subjectivity. If a man comes up to put the young man at his ease, the young man will at first be on the defensive. Because he is on the defensive, the young man has the lowest level of conversation *with* the other man. The other man is treated as much like an object as possible but the word "with" can apply only in a personal relationship. However, as the conversation progresses between the young man and the stranger, the stranger may reveal that he knew the young man's parents, or some other person intimately connected with the young man and then the "ice is broken." The mention of something else which they both have in common might have furthered the relationship to a certain extent. For Sartre it is common oppression that makes a human relationship as close as it can possibly be. However, Marcel affirms that "it is in the sort of case where I discover that a stranger has recognized the deep, individual quality of somebody whom I myself have tenderly loved and who retains a place in my heart, that true intersubjectivity arises."[31] It is this dimension of human relationships that Sartre has omitted from his discussion, most probably because he has never experienced it.

Marcel affirms that within a human relationship there is an ascending and descending scale from a practical and rigidly defined purpose to the mystical communion of souls in worship. This is clearly seen in a marriage relationship. "There may be moments of drought in marriage when the wife becomes for her husband merely that 'silly creature who should have been busy darning

[30]*Ibid.*, p. 177.
[31]*Ibid.*, p. 178.

socks, but there she was clucking round the tea table with a lot of old hens,' and there may be also mystical moments when the wife is acknowledged and loved as the bearer of a unique value to which eternal bliss has been promised."[32]

The notion of community has been a very confused one because the relationships between people begin almost as a mathematical sum of special tasks and can be treated as a chair beside a table. However, any measure of community, in a common effort or in a common situation is a basis on which persons can come to know each other more intimately—not purely externally but internally. Sartre, in his humanism, is at the fringe of this notion, but he fails to go on with Marcel into the consideration of the intimate relationships which make a third person an intruder. Marcel notes how some wives may be irritated when their husbands or sons speak with war comrades who have shared similar experiences or sufferings which the wife cannot appreciate. It is this suprapersonal unity which Marcel seeks to explain in his play *Quatuor en fa dièse*.

This suprapersonal unity is best seen in the true family relationship. However, the difficulty is that the modern outlook tends to repudiate the dignity of the family and life is no longer cherished as a gift. To be alive in such a distressing world is regarded as a penalty for a crime one has not committed. Furthermore, the act of begetting a child is often unpremeditated, with no sense of responsibility towards one who has not asked to be born. In Sartre, there is defiance against a life inflicted upon him, which he did not seek. As sons deny the rights of fathers, so do fathers reciprocally refuse to asknowledge any responsibility towards sons. Marcel notes how this tension is often covered up by ordinary tolerance and human decency and yet he sees this estrangement emerge in Sartre's works in a definite shape.

One might even say that Sartre's world is one where fatherhood, whether as a fact or a value has ceased to exist; it would be no exaggeration, in fact, to call this a world in which a man claims, in Sartre's slightly technical phraseology, to choose himself as the son of X, and therefore equally to reject himself as the son of X. But in relation to the general body of human traditions of feeling and behaviour, this is

32*Ibid.*, p. 179.

an innovation of a completely revolutionary sort. It is, in the most exact sense of the word, an impious innovation; and it is not by mere chance that Orestes, in Sartre's first play has the beau rôle just in that (not in spite of the fact that) he is the murderer of his mother."[33]

Sartre has no family and is frequently accused of living only a café life. Marcel substantiates his view of the anti-family attitude in Sartre's philosophy by quoting a remark Sartre himself made to Father Troisfontaines. "I am accused of spending my life in a café, and it is true that I can work only there. The café has the immeasurable advantage of being a place of indifference; I do not depend in any way on the people who are there and they depend in no way upon me. On the other hand, imagine if I had a home and family; I could not work because there a wife and children would weigh on my life and they would weigh even, and perhaps above all, if they made it too obvious that they would not weigh upon me or disturb me. This is to put things at their best, understand—let us not think about the most dismal possibilities."[34]

For Marcel, the spiritual relationship in the family cannot be treated as an object but as a presence. The answer to a selfish and nihilistic attitude must be by an appeal to a deep reality which Sartre and his followers have not recognized. Fatherhood or sonship is not to be considered as a purely legal term but as being on the deepest level of human behaviour. Nor is fatherhood or sonship to be regarded on a purely biological level. It is in the mystery of the family that the self takes pride in a community of which the self seeks to be worthy because in the family there is an embodiment of cherished ideals. Here is found a true authority which stands beyond the self: "I am accepted in it from birth, I am involved in it, I have put my roots there and my very being."[35] The traditions of the family preserve in the individual a reserve which makes true virtue in everyday life of society possible. It is this moral reserve which one gains in the family relationship which makes it possible for one to serve humanity and Marcel believes that the disregard for what Gustave Thibon has phrased

[33]*Ibid.*, p. 199.
[34]Marcel, "L'Existence et la liberté," p. 129.
[35]G. Marcel, *Homo viator*, p. 102.

"reserver pour mieux donner" has lead to the egotism and degeneration of modern life.[36]

Parellel to his distinction between being and having and between mystery and problem, Marcel draws a distinction between testimony and observation. Observation concerns a phenomenon which I am obliged to note, but my observation does not change the phenomenon at all. Anybody else could have observed the same thing. It is impersonal. Testimony involves the "I" who bears witness and is deeply personal. The essential fact of our lives is that we are witnesses and this is the expression of our mode of belonging to the world. "In the end there must be absolute commitment, entered upon by the whole of myself, or at least by something real in myself which could not be repudiated without repudiating the whole—and which could be addressed to the whole of Being and would be made in the presence of that whole. That is faith. Obviously, repudiation is still a possibility here, but cannot be justified by a change in the subject or object; it can only be explained by a fall."[37] We speak of a devoted and consecrated life as a testimony which is bound up with some form of fidelity. I bear witness as one who remembers—the testimony refers to something that has been received and to receive is in one sense an act— an act like that of the host who brings out the best in his guest and creates a genuine communication and exchange.

In an article at the conclusion of *Homo Viator* (p. 332), Marcel says that he finds in the German poet Rilke "one of the finest human witnesses." He believes that Rilke has reached a summit where the artist and the man can no longer be separated and this is the most authentic kind of genius, attained only by men such as Beethoven or Tolstoi. Rilke was not a Christian because he regarded the form of the Church as restrictive to being, and Marcel sees here much in common with the approach of Heidegger. Marcel does not believe that his own philosophy is valid only for Christians because the being to which the human individual witnesses is not restricted to the Christian fellowship. Rather, true being is that upon which all of creation depends, though the ontological Church is the highest corporate expression of this reality.

[36]*Ibid.*, p. 110.
[37]Marcel, *Being and Having*, p. 45–6.

However, Marcel realizes that Christians do not bear witness to the reality of the Church as they might, and he draws a distinction between orthodoxy and conformism.[38] Orthodoxy, in its truest sense, is fidelity to the Word of God whereas conformism is a submission to the rules of a group who decide what one must think and appreciate. Sometimes the orthodox, to substantiate their position, treat their orthodoxy as religious conformism, and often the Church is attacked as a mere conformism, and Christians disdained by unbelievers, as mimicking parrots.

Marcel feels that the greatest misunderstandings concerning the Church by Christians and non-Christians alike have come through the divisions in the empirical Church. It is in interconfessional relationships that Christians tend to regard orthodoxy, not as a fidelity, but as a superior conformism. In refuting heresy, Marcel believes that it is unwise to set one claim against another but rather one's own orthodoxy can only be revealed to the other through the light of charity. Marcel refers to Father Congar's *Divided Christendom*, in which he traces the shameful divisions among Christians.

If the Church is an organism, then to lose a part of it produces a fever. This fever is a hardening of heart against the heretical part. Heresy, says Marcel, should not be regarded as an external calamity but as an internal rupture for which each one of us in part is responsible. However, we cannot speak of a sin of the Church, as Berdyaev does, for the Church is the Body of Christ —the eternal mystery. This is the mystical body of which Christ is the Head and where "a Pope can be less near to Christ than a humble, ignorant woman." There is also the Church as an institution of society where there is an authority and subjects. Yet there is a unity between the two as between Christ's divine and human natures. This unity operates on the level of the sacraments where an outward and visible sign contains an inward and spiritual grace. Indeed, the Church is a sacrament supreme. This universality of the Church is not only compatible with an extreme diversity of religious experience and of ways to approach God—it requires it. It is interesting to note that Marcel's approach to the reality of the Church is essentially the same as that of E. L. Mascall in his *Christ, the Christian and the Church*.

[38]G. Marcel, *Du refus à l'invocation*, p. 237.

It is at this point that we make contact with the existentialist interpreters of St. Thomas Aquinas for whom every creature in its existence bears witness to its dependence on a self-existing Being. To speak of an authentic existence as Sartre does, is to regard one person as existing more than another and Gilson points out the fault of this in his *Being and Some Philosophers.* "It is true that we imagine that some existing things are more real than others and that we compare large things that exist to smaller ones, but we think less then of the fact of existence than of the nature of what exists. It is the existing thing which is large, not its existence itself because to every question about it one can only reply by a yes or a no deprived of degrees. In fact, brute existence is indivisible, and there is no intermediary position between it and nothingness."[39] Thus Sartre in speaking of authentic existence is really speaking of essence and the essence of which he speaks is not based on being itself but upon the psychological awareness of what the self is and can become by its own choice.

The original meaning of "to exist" is "to stand out" and thus the act of existing bears witness to an origin. Here again the psychological approach of Sartre is clearly seen in that for him the authentic existence of the "pour soi" depends on its transcendence by self-consciousness to the "en soi" world of brute being. What he should say is that the true essence of a human being is to be aware of his situation and of his choice in the situation and that the human essence is determined by this very self-conscious process of the mind. Thus the human mind is the "measure of all things." On the side of the Christian existentialists however, the act of existing constantly refers to its origin and the true essence of a creature, however it may develop, is to bear constant witness to this origin. E. L. Mascall writes:

It follows from this that not only does the existence of creatures declare to us that God exists, but their nature manifests to us God's nature. If, *per impossible,* they were related to him only in the order of existence, then the perfections which their natures imperfectly exemplify could only be alleged to exist virtually in God; God would cause the perfections in creatures but those perfections would not necessarily in any way resemble God. But the communication of existence to creatures

[39]E. Gilson, *L'Etre et l'essence,* p. 314–15.

is not one act and the communication of essence another. Finite essence is only the mode of finite existence, and in the order of essence, as in the order of existence, creatures are related to God by his one creative act which both makes them and makes them what they are.[40]

However, because God creates both human essence and existence in the one creative act, this is not to say that the whole world is intelligible by a human rational system. "The more we fully understand the world, the more clearly we can see that the world does not explain itself and that therefore its explanation must lie outside itself."[41] Thus E. L. Mascall points out the merit of Sartre and his followers in saying that the world does not make sense, because he believes that it is healthier for an atheist to find the world to be absurd than to find it to be a self-contained rational system. "It may well be that the doctrine of the absurdity of the world is simply what the doctrine of contingency becomes when it is transposed from a theistic to an atheistic setting."[42] God does not create by a logical necessity but by an act of unconditioned creative will.

Though God's intellect and will are identical, the creature as an object of knowledge and as an object of will are not identical because the creature's ability to be known arises from its necessary existence as an idea in the mind of God and its ability to be willed from its contingent existence as a creature. Gilson writes: "Between pure existing, from which all intelligibility is born, and the finite acts of existing passes the break which separates the infinite from the finite."[43]

The human being then, though aware of its existence and its finite essence, realizes itself to be still in a process of creation as it moves through a world of space and time. God continues to will its continued existence, though its nature as a whole remains unintelligible because it is becoming. In response to this continuous act of creation, the individual bears witness to the being upon whom he depends in "attestation créatrice." Here we see a further similarity in the philosophical approach of Gabriel Marcel and that of the existentialist interpreters of St. Thomas. Marcel writes: "At the beginning of all creation, visible or not, one discovers the

[40]E. L. Mascall, *Existence and Analogy*, p. 123.
[41]*Ibid.*, p. 126.
[42]*Ibid.*, p. 126.
[43]Gilson, *L'Etre et l'essence*, p. 327.

same presence, and, I will add, the same demand of Being to the soul that it surrounds, but also the act, identical in its infinite specifications, by which the soul bears witness to this same presence that is given to him nevertheless to be able to deny, that is, to make void, in the very measure in which it is soul, that is to say freedom."[44]

The degradation of man in the modern world has been caused by a refusal or a denial of being. The Christian existentialists believe that it is only after a sense of God's Being has been restored to men that the full dignity of human being will be recovered.

Let us summarize:

1. All of the existentialists agree that the human reality in this century has been degraded to an unusual degree. Gabriel Marcel sees the chief evidence of this in the techniques of degradation used in the concentration camps, in propaganda, in man's subjugation to the machine and in the totalitarian state, Marcel feels that the tendency to mass-consciousness encourages fanaticism, even in Church members. Sartre adds Christianity and Communism to the lists of agents that degrade the human reality as well as the bourgeois mentality which he feels has been largely developed through Christian principles.

2. The answer of the existentialists to human degradation lies in transcendence, but they conceive of transcendence in radically different ways. For Camus, transcendence is in revolt. For Sartre, transcendence is in the self-conscious self and he encourages this self to live in good faith which is distinguished from sincerity which he feels is impossible. Self-consciousness put the self in isolation and yet Sartre finds a measure of community when free individuals fight together against a common oppressor, and when the mind can imagine the perfect society.

3. For Marcel and for the existentialist interpreters of St. Thomas, transcendence is in Being by which and from which all things are. It is through this Being which transcends all evil and oppression that the human individual in loving community with others is able to attain to the sacred character of his personality and of his dignity.

[44]Marcel, *Du refus à l'invocation*, p. 16.

Chapter Ten

CONCLUSION

THERE is a common tendency to regard existentialism as a passing fad rather than as a valid philosophy. This has been largely due to the existentialist writers' presentation of certain *risqué* themes as well as to the wide distribution of Sartre's journalistic and artistic writings. However, this popularizing is due not to a desire for scandal only, but, more fundamentally, to the moral mission which Sartre has assigned himself, to bring as many men as possible to an awareness of themselves and of their freedom. Though there are elements in the philosophies of the non-Christian existentialists which encourage scandal and faddism, these are not sufficiently important to justify casting aside their work as void of any deeply philosophical thought. The writings of Merleau-Ponty alone should prove that this is not so.

Furthermore, though it might well appear that the group of Thomists who call themselves existentialists are more desirous of reaping the benefits of the current popularity of existentialism than they are of presenting a valid interpretation of the writings of St. Thomas Aquinas, the scholarly writings of Gilson, Mascall and Maritain are sufficient to refute such a conclusion. E. L. Mascall when questioned on this point affirmed that it seemed to him very surprising that no one had interpreted the writings of

St. Thomas in such a way before, but, as far as he could see, his interpretation was the correct one. In *Existence and Analogy*, Mascall introduces the possibility that Gilson may be unduly influenced by the intellectual climate of his time, but he concludes (p. 45): "Further reflection and examination, however, seem to make it plain that, whatever suggestive power his environment may have exercised, Gilson's new presentation has in fact brought out the true nature of St. Thomas' thought and has given his own exposition a force and a coherence far greater than it had before."

The authenticity of the writings of Gabriel Marcel cannot be disputed since he developed his basic philosophical approach prior to a knowledge of Kierkegaard's writings and prior to the development of phenomenology and existentialism in both France and Germany.

Existentialism, then, as a whole is to be regarded as a new and valid school of philosophy which has a positive contribution to make in the development of human understanding. Nevertheless, it is not to be regarded as something entirely new; for, as we have seen, it has deep roots in the wisdom of philosophers of the past.

What are the positive contributions of existentialism as a whole to philosophy?

One of the oustanding contributions of existentialism has been to deal a shattering blow to absolute idealism by clearly pointing out that the rational concept and law are products of the human mind in its search for an understanding of the world that exists outside of the mind. Furthermore, man himself is existing in this world and therefore he is unable to detach himself completely to study objectively the world of being as a whole. That privilege is reserved for God alone if He exists.

Furthermore, the existentialists by pursuing a phenomenological method point out that the rational concept is in a way an inferior way to knowledge, subordinate to sense experience, because it is through sense experience that the self finds the existential index of the natural world. A weakness of the non-Christian existentialists is that they recognize sense experience as the only check to the rational concept. On the other hand, the Christian existentialists pursue a third and primary method to knowledge which is contemplation. They affirm that it is only through contemplating that one obtains a healthy approach to existing and being and that one begins to have a valid knowledge of the world that is. It is the absence of contemplation in philosophy since the time of Descartes that has marked the essential weakness of all modern epistemology.

A temptation for anyone who reacts against a system of thought is to assume its postulates in order to deny it. If this is done, one preserves certain characteristics of the old system in one's own thought. Thus Gabriel Marcel in his first work, his *Metaphysical Journal*, has assumed the postulates of the idealism against which he reacts by opposing emotion to reason and by considering religious truth as the object of emotion. However, he has escaped this position in the closing essay of the *Journal* on "Existence and Objectivity" and in his later writings. On the other hand, Sartre and his followers, influenced by Bergson, have never escaped some of the postulates of the idealism against which they react. Since their only epistemological check to the rational is the empirical, and since they affirm that only that which can be seen exists, then moral, political and religious truths which cannot be seen are void of any existential index and they are treated as ideal concepts.

The inherent weakness in the writings of Sartre and his followers is the failure to develop any healthy approach to existence and being. They accept existence and being as mysteries and go on from there to analyse their own consciousness without seeking to probe further into these mysteries which necessarily transcend rational thought and sense experience. It is only by pursuing the mystery of being as a whole, as the Christian existentialists have done, that there can be any hope of an adequate epistemology in which the being of reason and the being of sense experience can be seen in their true perspective. In this sense, the approach of Heidegger can be seen to be far more profound than that of Sartre and his followers.

The question is often asked concerning Sartre's authentic man as to why he should be authentic, because to be authentic leads to anguish and isolation, and there seems to be no reason for being authentic. One might also ask a Christian existentialist why he advocated contemplation. However, to ask an existentialist the question "Why?" is, probably, an invalid question since it assumes the idealist postulates whereby a rational answer can be given. The existential appeal is to a truth which precedes any rational explanation. It is true that a Christian existentialist can assert that he exists because God wills him to exist, but the question why God wills him to exist is unanswerable by any creature. The fulness or inadequacy of an existentialist philosophy cannot be determined by rational means but by the test of experience. Therefore, one cannot say that Sartre's philosophy is incorrect since it is undoubtedly largely true as far as Sartre's experience is concerned. What a Christian should say is that Sartre's philosophy is inadequate since it fails to take into account the greater fulness of reality that I have experienced in my life.

A weakness in the writings of Gabriel Marcel, which has been noted by several commentators, has been his failure to discuss the place of reason in his philosophy. Apart from a few casual references to reason in relation to language and apart from the fact that he frequently expresses himself in philosophical essays, his references to reason are made in radical opposition to its misuse. This is accounted for in part by his strong reaction to the untruths of idealist philosophy and of positivism and also by his constant awareness that the rational concept, which is necessarily secondary and abstract, cannot deal at all adequately with concrete situations. However, this weakness in Marcel may be regarded more as an omission, since from his study of *The Mystery of Being* he has been able to see the being of reason in relation to Being as a whole, but he has failed to expound what the function of reason and of the concept may be. It is because of this that Marcel's philosophy may appear to be one of extreme impracticability and other-worldliness with little guidance for persons in the everyday activities of human existing. It is for this reason that the writings of St. Thomas and his existentialist interpreters (Gilson, Mascall and Maritain) are more intellectually satisfying than the works of Marcel.

Closely related to the revolt against philosophical idealism is the revolt against an interpretation of St. Thomas in which the Aristotelian references in St. Thomas's writings are related to Cartesian thought and given predominance over existing, and being. For

Gilson, Mascall, and Maritain, the answer has been to interpret the writings of St. Thomas as he intended them to be interpreted and thereby to point out the errors of the essentialists. In doing so, they have brought forth several important truths in St. Thomas's writings which have been hidden since the time of Descartes. Gabriel Marcel has come to Christianity through his own philosophical approach. The only Thomism he has known in France has been the essentialist interpretation and he repudiates much in this because it seems to encourage a strictly impersonal approach by the clergy and a general reactionary position by the Church as a whole. This leads Marcel to appeal to the ontological reality of Christian truth which transcends its rational exposition, and, here, his views are strikingly similar to those of Gilson and Mascall.

Again, the Catholic Christianity which Sartre and his followers have known in France has been dominated by an essentialist Cartesian Thomism.[1] The God of Descartes is equated with the God of the Christians, and consequently, Sartre's revolt against idealism ties in very closely with his revolt against Christianity. This revolt against Christianity has a peculiar appeal for Sartre. Troisfontaines writes in his *Le Choix de J.-P. Sartre*: "Sartre—if I can believe his friends—is aware and proud of his opposition to Christianity" (pp. 66–7). For Sartre, Christianity is not only a religion, a Church, but it also is responsible for many of the characteristics of contemporary French society. Thus the bourgeois is a product of Christian civilization, and Sartre's moral and political views must be understood in relation to the society in which Sartre finds himself. In this sense, Sartre's works are seen to grow out of a society dominated by a Christianity preached in essentialist Cartesian terms.

As we have seen, in his reaction to idealism, Sartre has preserved many basic hypotheses of idealism and this is also true in his reaction to Christianity as he has experienced it. This accounts for

---

[1]This is evident throughout Simone de Beauvoir's recently published autobiography, *The Memoirs of a Dutiful Daughter*. Brought up in a Catholic home, she reacted against the very strict atmosphere. When a new girl came to her school who knew how to laugh heartily, she writes that "her sporty manner and her uninhibited voice were obvious signs that she had not been brought up under the influence of Saint Thomas Aquinas" (p. 152).

the surprising number of religious terms in Sartre's militantly atheistic philosophy. Sartre validly affirms that Descartes' idea of God was only Descartes' idea of perfection which could have no existence in itself. However, every man still preserves his own idea of perfection and the mission of the human being is to try to realize this ideal. Since there is no pre-established rational order in things, each man has his own particular idea of perfection. If God does not exist, then man must try to be God. If values which would be assured by the existence of a perfect being do not exist, then man must try to give them existence. Accompanying the desire to achieve the ideal is a sense of sin and guilt, because the individual is always aware of how far short he is of the ideals he has in mind. Sartre even recognizes a form of hell. It is under the gaze of other people that the self is objectified and can truly see itself for what it is, through the objective judgment of others. When the self truly sees itself for what it is, it, at the same time, realizes most clearly how far short it falls of the ideals it has in mind. Furthermore, since the objective gaze of others upon the self creates an opinion which is irrevocable, this gaze brings a form of eternal hell to the self. This eternity of hell is achieved in death when the self has lost its consciousness and can no longer escape the opinions of others. In this sense, every man in a human world is condemned both in life and in death to hell. This is a form of predestination to damnation which goes hand in hand with a completely rational, not existential, way of presenting theological truth.

Accompanying this sense of guilt and hell in Sartre's philosophy is a sense of original sin and responsibility. The authentic individual finds himself to be responsible for every existential situation. Since God is only an idea in the mind, then the self, realizing that it is aware of the situation and that, by its existence, it has a certain power to change the situation, feels that the responsibility falls upon its shoulders to make the world as God would have it if He existed.

A philosopher who reaches such a position is one who has carefully reflected on Christianity as it has been presented to him. It reflects an admiration for the ideal which Christians have presented, but also a valid awareness that this ideal is only a product of human aspiration and thought. The world as it exists, as Sartre presents it, appears so much the more sordid in relation to the ideal of what the world might be like if the Cartesian God existed.

However, for this very reason, the existential presentation of Christian truth by Gabriel Marcel, and by Gilson, Mascall and Maritain in their interpretation of St. Thomas, completely undercuts Sartre's criticisms of Christianity and, if Sartre is willing to appreciate these presentations, they may very well lead him to a completely new outlook on our universe where He Who Is grants existing and being to every creature. On the other hand, if Sartre refuses to consider seriously the Christian existentialist presentation, then it seems very likely that he will seek ever closer affiliation with Communist materialism. Since for Sartre only that which he can see, exists, and since only material things can be seen, then in the present terms of his philosophy, he is already on the path to a completely materialistic position, whether Communist or something else.

A third contribution of existentialism as a whole has been to reveal the evils and errors of mass movements of society whether in terms of historical determinism, scientific determinism, mass hysteria, fanaticism, or political absolutism. In this century, more than ever before, dehumanizing forces threaten men in their most personal everyday experiences. Because of this, human beings are faced with tragedy as never before and this leads many men to shirk their responsibilities in an unworthy desire for security at any price. In opposition to this unwarranted escapism which has been encouraged by the contemporary emphasis on pleasure and efficiency, the existentialists make an appeal to men to face the truth of their situation and the truth of themselves as existing individuals. What the individual thinks and believes and does is of far greater significance than any mass movements of society.

Nevertheless, though all existentialists seek to recover the dignity and importance of the self-conscious existing human individual, the Christian and non-Christian existentialists differ in their presentation of what the human reality is. According to Sartre, the authentic individual is isolated in his self-consciousness with no possibility of uniting with fellow-men except in the face of a common oppressor.

Other efforts for unity are made through conceptual language and values, but unity by concepts cannot be realized, because a concept is created by the individual mind. There is no assurance that another individual will create an exactly similar concept. On the other hand, the Christian existentialists are vitally concerned to make men aware of their unity in Being. Moreover, they maintain that it is only through this unity that a human individual is in reality a person who participates in the godly virtues of Faith, Hope and Love.

The existentialists have in their separate ways made a very telling analysis of the evils that confront modern society. In particular, the non-Christian existentialists have written most enlightening studies of Russian Communism. Though they admire the ultimate end of Communist theory, they feel that the means used by the Party will destroy that end and they believe that, first and last, one must seek to restore the individual human reality to a true sense of freedom. However, their prescriptions have been commonly accused of quietism.

To accuse Sartre of quietism in politics might seem at first to be absurd. Does he not hold up the man of action as the ideal? Has he not expounded the glories of the French Resistance Movement? Nevertheless, there does seem to be some justification in this charge of quietism. For Sartre, the isolated consciousness must bear the responsibilities of the world upon its shoulders. There is no guide for action but the consciousness must choose a course of action from an infinite number of possibilities which the imagination sets forth. In such a world, there is is a strong temptation for the self to sink into lethargy, burdened by the anguish of its situation. To Orestes, the man of action, in *The Flies* we must contrast Mathieu of *The Roads to Freedom* who does little to startle the world and who spends most of his time worrying about himself. In his *Existentialism and Humanism*, Sartre strongly denies that his philosophy is one of quietism because he affirms that man is defined by his actions. However, in a system in which man is constantly worried how his actions will define him and in which the powerless isolated consciousness must assume the burden of the world, the temptation to quietism is inherently a strong one. It is a world in which the strong man might come out on top but one in which his weaker brothers would inevitably fall away to suicide or to utter despair.

Gabriel Marcel has also been accused of quietism and there seems to be a measure of justification in this. A philosopher who prescribes departure from the world in contemplation, whose world is one of personal relationships, and who preserves a respect for the old traditions and looks for the restoration of the French monarchy is inevitably open to such a charge. However, Marcel is one of the few who take an eternal view of world affairs, and in the long run it is only after men have recovered their dignity in a communion with reality that any sort of permanent solution to the world's problems can be realized. Furthermore, it is only after man has recognized a power beyond him which is available to him that he can exert effective power in human affairs. The great tendency today is for men to undertake numerous activities without seeing the significance of their acts. Science has put enormous power at man's disposal, but it is only if man maintains a communion with reality that these scientific powers can be used for man's well-being rather than for his destruction.

Marcel has used a phrase of Thibon, "reserver pour donner." It is only after contemplation and prayer, and after making the self available to spiritual grace, that the self is really suited to be offered in service to humanity. Marcel's writings up to the present have laid the basis for guiding men to Being and to an appreciation of their relationships. It is to be hoped that in the future he may offer his guidance as to how this personal communion with Being is to become an effective force in the chaotic world of everyday human experience.

Finally, what may we say about the merits or demerits of the particular schools of existentialism with which we have been concerned?

Many Christians have denounced Sartre and his followers as devils incarnate, thereby failing to seriously estimate the worth of the contributions which Sartre, Merleau-Ponty and Simone de Beauvoir have made to human thought. Perhaps the greatest contribution of Sartre and his followers has been in the realm of psychology. To speak of creating the self in psychological terms makes sense. Beginning as they do from the *cogito* of Descartes, the non-Christian existentialists have made an exhaustive analysis of the human consciousness and their interest in imagination and emotion has coloured all their writings. Throughout this study, emphasis has been laid upon the fact that the non-Christian existentialists have been dealing in a realm of psychology, not of ontology. Psychologically, their works have great meaning but considered ontologically they are absurd.

Their ontological inadequacy is clearly seen in their treatment of existence. Existence is considered in isolation from being and separated from essence. This is of course pure abstraction because there is no such thing as pure existence; there must be something existing. They are guilty of the same fallacy as Kierkegaard.

It is in the inadequacy of their own ontology that the inadequacies of absolute idealism, of absolute materialism and of modern scientism may be clearly seen. As non-Christian existentialism is seen to be predominantly psychological, both idealist, materialist and scientific hypotheses are also seen to be products of human consciousness without relation to the mysteries of being. Christians oppose Sartre's interpretation of the "en soi," not, as Merleau-Ponty declares, because they want to idealize matter, but because the being of any object of experience can only be understood in relation to Being as a whole. Sartre's treatment of the "en soi" fails to consider material things as created.

With regard to their political views, we have already referred to the excellent analysis of Communism in Russia by Sartre and his followers. However, they have failed to gain any adequate understanding of the United States. Sartre's play *The Respectable Prostitute* is largely anti-American propaganda.

One of the great dangers of Sartre's writings is that they have an inherent tendency to negation and destruction. It is true that, in this attitude of negation, Sartre is able to analyse the world around him with a certain measure of detachment, and he has been able to offer valid criticisms to certain beliefs in politics, ethics and religion. However, such a dominantly negative attitude leads very easily to self-satisfaction and conceit. Furthermore, because so many of his themes seem so relevant to the contemporary world, Sartre has a great attraction for young people, not only in France but in other parts of the world. It is because of the possible harmful influence that Sartre might have upon young people that Gabriel Marcel has taken a particular interest in Sartre's writings in order to point out their inadequacies.[2]

One of the greatest contributions to philosophy by Marcel, in an age when the misuse of reason has made the world appear so cut and dried, is his presentation of the truth that the world and life itself are still full of mystery. In opening up to us the mysteries of life, he has rediscovered contemplation, a method which has been virtually lost in philosophy since the sixteenth century. Epistemology has been the most pressing problem of modern philosophy precisely because the empirical and rational means which philosophers recognized were inherently inadequate in themselves for the job in hand. Marcel clearly points out that it is only through contemplation that we can come to a valid understanding of reality.

Far more profoundly than Sartre, Marcel has shown us what it means to be a human being. For the human individual existing in space and time, there is always a temptation to isolation and despair. However it is as the individual makes himself available to other beings and to Being that he can realize not only his created nature but also his communion with reality. The reality of a human being is not to be an isolated self-conscious atom, as Sartre regards it, but rather it is to be a person in the fullest sense. A person is one who participates in virtue and virtue is not an abstract ideal but a living reality. The fulness of human life is most clearly shown in virtue and Marcel's writings have done much to clarify what human virtues really are. Almost every choice with which a man is confronted in a finite existence is an invalid one because a decision either way is a decision against beings. Love is not a decision against beings but a decision for beings and, therefore, the only valid decision for a human being to make is a decision against evil and negation.

Marcel's treatment of reality is not a popular one and his writings

[2]G. Marcel, "L'Existence et la liberté humaine chez J.-P. Sartre," in *Les Grands Appels de l'homme contemporain*, pp. 114–15.

will not be read by the large numbers of people who read Sartre. In many ways his delicate thoughts are very foreign to the tempo of contemporary society. However, one cannot doubt that Marcel is in touch with a reality that is greatly needed by modern man. Marcel himself began writing as an unbeliever and he feels that his salvation cannot be totally achieved until his fellow human beings are able to share his joy with him. His interest in art and in life as a work of art makes possible a continuous growth in creative fidelity to an appreciation and understanding of reality.

Marcel's thought has strong mystical qualities and as such it is vague on the relations between existence and being and between being and God. Nevertheless, he has made many vividly aware of the transcendence of existing and being to human consciousness and of our dependence upon a reality which lies far beyond our comprehension.

Though Marcel has reached his position through personal contemplation, there are many striking similarities between his writings and those of the existentialist interpreters of St. Thomas Aquinas.[3] Among these, the importance of the writings of Gilson, Mascall and Maritain cannot be overestimated. They have revealed many truths in St. Thomas's writing which have been overlooked for hundreds of years. Kierkegaard in the name of existence had denied any possibility of philosophy. Gilson, Mascall and Maritain have reinstated being and existing to their rightful place in philosophy. Men may think of reality, but their thoughts in no way determine reality because being and existing infinitely transcend human thought. Therefore, all human thought is analogical in character.

This conclusion by Gilson, Mascall and Maritain may have extremely important consequences in inter-Christian relationships. Catholic philosophy has been so dominated in the past by essentialist interpretations that the approach to theology has appeared as an integral part of an idealist rational system of philosophy. Divine immanence has been so stressed that the approach to divine transcendance has immeasurably suffered. On the other hand, traditional

---

[3]In the work by M. Pontifex and I. Trethowan, *The Meaning of Existence* (pp. 149 f.), Trethowan notes the measure of similarity between Marcel and the existentialist Thomists.

Protestant theology has so stressed divine transcendance in contrast to human sin that small attention has been paid to divine immanence. The result has been that Protestant and Catholic approaches have been poles apart and, indeed, it has been extremely difficult for Protestants to see that Catholics are talking about the same things. However, through the existentialist interpretation of St. Thomas, it is now possible to see that Catholic philosophy is centred on the same problems as Protestant writings and a far greater measure of understanding seems possible. Kierkegaard has had an even greater influence upon contemporary Protestant thought than he has had upon Gilson and Mascall.

Doctrine in the Roman Church has been frequently presented in the manuals by a series of set questions and answers with little or no recognition being given to the analogical character of Christian teaching. It remains to be seen what influence the existentialist interpreters of St. Thomas will have on the Roman church as a whole, but the validity of their writings cannot but have a marked effect. If this be true, non-Roman Christians may have a far greater appreciation of Roman doctrinal beliefs and, on the other hand, Roman Christians may come to a far greater understanding of the validity in much of Protestant theology. In a world where the existence of the Church is so threatened, it is of added importance that Christian truth should be presented in a clear and valid way. Furthermore, the possibility that an existential presentation of Christian truth will lead to a greater understanding among all Christians cannot be overestimated.[4]

Nothing leads to a stronger case for atheism whether in Sartrian, Marxist or any other form, than a divided Christendom which presents its claim in a self-satisfied, invalid and untrue way.

[4]For an account of significant developments along this line, see E. L. Mascall's *The Recovery of Unity*.

Bibliography

PRIMARY SOURCE

Philosophical Works

BEAUVOIR, SIMONE DE. *Le Deuxième Sexe.* 2 volumes. Paris: Gallimard, 1949. (Translated into English as *The Second Sex* by H. M. PARSHLEY, New York: Knopf, 1953.)
    L'Existentialisme et la sagesse des nations. Paris: Nagel, 1948.
    Pour une morale de l'ambiguité. Paris: Gallimard, 1947.
    Pyrrhus et Cinéas. Paris: Gallimard, 1944.
CAMUS, A. *Actuelles-Chroniques, 1944–1948.* Paris: Gallimard, 1950.
    Lettres à un ami allemand. Paris: Gallimard, 1948.
    L'Homme révolté. Paris: Gallimard, 1951. (Translated into English as *The Rebel* by A. BOWER, foreword by Sir H. READ, London: Hamish Hamilton, 1953.)
    Le Mythe de Sisyphe. Paris: Gallimard, 1942. (Translated into English as *The Myth of Sisyphus and Other Essays* by J. O'BRIEN. London: Hamish Hamilton, 1955.)
    Noces. Paris: Gallimard, 1947.
GILSON, E. *Le Réalisme méthodique.* Paris: Téqui, 1948.
    L'Esprit de philosophie médiévale. Paris: Vrin, 2nd ed., 1948.
    Le Thomisme: Introduction à la philosophie de saint Thomas d'Aquin. Paris: Vrin, 5th ed., 1947.
    L'Etre et l'essence. Paris: Vrin, 1948. (English version by Gilson, *Being and Some Philosophers*, Toronto: Pontifical Institute of Medieval Studies, 1949. This does not contain the Introduction to the French original.)
HEIDEGGER, M. *Existence and Being.* Introduction and English translation by W. BROCK. London: Vision Press, 1949.
    Sein und Zeit. Erste Hälfte. Tübingen: Neomarius, 6th ed., 1949.
HUSSERL, E. *Ideas: General Introduction to Pure Phenomenology.* English translation by W. R. B. GILSON. London: Macmillan, 1931. (German original *Ideen zu einer reinen Phänomenologie und phänomenologischen Philosophie*, Halle, 1913.)

KIERKEGAARD, S.   *A Kierkegaard Anthology.* ed. R. BRETALL. Princeton University Press, 1947.

Concluding Unscientific Postscript. English translation by D. SWENSON. Introduction by W. LOWRIE. Oxford: Oxford University Press, 1941.

Fear and Trembling. English translation by R. PAYNE. Oxford: Oxford University Press, 1939.

Journals. Translated and edited by A. DRU. Oxford: Oxford University Press, 1938.

Philosophical Fragments. English translation by D. SWENSON. Princeton: Princeton University Press, 1944.

MARCEL, G.   *Being and Having.* English translation by K. FARRER. London: Dacre, 1949. (French original, *Etre et Avoir*, Paris: Aubier, 1935.)

Du refus à l'invocation. Paris: Gallimard, 1940.

Homo viator. Paris: Aubier, 1944. (Translated into English as *Homo Viator* by E. CRAUFURD. London: Gollancz, 1951.)

Journal métaphysique. Paris: Gallimard, 1935. (Translated into English as *Metaphysical Journal* by B. WALL, preface by G. MARCEL, London: Rockliff, 1952.)

La Métaphysique de Royce. Paris: Aubier, 1945. Written in 1917. (Translated into English as *Royce's Metaphysics* by V. and G. RINGER, New York: Regnery, 1956.)

Le Déclin de la sagesse. Paris: Plon, 1954.

Les Hommes contre l'humain. Paris: La Colombe, 1951. (Translated into English as *Men against Humanity* by G. S. FRASER. Introduction by D. MACKINNON. London: Harvill, 1952.)

Position et approches concrètes du mystère ontologique. Louvain: E. Nauwelaerts; Paris: Vrin, 1949.

The Mystery of Being. Part I. English translation by G. S. FRASER. London: Harvill. 1950. Part II. English translation by R. HAGUE. London: Harvill, 1951. (French original: *Le Mystère de l'être,* I and II, Paris: Aubier, 1950.)

The Philosophy of Existence. English translation by M. HARARI. London: Harvill, 1948.

MARITAIN, J.   *A travers le désastre.* New York: Collection Voix de France, 1941. (Published in English as *France, My Country, through the Disaster*, New York: Longmans, 1941.)

Approaches to God. English translation by P. O'REILLY. New York: Harper, 1954. (French original, *Approches de Dieu*, Paris: Alsatia, 1953.)

A Preface to Metaphysics: Seven Lectures on Being. New York: Sheed and Ward, 1948. First published 1939.

Court Traité de l'existence et de l'existant. Paris: Hartmann, 1947. (Translated into English as *Existence and the Existent* by L. GALANTIERE and G. B. PHELAN, New York: Pantheon, 1948.)

The Degrees of Knowledge. Newly translated from the fourth French edition under the supervision of G. B. PHELAN. London: Geoffrey Bles, 1959.

True Humanism. London: Geoffrey Bles, 1938.

MASCALL, E. L. *Christ, the Christian and the Church.* London: Longmans, 1946.

Existence and Analogy. London: Longmans, 1949.

He Who Is. London: Longmans, 1943.

The Importance of Being Human. New York: Columbia University Press, 1958.

The Recovery of Unity. London: Longmans, 1958.

Words and Images. London: Longmans, 1957.

MERLEAU-PONTY, M. *Humanisme et terreur.* Paris: Gallimard, 1947.

La Structure du comportment. Paris: Presses Universitaires de France, 1942.

Phénoménologie de la perception. Paris: Gallimard, 1945.

Sens et non-sens. Paris: Nagel, 1948.

SARTRE, J.-P. *Baudelaire.* Paris: Gallimard, 1947. (Translated into English as *Baudelaire* by M. TURNELL, London: Horizon, 1949.)

Descartes. Paris: Editions des Trois Collines, 1946.

Esquisse d'une théorie des émotions. Paris: Hermann, 2nd ed., 1948. (Translated into English as *The Emotions: Outline of a Theory* by B. FRECHTMAN, New York: Philosophical Library, 1948.)

L'Etre et le Néant (Essai d'ontologie phénoménologique). Paris: Bibliothèque des Idées, 1943. (Translated into English as *Being and Nothingness* by HAZEL BARNES, New York: Philosophical Library, 1956.)

Existentialism and Humanism. Introduction and English translation by P. MAIRET. London: Methuen, 1948. (French original, *L'Existentialisme est un humanisme*, Paris: Nagel, 1946.)

L'Imagination. Paris: Presses Universitaires de France, 1950. (First published in 1936.)

L'Imaginaire: Psychologie phénoménologique de l'imagination. Paris: Bibliothèque des Idées, 7th ed., 1948. (Translated into English as *The Psychology of Imagination*, London: Rider, 1950.)

Portrait of the Anti-Semite. English translation by E. DE MAUNY.

London: Secker and Warburg and Lindsay Drummond, 1948. (French original, *Réflections sur la question juive*, Paris: Morihien, 1946.)

Situations, I. Paris: Gallimard, 1947.

Situation, II. Paris: Gallimard, 1948. (Translated into English as *What is Literature?* by B. FRECHTMAN, London: Methuen, 1950.)

Situations, III. Paris: Gallimard, 1949.

SARTRE, J.-P. ROUSSET, D., and ROSENTHAL, G. *Entretiens sur la politique*. Paris: Gallimard, 1949.

Literary Works

BEAUVOIR, S. DE. *Le Sang des Autres*. Paris: Gallimard, 1945.

L'Invitée. Paris: Gallimard, 1943. (Translated into English as *She Came to Stay* by Y. MOYSE and R. SENHOUSE. London: Secker and Warburg, 1949.)

Memoirs of a Dutiful Daughter. English translation by J. KIRKUP. London: Andre Deutsch and Weidenfeld and Nicolson, 1959. (French original, *Mémoires d'une jeune fille rangée*, Paris: Gallimard, 1958.)

The Mandarins. English translation by L. FRIEDMAN. London: Collins, 1957.

Tous les hommes sont mortels. Paris: Gallimard, 1947. (Translated into English as *All Men Are Mortal* by L. FRIEDMAN. London: World Publishing Co., 1955.)

CAMUS, A. *Le Malentendu, Caligula*. Paris: Gallimard, 1947. (Translated into English as *Caligula and Cross Purpose* by S. GILBERT, London: Hamish Hamilton, 1947.)

La Peste. Paris: Gallimard, 1947. (Translated into English as *The Plague*, by S. GILBERT. London: Hamish Hamilton, 1948.)

Les Justes. Paris: Gallimard, 1950.

L'Etat de siège. Paris: Gallimard, 1948.

L'Etranger. Paris: Gallimard, 1942. (Translated into English as *The Outsider* by S. GILBERT, London: Hamish Hamilton, 1946.)

MARCEL, G. *La Chapelle ardente*. Paris: La Table Ronde, 1950.

La Soif. Paris: Desclée de Brouwer, 1937.

Le Chemin de Crête. Paris: Grasset, 1936.

Le Dard. Paris: Plon, 1936.

Le Monde cassé. Paris: Desclée de Brouwer, 1933.

Le Quator en fa dièse. Paris: Plon. 1925.

L'Iconoclaste. Paris: Stock, 1923.

Rome n'est plus dans Rome. Paris: La Table Ronde, 1951.

Théâtre comique. Paris: A. Michel, 1947.

Un Homme de Dieu. Paris: La Table Ronde, 1950. (Translated into English as *Man of God* with *Ariadne* and *The Funeral Pyre* by M. GABAIN, London: Secker and Warburg, 1952.)

Vers un autre royaume (L'Emissaire, Le Signe de la Croix). Paris: Plon, 1949.

SARTRE, J.-P. *Intimacy and Other Stories* (including "The Childhood of a Leader"). English translation by L. Alexander. London: Peter Nevill, 1949.

La Nausée. Paris: Gallimard. 1938. (Translated into English as *The Diary of Antoine Roquentin* by L. ALEXANDER, London: Lehman, 1949.)

Le Diable et le bon Dieu. Paris: Gallimard, 1951. (Translated into English as *Lucifer and the Lord* by K. BLACK, London: Hamish Hamilton, 1952.)

Les Chemins de la liberté (Roads to Freedom). I. *L'Age de raison.* Paris: Gallimard, 1945. (Translated into English as *The Age of Reason* by E. SUTTON, London: Hamish Hamilton, 1947.) II. *Le Sursis.* Paris: Gallimard, 1945. (Translated into English as *The Reprieve* by E. SUTTON, London: Hamish Hamilton, 1947.) III. *La Mort dans l'âme.* Paris: Gallimard, 1949. (Translated into English as *Iron in the Soul* by G. HOPKINS, London: Hamish Hamilton, 1950.)

Le Mur. Paris: Gallimard, 1939.

Théâtre I (Les Mouches, Huis-clos, Morts sans sépulture, La Putain respectueuse). Paris: Gallimard, 1947.

Les Mains Sales. Paris: Gallimard, 1948.

The Chips are Down (Les Jeux sont faits). English translation by L. VARÈSE. London: Rider, 1951.

Three Plays: Crime passionelle (Les Mains Sales), *Men Without Shadows* (Morts sans sépulture), *The Respectable Prostitute* (La Putain respectueuse). English translation by K. BLACK. London: Hamish Hamilton, 1949.

Two Plays: In Camera (Huis-clos) and *The Flies (Les Mouches).* English translation by S. GILBERT. London: Hamish Hamilton, 1946.

Articles

BEAUVOIR, S. DE. "L'Amérique au jour le jour," *Les Temps Modernes,* December, 1947, January, 1948. (Published in English as *America Day by Day,* translated by P. DUDLEY, London: Duckworth. 1952.)

"Littérature et métaphysique," *Les Temps Modernes,* April, 1946, pp. 1153 f.

CAMUS, A.   "Prometheus in Torment," *World Review*, May, 1952, pp. 53 f.

CAMUS, A., SARTRE, J.-P., JEANSON, F.   Dispute re Jeanson's review of Camus' *L'Homme révolté*, *Les Temps Modernes*, August, 1952.

GILSON, E.   "Le Thomisme et les philosophies existentielles," *La Vie Intellectuelle*, June, 1945.

"Lettre à Albert Béguin," *Esprit*, April, 1951.

"Philosophical Movements in France," *The Listener*, February 6, 1947.

"Religious Wisdom and Scientific Knowledge," *Christianity and Modern Science*, Canadian Broadcasting Corporation, 1952.

HUSSERL, E.   "Phenomenology," *Encyclopaedia Britannica*, vol. 17.

MARCEL, G.   "Autour de Heidegger," *Dieu Vivant*, no. 2, pp. 89 f.

"Le Drame de l'humanisme athée," *La Vie Intellectuelle*, December, 1945.

"L'Existence et la liberté humaine chez J.-P. Sartre," *Les Grands Appels de l'homme contemporain*. Paris: Editions du Temps Présent, 1947.

"Pessimisme et conscience eschatologique," *Dieu Vivant*, no. 10.

"Réflexions sur les exigences d'un théâtre chrétien," *La Vie Intellectuelle*, March 25, 1937, pp. 458 f.

Review of J.-P. Sartre's *La Putain Respectueuse* and *Morts sans sépulture*, Theatre Arts, May, 1947, p. 44.

MASCALL, E.   Review of Gilson's *Being and Some Philosophers*, *Journal of Theological Studies*, 1949, pp. 199–200.

Review of Maritain's *The Degrees of Knowledge* (new translation), *Church Quarterly Review*, April-June, 1960, pp. 228 f.

MERLEAU-PONTY, M.   "Le langage indirect et les voix du silence," *Les Temps Modernes*, June and July, 1952.

"Note sur Machiavel," *Les Temps Modernes*, October, 1949, p. 577 f.

"Sur la phénoménologie du langage," *Problèmes actuels de la phénoménologie*. Paris: Desclée de Brouwer, 1952.

SARTRE, J.-P.   "Les Américains dans le souci," *Le Combat*, February 4 and 5, 1945.

"Orphée noir," *Les Temps Modernes*, October, 1948.

"Un Promeneur dans Paris insurgé," *Le Combat*, August to October, 1944.

SECONDARY SOURCES

Works

ALLEN, E. L.   *Existentialism from Within*. London: Routledge and Kegan Paul, 1953.

BARRETT, W. *Irrational Man.* New York: Doubleday, 1958.

BEIGBEDER, M. *L'Homme Sartre.* Paris: Bordas, 1947.

BERGSON, H. *Creative Evolution.* English translation by A. MITCHELL. London: Macmillan, 1913.

BERDYAEV, N. *The Origin of Russian Communism.* English translation by R. M. FRENCH. London: Centenary Press, 1937.

Towards a New Epoch. English translation by O. F. CLARKE. London: Geoffrey Bles, 1949.

BLACKHAM, H. J. *Six Existentialist Thinkers.* London: Routledge and Kegan Paul, 1952.

BOBBIO, N. *The Philosophy of Decadentism: A Study in Existentialism.* English translation by D. MOORE. Oxford: Blackwell, 1948.

BOUTANG, P. and PINGAUD, B. *Sartre, est-il un possédé?* Paris: La Table Ronde, 1946.

CAMPBELL, R. *Jean-Paul Sartre ou une littérature philosophique.* Paris: Editions Pierre Ardent, 1945.

CHENU, J. *Le Théâtre de Gabriel Marcel et sa signification métaphysique.* Paris: Aubier, 1948.

Christianity and the Existentialists, ed. C. MICHALSON. New York: Scribners, 1956.

CORTE, M. DE. *La Philosophie de Gabriel Marcel.* Paris: Téqui, n.d.

DEMPSEY, P. J. R. *The Psychology of Sartre.* Cork: Cork University Press. 1950.

DE WAELHENS, A. *Une Philosophie de l'ambiguité: L'Existentialisme de Maurice Merleau-Ponty.* Publications Universitaires de Louvain, 1951.

Etienne Gilson: Philosophe de la Chrétienté. Paris: Les Editions du Cerf, 1949.

Existentialisme chrétien: Gabriel Marcel. Présentation de E. Gilson. Paris: Plon, 1947. (This work includes an essay "Regard en arrière" by GABRIEL MARCEL.)

FOULQUIE, P. *L'Existentialisme.* Paris: Presses Universitaires de France, 6th ed., 1951.

HEINEMANN, F. H. *Existentialism and the Modern Predicament.* New York: Harper, 1958.

JEANSON, F. *Le Problème moral et la pensée de Sartre.* Paris: Editions de Myrte, 1947.

JOLIVET, R. *Le Problème de la mort chez M. Heidegger et J.-P. Sartre.* Editions de Fontenelle, 1950.

Les Doctrines existentialistes de Kierkegaard à J.-P. Sartre. Editions de Fontenelle, 1948.

KUHN. H. *Encounter with Nothingness.* Hinsdale, Ill.: Regnery, 1949.

L'Activité philosophique contemporaine en France et aux Etats-Unis. Tome Second. *La Philosophie française.* Ed. by M. FARBER. Paris: Presses Universitaires de France, 1950.

LAVELLE, L.   *La Philosophie française entre les deux guerres.* Paris: Aubier, 1947.

LEFEBVRE, H.   *L'Existentialisme.* Paris: Sagittaire, 1946.

LEWIS, C. S.   *The Problem of Pain.* London: Centenary Press, 1940.

LUKACS, G.   *Existentialisme ou marxisme?* Paris: Nagel, 1948.

MASARYK, T. G.   *Modern Man and Religion.* London: Allen and Unwin, 1938 (Written in 1896–8.)

MOUGIN, H.   *La Sainte Famille existentialiste.* Paris: Editions Sociales, 1947.

MOUNIER, E.   *Introduction aux existentialismes.* Paris: Société des Editions Denoël, 1947. (Translated into English as *Existentialist Philosophies* by E. BLOW, London: Rockliff, 1948.)

MURDOCH, I.   *Sartre.* Cambridge: Bowes and Bowes, 1953.

PAILLOU, P.-H.   *Arthur Rimbaud: Père de l'existentialisme.* Paris: Librairie Académique Perrin, 1947.

PATON, H. J.   *In Defence of Reason.* London: Hutchinson's University Library, 1951.

PHILLIPS, R. P.   *Modern Thomistic Philosophy.* 2 volumes. London: Burns Oates, 1935.

PONTIFEX, M. and TRETHOWAN, I.   *The Meaning of Existence.* London: Longmans, 1953.

PRINI, P.   *Gabriel Marcel et la méthodologie de l'invérifiable.* Préface de GABRIEL MARCEL. Paris: Desclée de Brouwer, 1953.

RICOEUR, P.   *Gabriel Marcel et Karl Jaspers.* Paris: Editions du Temps Présent, 1947.

ROBERTS, D. E.   *Existentialism and Religious Belief.* Ed. R. HAZELTON. New York: Oxford University Press, 1959.

RUGGIERO, G. DE.   *Existentialism.* Ed. R. HEPPENSTALL. English translation by E. M. COCKS. London: Secker and Warburg, 1946.

SCIACCA, M. F.   *L'Existence de Dieu.* Paris: Aubier, 1951.

SERTILLANGES, A. D.   *L'Idée de création.* Paris: Aubier, 1945.

TROISFONTAINES, R.   *Le Choix de J.-P. Sartre.* Paris: Aubier, 1951.
   De l'existence à l'être. Lettre-Préface de GABRIEL MARCEL. Deux tomes. Namur: Secrétariat des Publications, 1953.

TRUC, G.   *De J.-P. Sartre à L. Lavelle ou désagrégation et réintégration.* Paris: Tissot, 1946.

VARET, G.   *L'Ontologie de Sartre.* Paris: Presses Universitaires de France, 1948.

VERNEAUX, R.   *Leçons sur l'existentialisme et ses formes principales.* Paris: Téqui, 1948.

WAHL, J. *Esquisse pour une histoire de l'existentialisme.* Paris: L'Arche, 1949.
Vers le concret. Paris: Vrin, 1932.

Articles

ALBERES, R. M. "Is There a New Ethic in Fiction?," *Yale French Studies,* no. 8.

BATAILLE, G. "Discussion sur le péché," *Dieu Vivant,* no. 4, pp. 83 f.

BLANCHET, A. "La Querelle Sartre-Camus," *Etudes,* November, 1952.

BURGELIN, P. Review of G. Marcel's *Homo viator, Dieu Vivant,* no. 2.

CHASTAING, M. "La Pensée engagée, sur le sens de l'alterité dans le théâtre de Gabriel Marcel," *Esprit,* March, 1937.

CHASTAING, M. and TOUCHARD, P.-A. "Autour du théâtre de Gabriel Marcel," *Esprit,* June, 1939.

COLIN, P. "La Philosophie de l'existence en Allemagne et en France," *La Vie Intellectuelle,* January, 1952.

DELHOMME, J. "J.-P. Sartre—*Existentialisme est un humanisme,*" *La Vie Intellectuelle,* June, 1946.

DUMERY, H. "La Méthode complexe de Jean-Paul Sartre," *La Vie Intellectuelle,* July, 1948.

FOSTER, M. B. "The Christian Doctrine of Creation and the Rise of Modern Natural Science," *Mind,* vol. XLIII, no. 172, October, 1934, pp. 446 f. "Christian Theology and Modern Science of Nature," *Mind,* vol. XLIV, no. 176, October, 1935, pp. 439 f.

GAUTHIER, H. Review of Sartre's *Les Mains sales, La Vie Intellectuelle,* July, 1948.

HIPPOLITE, J. "Du Bergsonisme à l'existentialisme," *Mercure de France,* July, 1949.

JEANSON, F. "Albert Camus ou l'âme révoltée," *Les Temps Moderns,* May, 1952.

LACROIX, J. "Conscience religieuse et conscience politique," *Esprit,* May, 1952, pp. 872 f.
"L'Affaire Gilson," *Esprit,* April, 1951, pp. 590 f.

LE BLOND, J. M. "L'Humanisme athée au Collège de France," *Etudes,* March, 1953.

LEMARCHAND, J. Review of Sartre's *Morts sans sépulture* and *La Putain Respectueuse, Le Combat,* November 9, 1946.

MESNARD, P. "Gabriel Marcel, dialecticien de l'esperance," *La Vie Intellectuelle,* June, 1946.

NEWMAN, J. "The Ethics of Existentialism," *The Irish Ecclesiastical Record,* Fifth Series, vol. LXXVII, May, 1952.

PETIT, L. Review of Sartre's *Les Jeux sont faits, La Vie Intellectuelle,* July, 1948.

RAU, C. "The Ethical Theory of Jean-Paul Sartre," *Journal of Philosophy*, August, 1949, pp. 536 f.

Revue de Philosophie—L'Existentialisme. Année 1946. Articles by F. COYRÉ, M. DE CORTE, P. DESCOQS, D. DUBARLE, R. JOLIVET, G. THIBON, R. VERNEAUX. Paris: Téqui, 1947.

ROYNET, L. "A. Camus chez les chrétiens," *La Vie Intellectuelle*, April, 1949.

SPEAIGHT, R. "Philosophy in the French Theatre To-day," *The Listener*, February 19, 1953, pp. 308 f.

TOYNBEE, P. "Sartre and the Absolute," *The Observer*, February 15, 1953, Review of *Lucifer and the Lord.*

TULLOCH, D. M. "Sartrian Existentialism," *Philosophical Quarterly*, January, 1952.

"Un Débat sur la philosophie de l'existence," *Dieu Vivant*, no. 6.

Index